YASMEEN

Creator and Writer
SAIF A. AHMED

Artist
FABIANA MASCOLO

Letterer
ROBIN JONES

Script Editor
TRAVIS CZAP

Logo Design
TOBEN RACICOT

Scout Editor
JAMES PRUETT

Scout Production
KURT KNIPPEL

Chief Executive Officer
Brendan Deneen

Chief Creative Officer
James Pruett

Chief Strategy Officer
Tennessee Edwards

President
James Haick III

Chief Media Officer
Don Handfield

Publishers
David A. Byrne and
Charlie Stickney

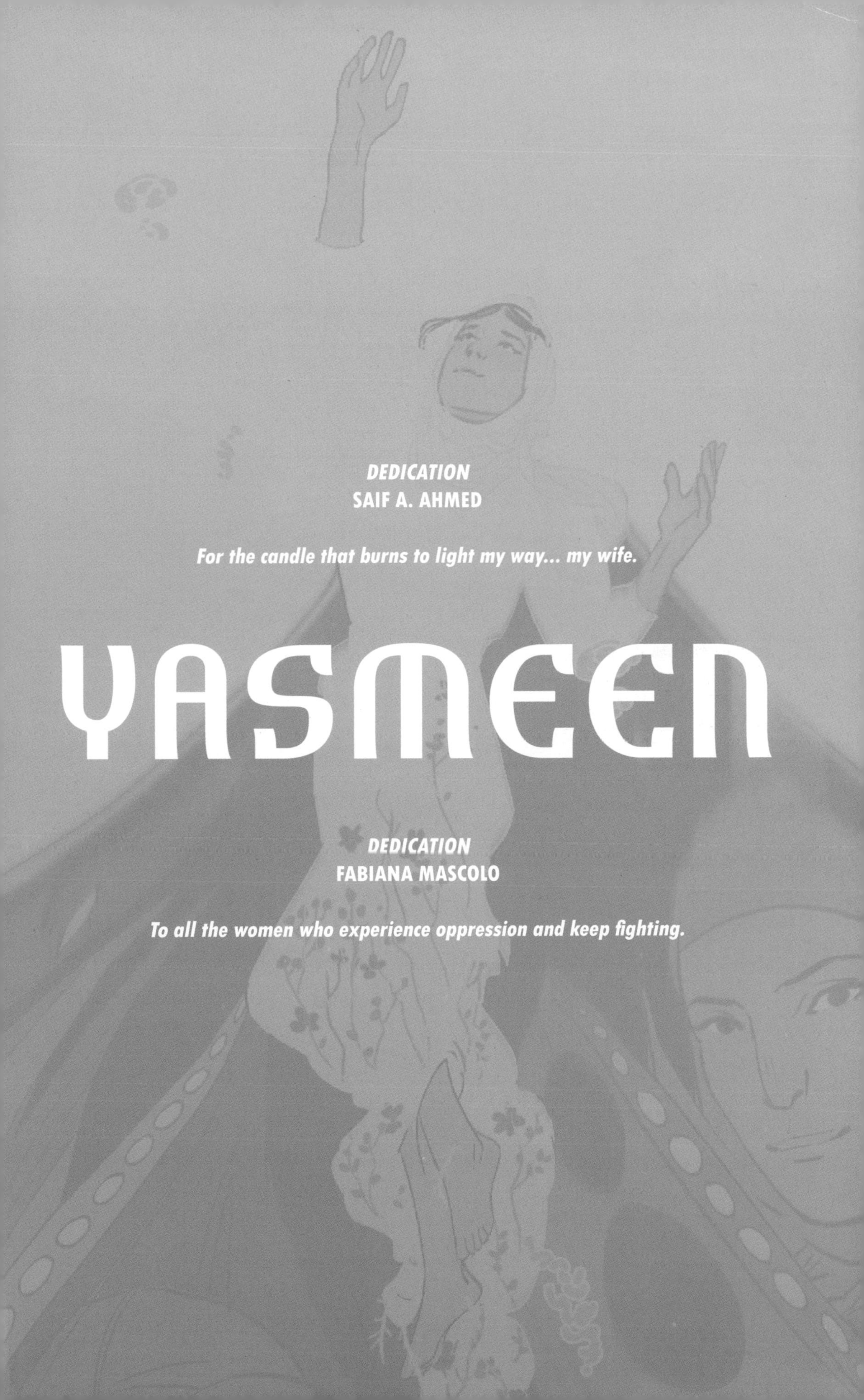

DEDICATION
SAIF A. AHMED

For the candle that burns to light my way... my wife.

YASMEEN

DEDICATION
FABIANA MASCOLO

To all the women who experience oppression and keep fighting.

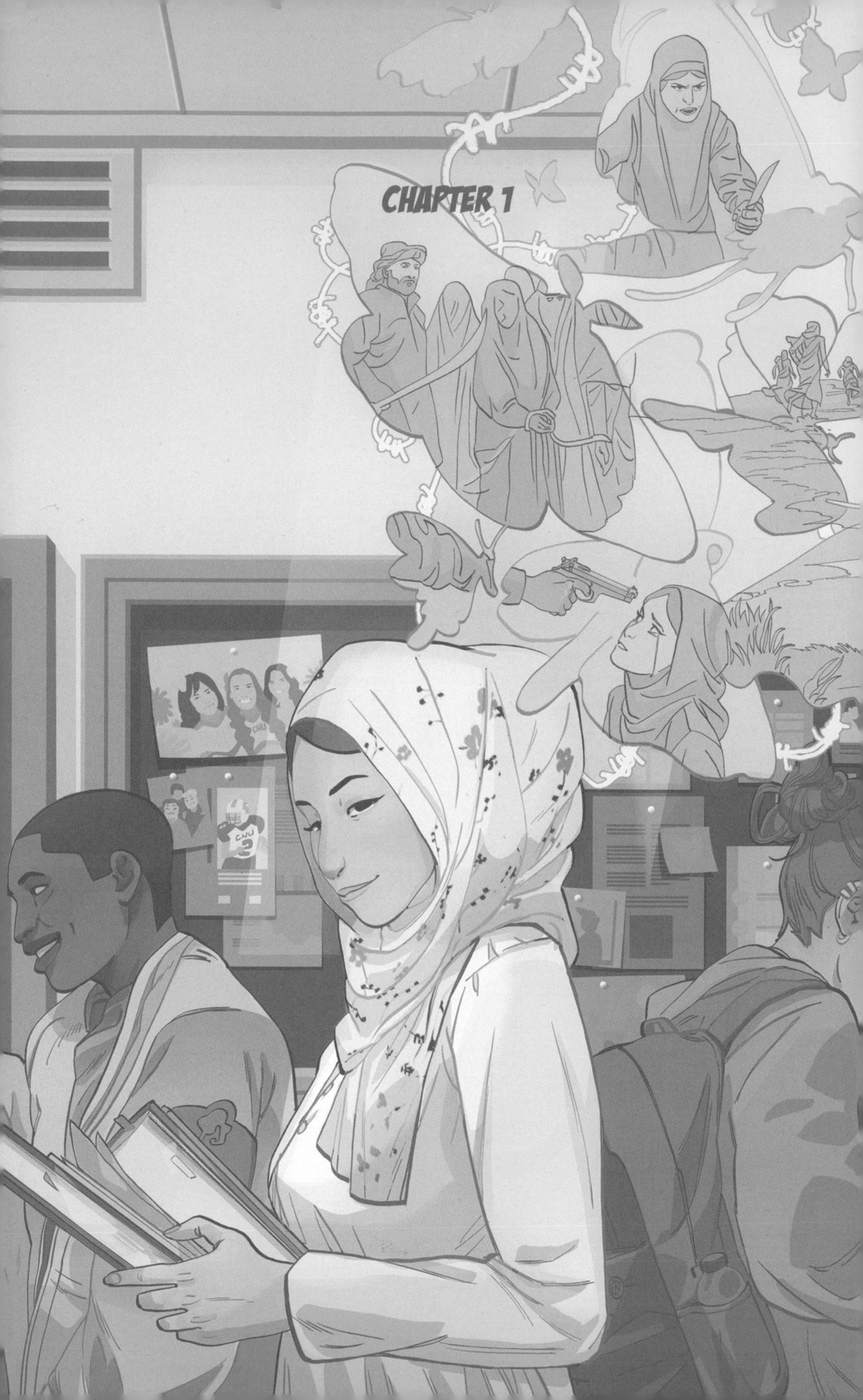
CHAPTER 1
CNU

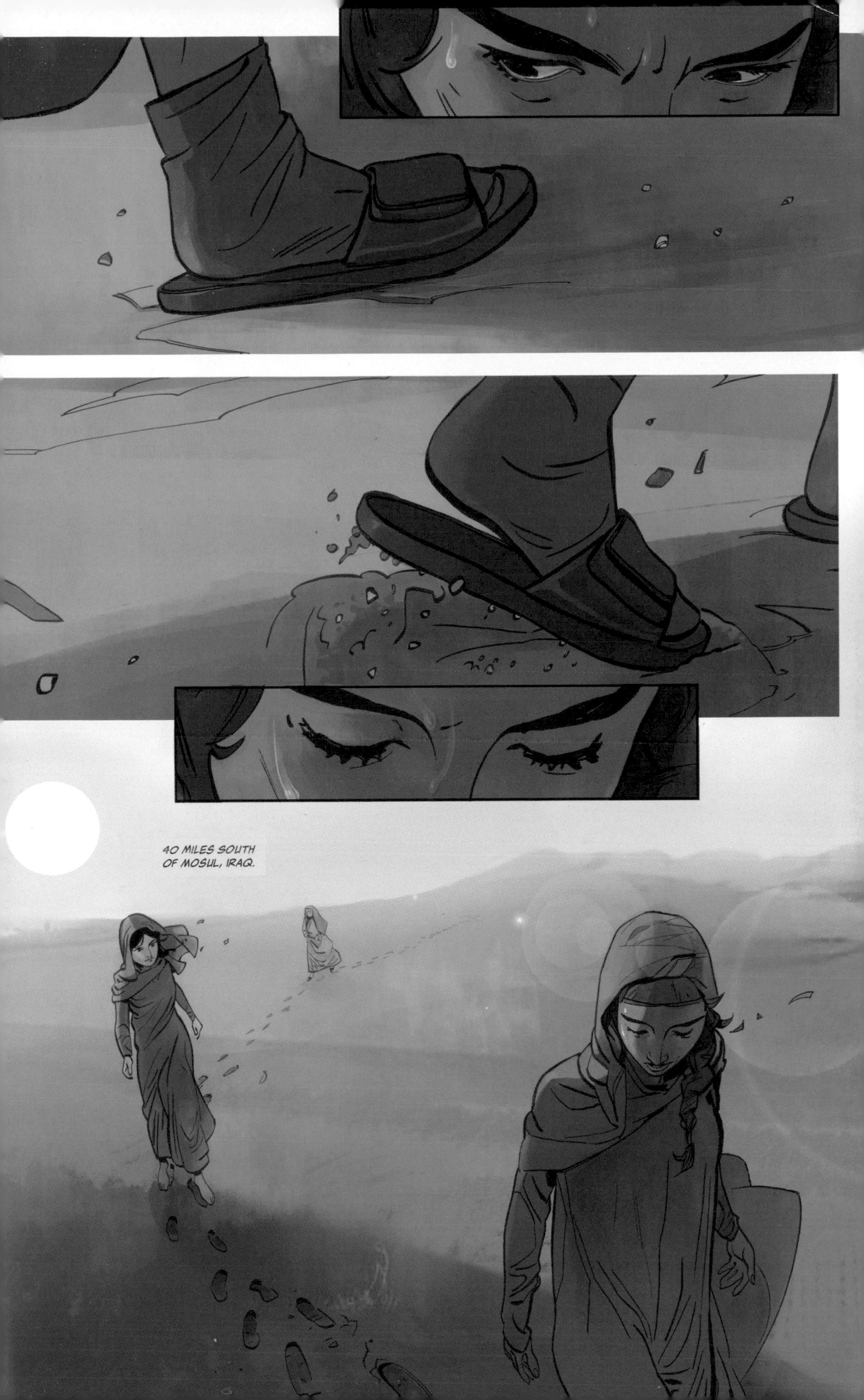
40 MILES SOUTH
OF MOSUL, IRAQ.

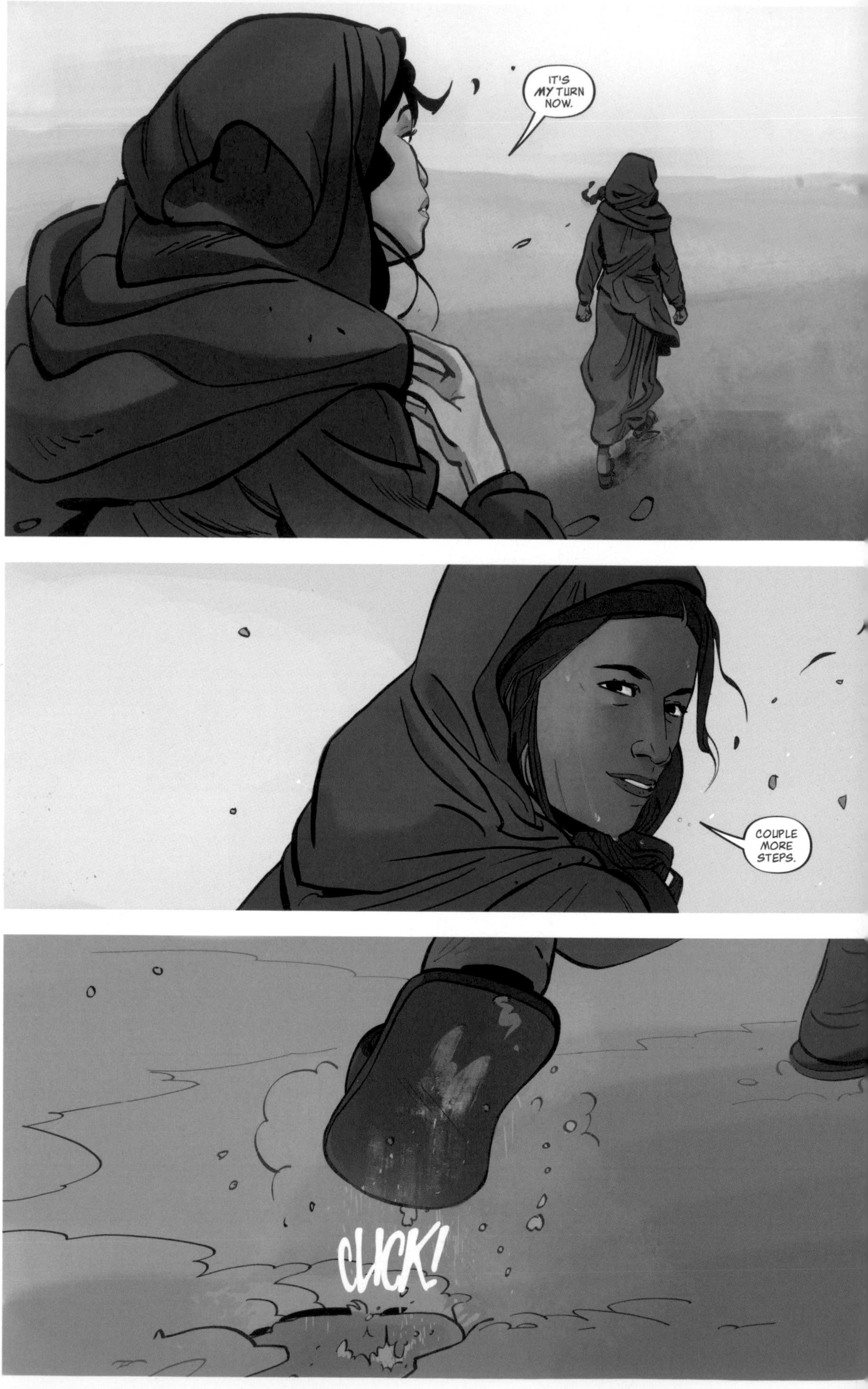
IT'S MY TURN NOW.
COUPLE MORE STEPS.
CLICK!

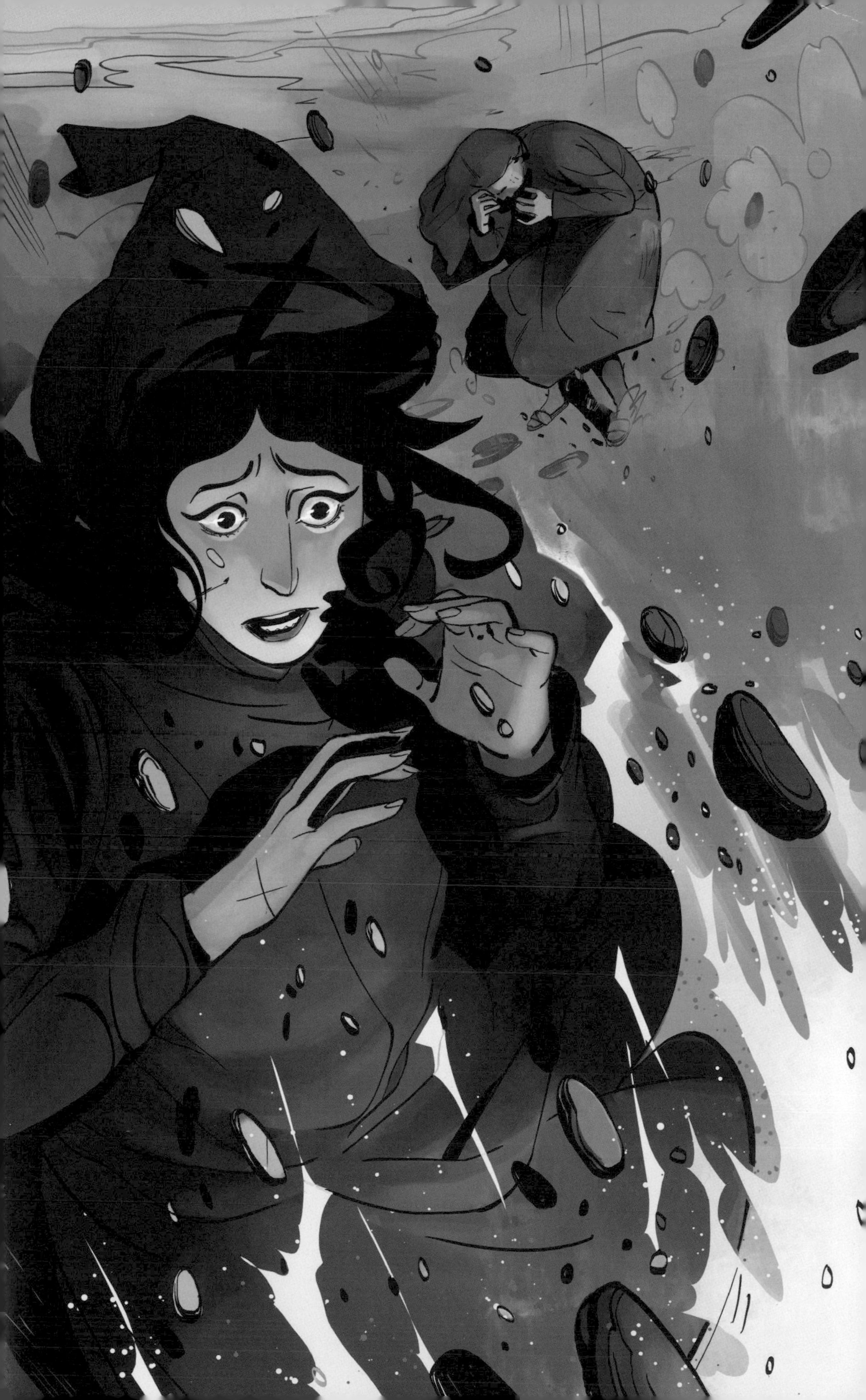

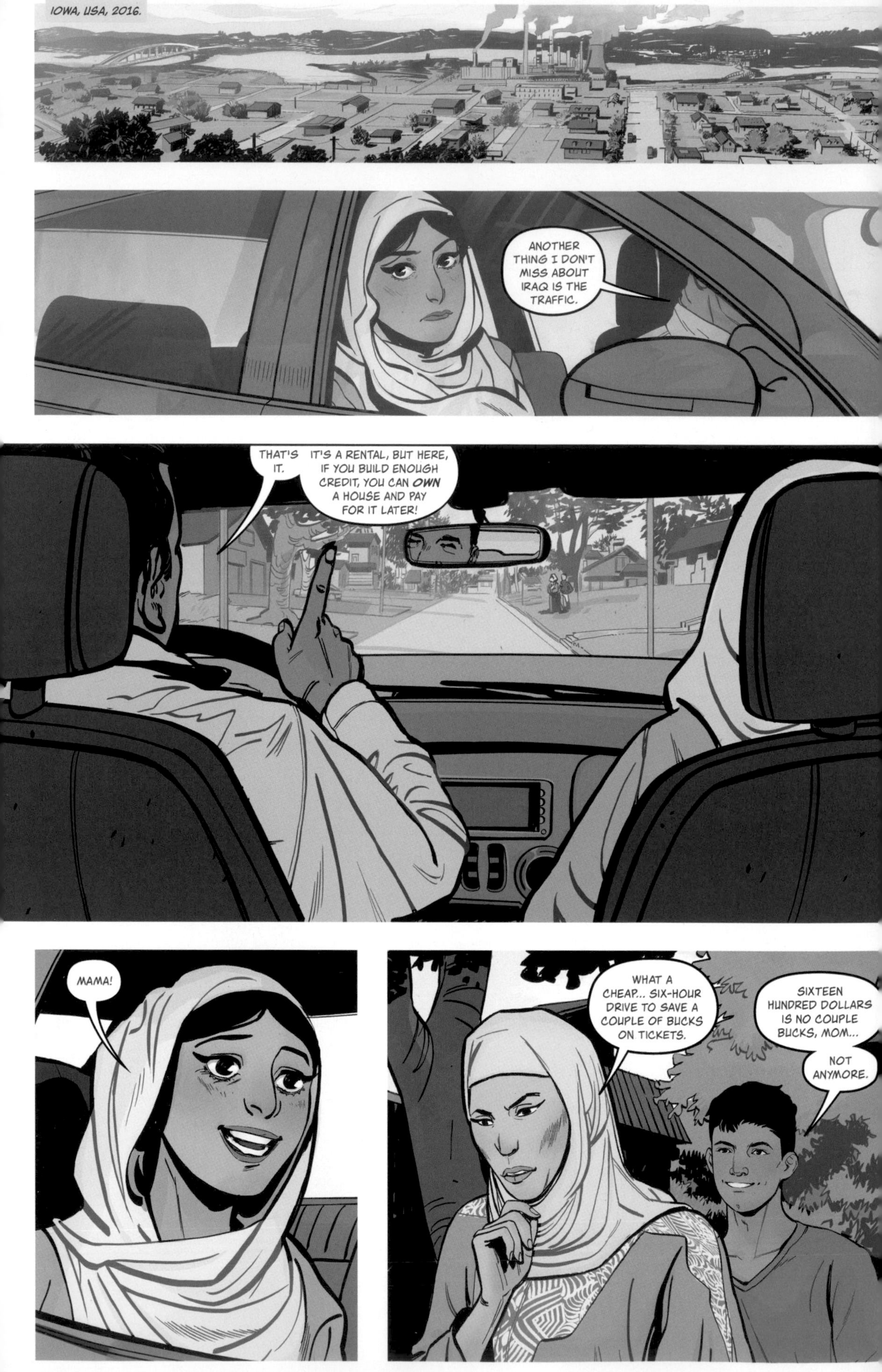
IOWA, USA, 2016.
ANOTHER THING I DON'T MISS ABOUT IRAQ IS THE TRAFFIC.
THAT'S IT.
IT'S A RENTAL, BUT HERE, IF YOU BUILD ENOUGH CREDIT, YOU CAN OWN A HOUSE AND PAY FOR IT LATER!
MAMA!
WHAT A CHEAP... SIX-HOUR DRIVE TO SAVE A COUPLE OF BUCKS ON TICKETS.
SIXTEEN HUNDRED DOLLARS IS NO COUPLE BUCKS, MOM...
NOT ANYMORE.

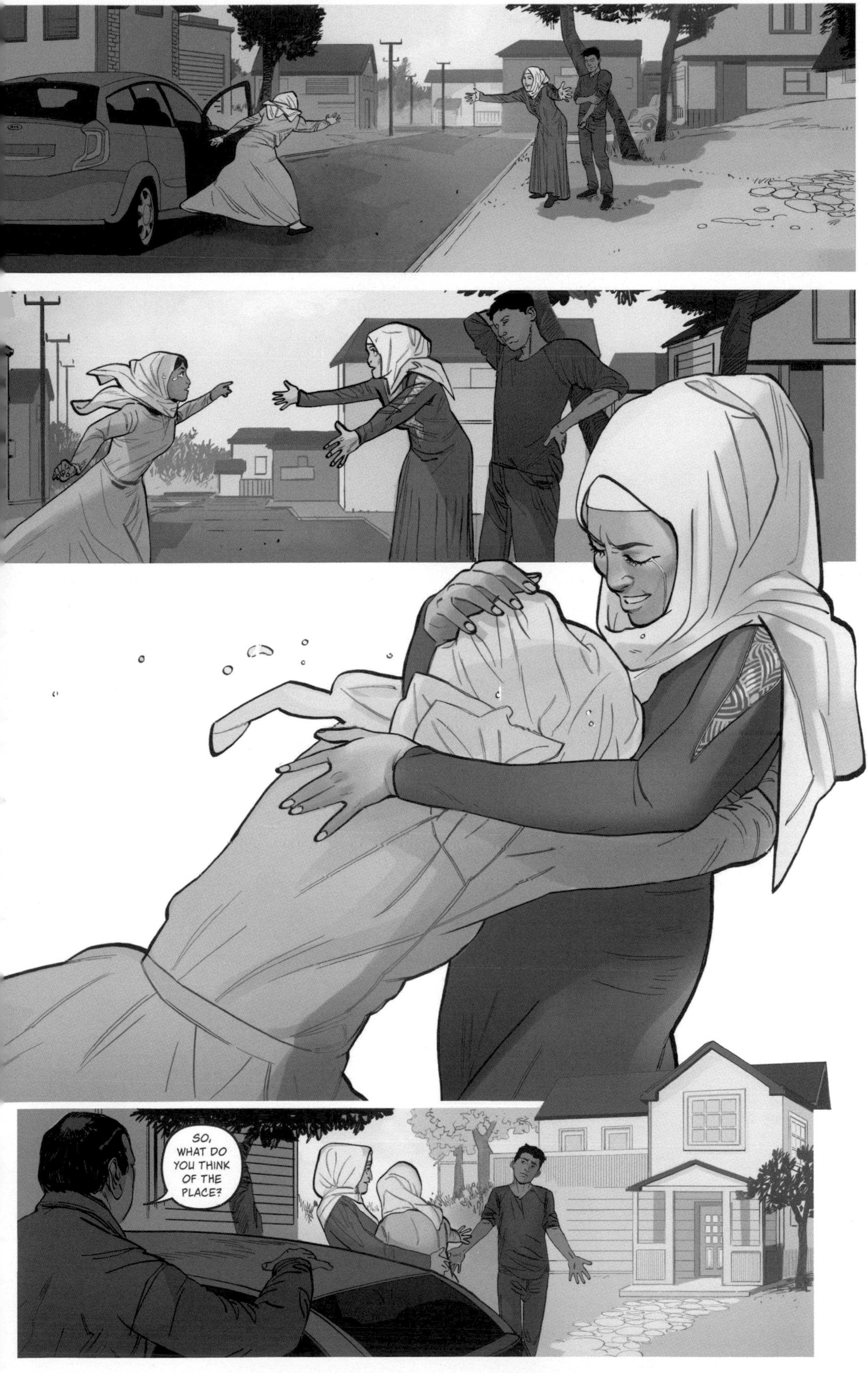
SO, WHAT DO YOU THINK OF THE PLACE?

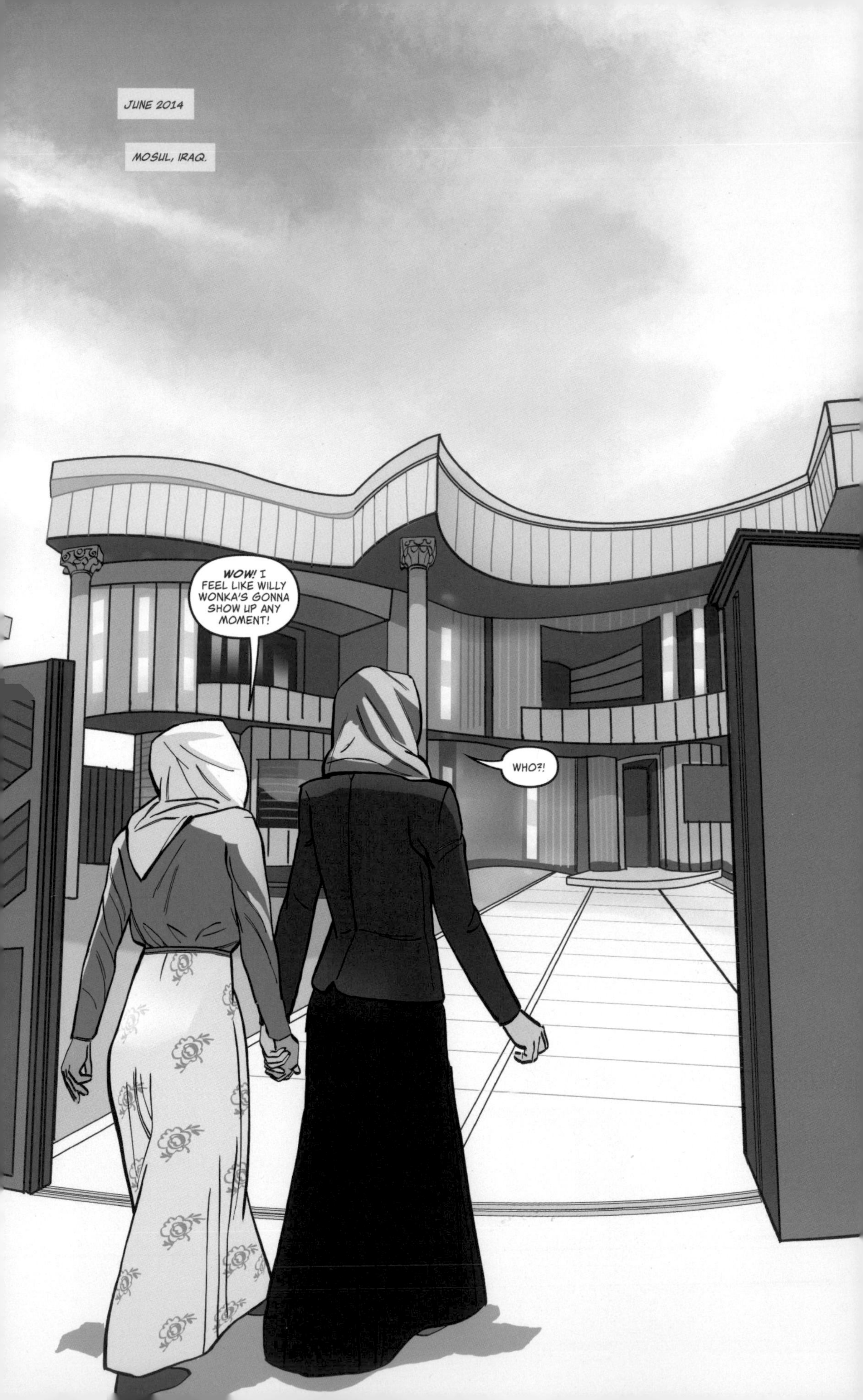
JUNE 2014
MOSUL, IRAQ.
WOW! I FEEL LIKE WILLY WONKA'S GONNA SHOW UP ANY MOMENT!
WHO?!

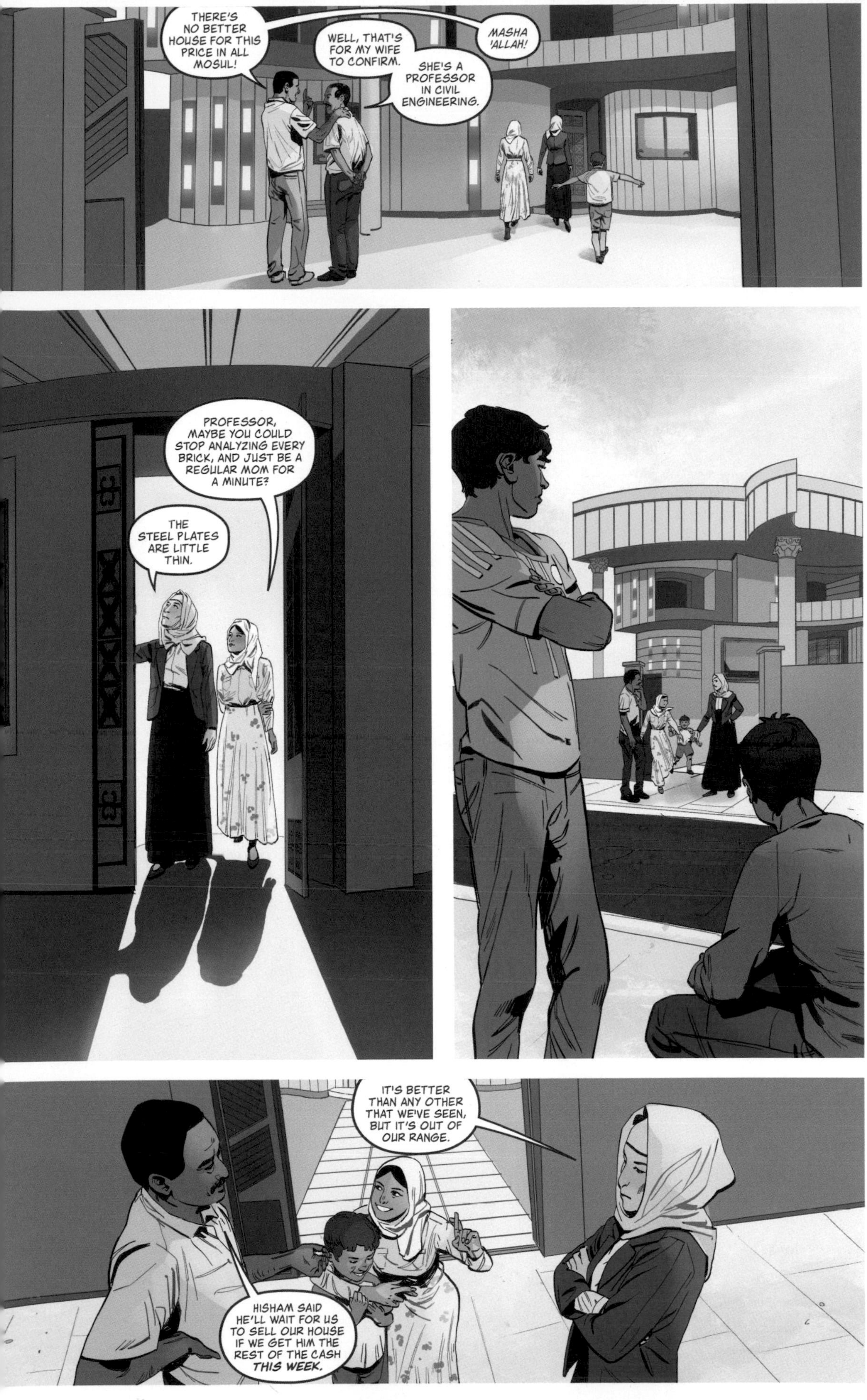
THERE'S NO BETTER HOUSE FOR THIS PRICE IN ALL MOSUL!
MASHA 'ALLAH!
WELL, THAT'S FOR MY WIFE TO CONFIRM.
SHE'S A PROFESSOR IN CIVIL ENGINEERING.
THE STEEL PLATES ARE LITTLE THIN.
PROFESSOR, MAYBE YOU COULD STOP ANALYZING EVERY BRICK, AND JUST BE A REGULAR MOM FOR A MINUTE?
IT'S BETTER THAN ANY OTHER THAT WE'VE SEEN, BUT IT'S OUT OF OUR RANGE.
HISHAM SAID HE'LL WAIT FOR US TO SELL OUR HOUSE IF WE GET HIM THE REST OF THE CASH *THIS WEEK.*

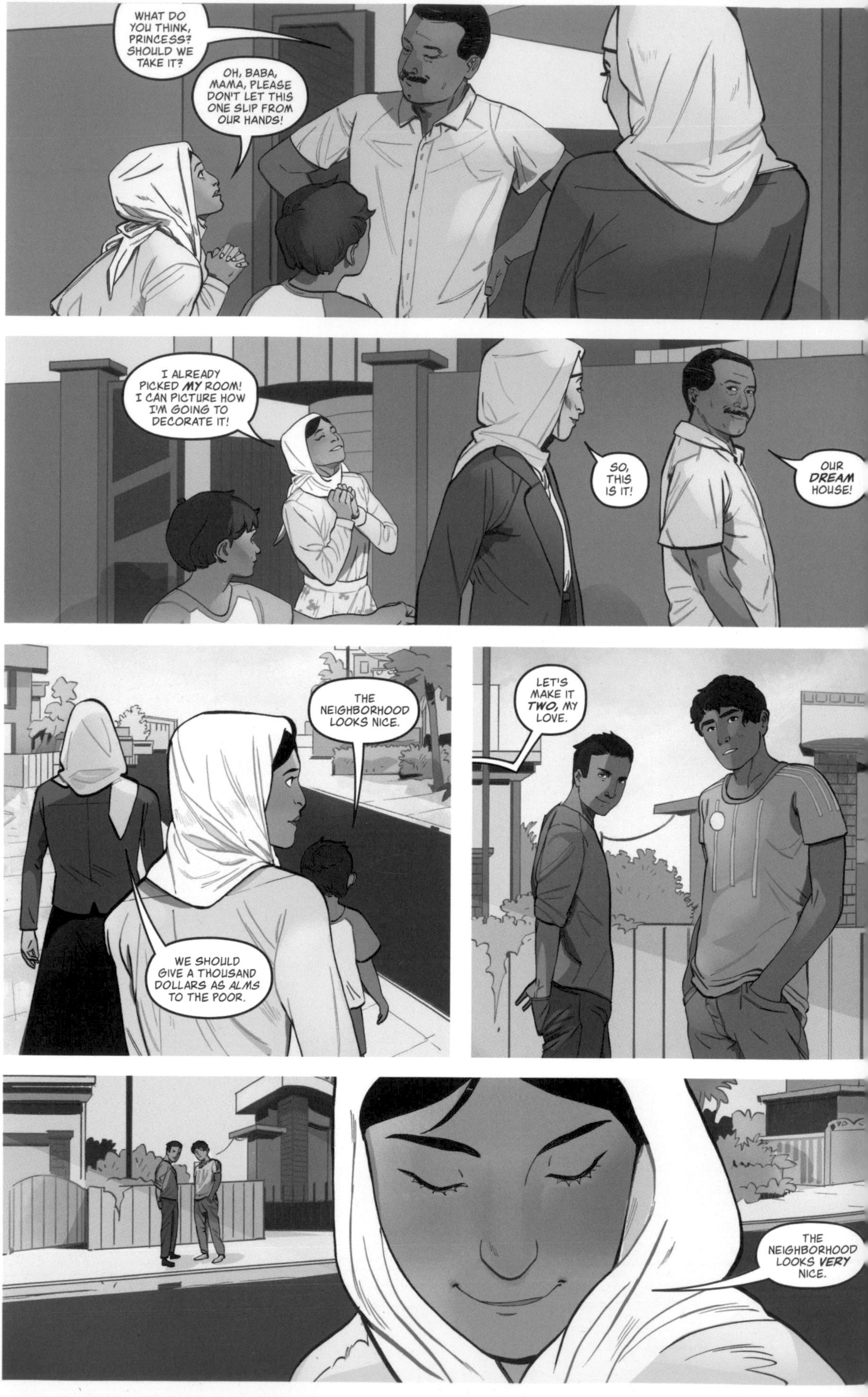
WHAT DO YOU THINK, PRINCESS? SHOULD WE TAKE IT?
OH, BABA, MAMA, PLEASE DON'T LET THIS ONE SLIP FROM OUR HANDS!
I ALREADY PICKED MY ROOM! I CAN PICTURE HOW I'M GOING TO DECORATE IT!
SO, THIS IS IT!
OUR DREAM HOUSE!
THE NEIGHBORHOOD LOOKS NICE.
WE SHOULD GIVE A THOUSAND DOLLARS AS ALMS TO THE POOR.
LET'S MAKE IT TWO, MY LOVE.
THE NEIGHBORHOOD LOOKS VERY NICE.

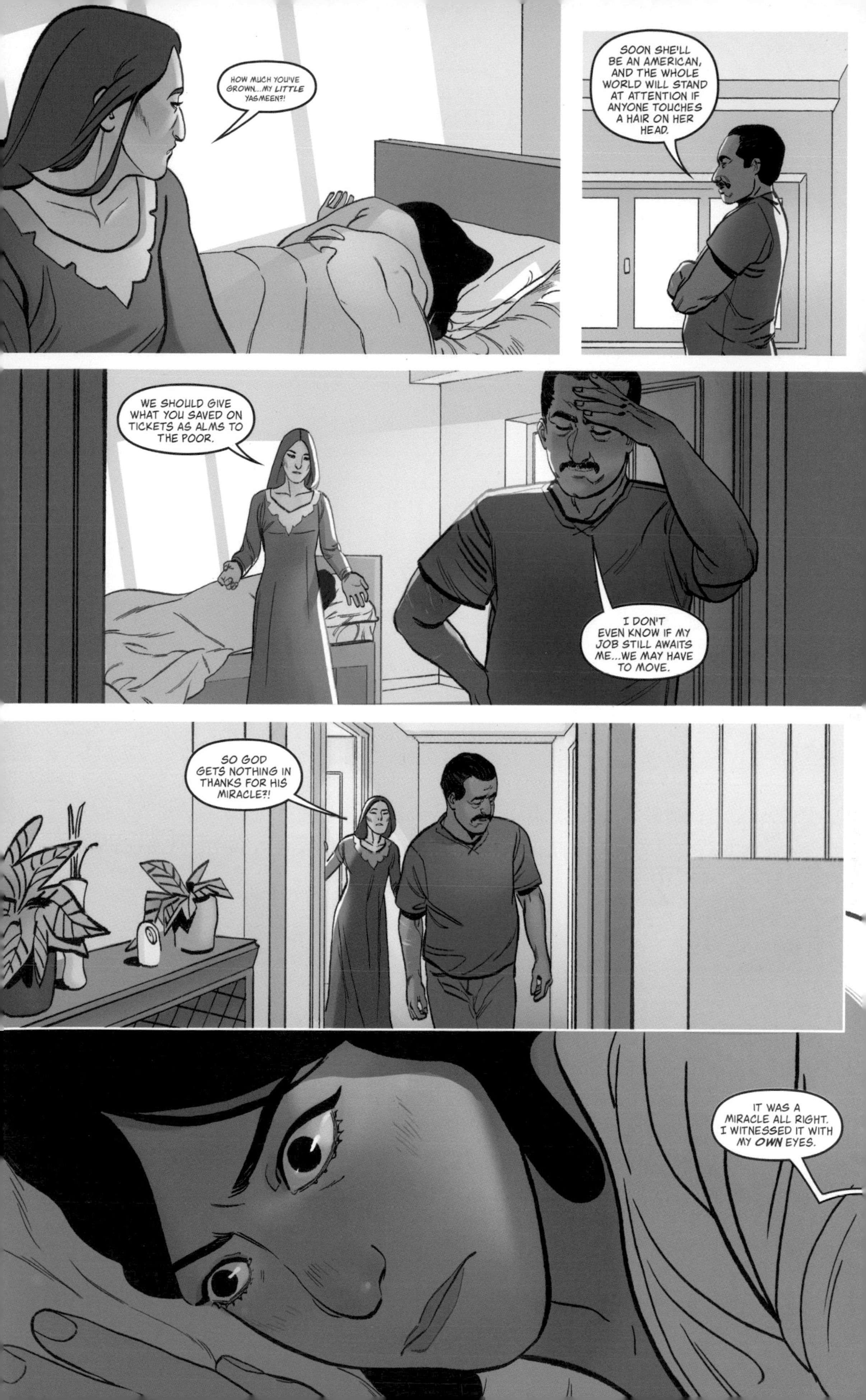
HOW MUCH YOU'VE GROWN...MY *LITTLE* YASMEEN?!
SOON SHE'LL BE AN AMERICAN, AND THE WHOLE WORLD WILL STAND AT ATTENTION IF ANYONE TOUCHES A HAIR ON HER HEAD.
WE SHOULD GIVE WHAT YOU SAVED ON TICKETS AS ALMS TO THE POOR.
I DON'T EVEN KNOW IF MY JOB STILL AWAITS ME...WE MAY HAVE TO MOVE.
SO GOD GETS NOTHING IN THANKS FOR HIS MIRACLE?!
IT WAS A MIRACLE ALL RIGHT. I WITNESSED IT WITH MY *OWN* EYES.

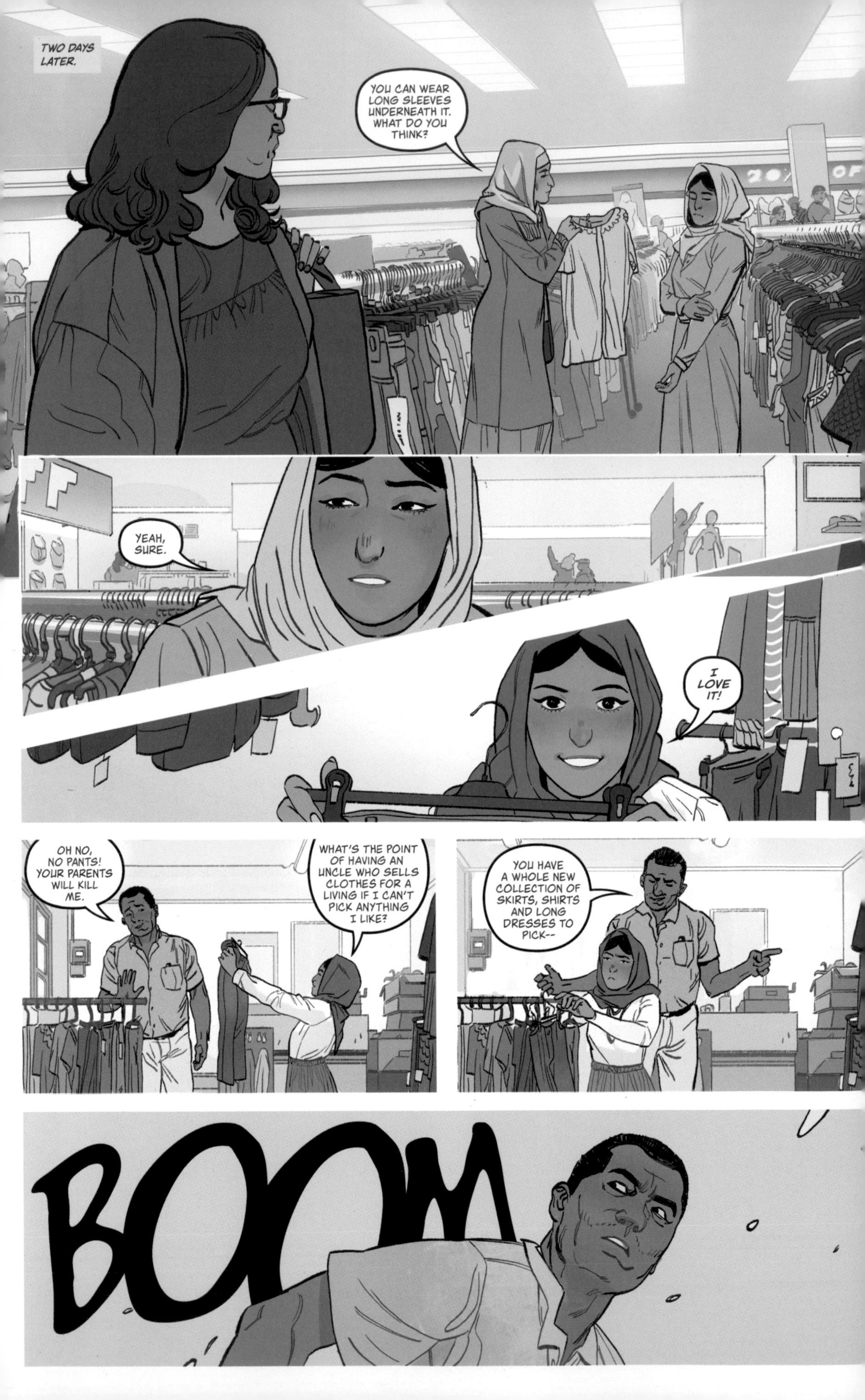
TWO DAYS LATER.
YOU CAN WEAR LONG SLEEVES UNDERNEATH IT. WHAT DO YOU THINK?
YEAH, SURE.
I LOVE IT!
OH NO, NO PANTS! YOUR PARENTS WILL KILL ME.
WHAT'S THE POINT OF HAVING AN UNCLE WHO SELLS CLOTHES FOR A LIVING IF I CAN'T PICK ANYTHING I LIKE?
YOU HAVE A WHOLE NEW COLLECTION OF SKIRTS, SHIRTS AND LONG DRESSES TO PICK--
BOOM

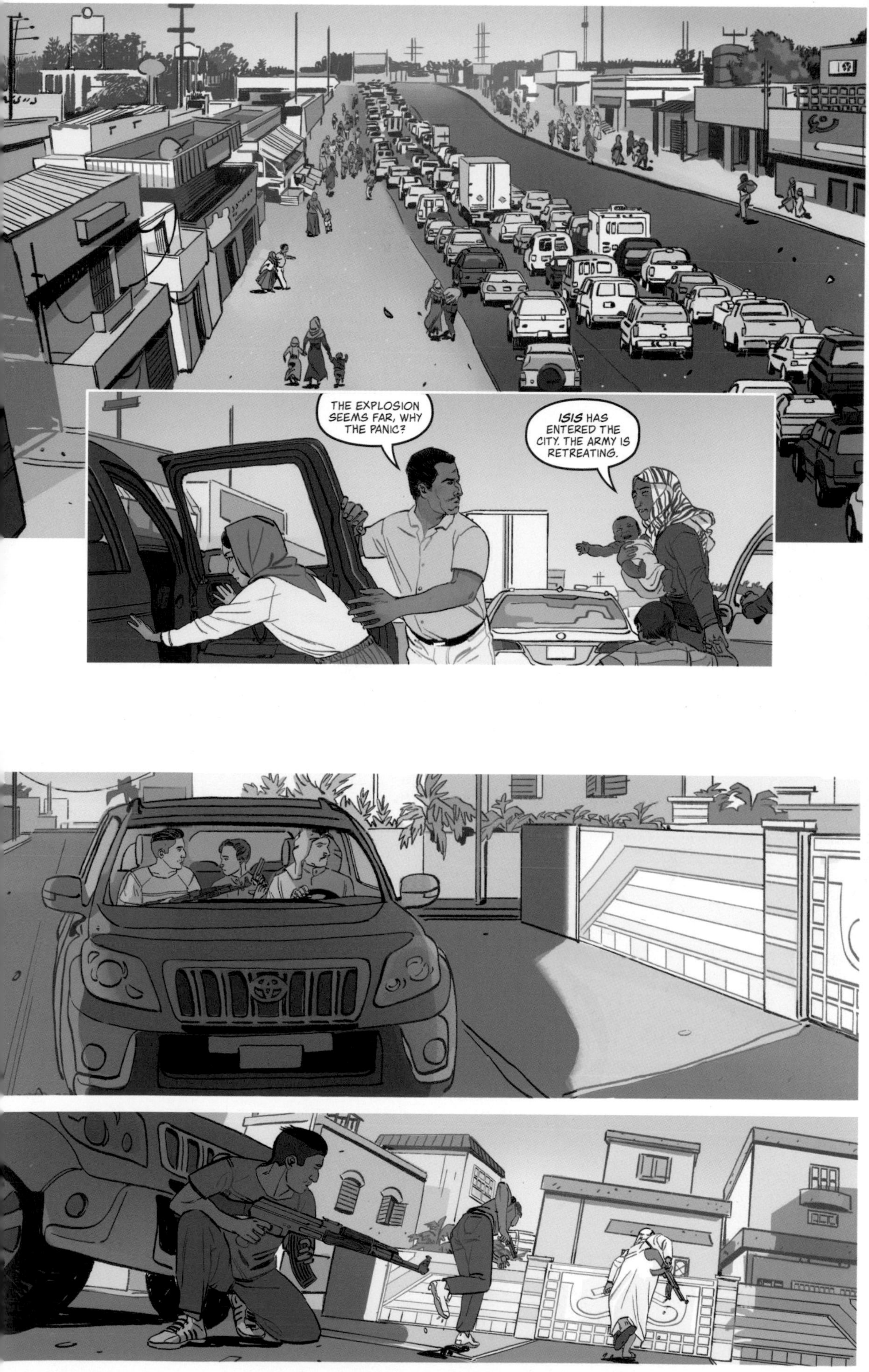
THE EXPLOSION SEEMS FAR, WHY THE PANIC?
ISIS HAS ENTERED THE CITY. THE ARMY IS RETREATING.

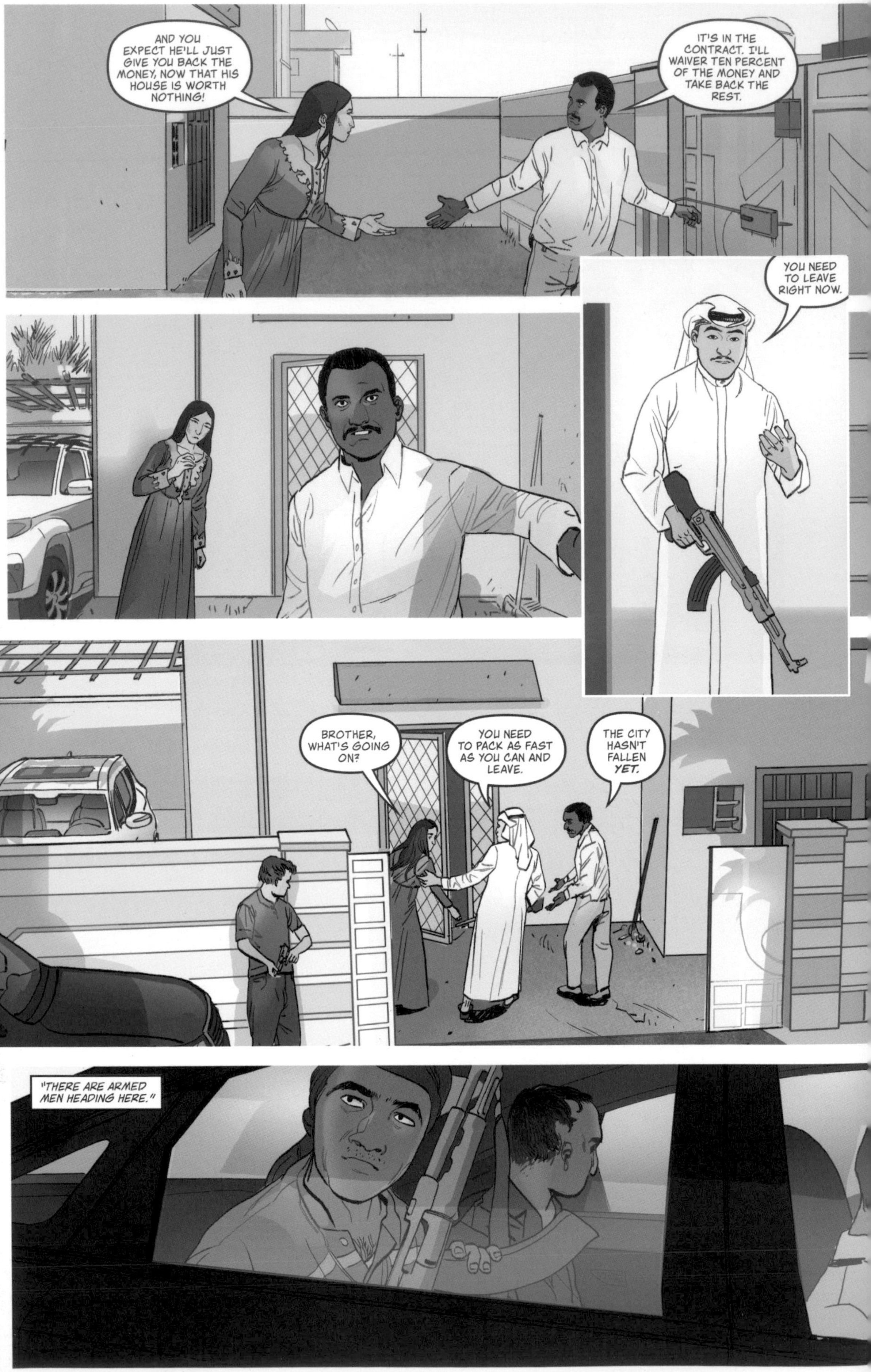
AND YOU EXPECT HE'LL JUST GIVE YOU BACK THE MONEY, NOW THAT HIS HOUSE IS WORTH NOTHING!
IT'S IN THE CONTRACT. I'LL WAIVER TEN PERCENT OF THE MONEY AND TAKE BACK THE REST.
YOU NEED TO LEAVE RIGHT NOW.
BROTHER, WHAT'S GOING ON?
YOU NEED TO PACK AS FAST AS YOU CAN AND LEAVE.
THE CITY HASN'T FALLEN *YET.*
"THERE ARE ARMED MEN HEADING HERE."

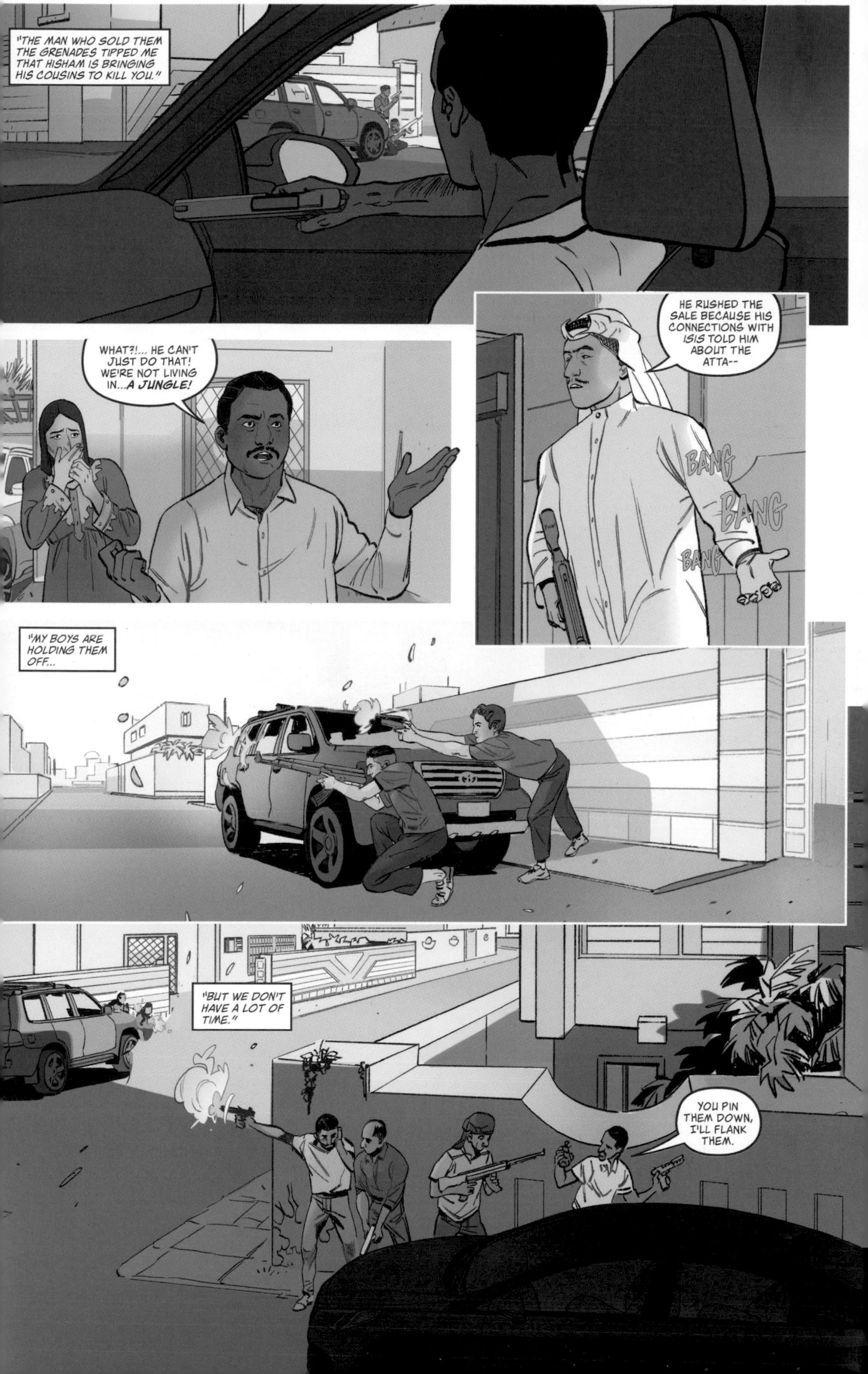
"THE MAN WHO SOLD THEM THE GRENADES TIPPED ME THAT HISHAM IS BRINGING HIS COUSINS TO KILL YOU."
WHAT?!... HE CAN'T JUST DO THAT! WE'RE NOT LIVING IN...A JUNGLE!
HE RUSHED THE SALE BECAUSE HIS CONNECTIONS WITH ISIS TOLD HIM ABOUT THE ATTA--
BANG
BANG
BANG
"MY BOYS ARE HOLDING THEM OFF...
"BUT WE DON'T HAVE A LOT OF TIME."
YOU PIN THEM DOWN, I'LL FLANK THEM.

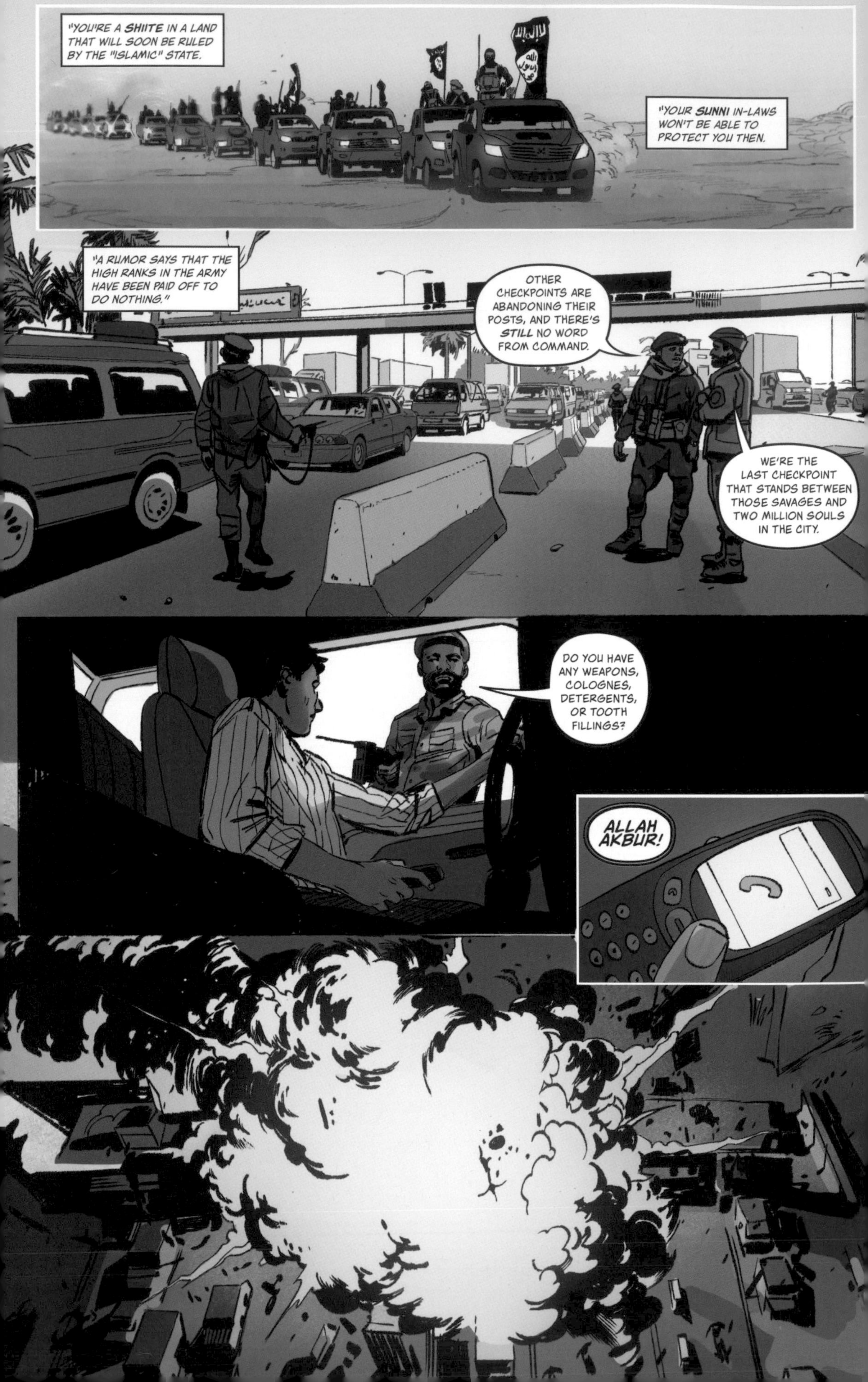
"YOU'RE A SHIITE IN A LAND THAT WILL SOON BE RULED BY THE "ISLAMIC" STATE.
"YOUR SUNNI IN-LAWS WON'T BE ABLE TO PROTECT YOU THEN.
"A RUMOR SAYS THAT THE HIGH RANKS IN THE ARMY HAVE BEEN PAID OFF TO DO NOTHING."
OTHER CHECKPOINTS ARE ABANDONING THEIR POSTS, AND THERE'S STILL NO WORD FROM COMMAND.
WE'RE THE LAST CHECKPOINT THAT STANDS BETWEEN THOSE SAVAGES AND TWO MILLION SOULS IN THE CITY.
DO YOU HAVE ANY WEAPONS, COLOGNES, DETERGENTS, OR TOOTH FILLINGS?
ALLAH AKBUR!

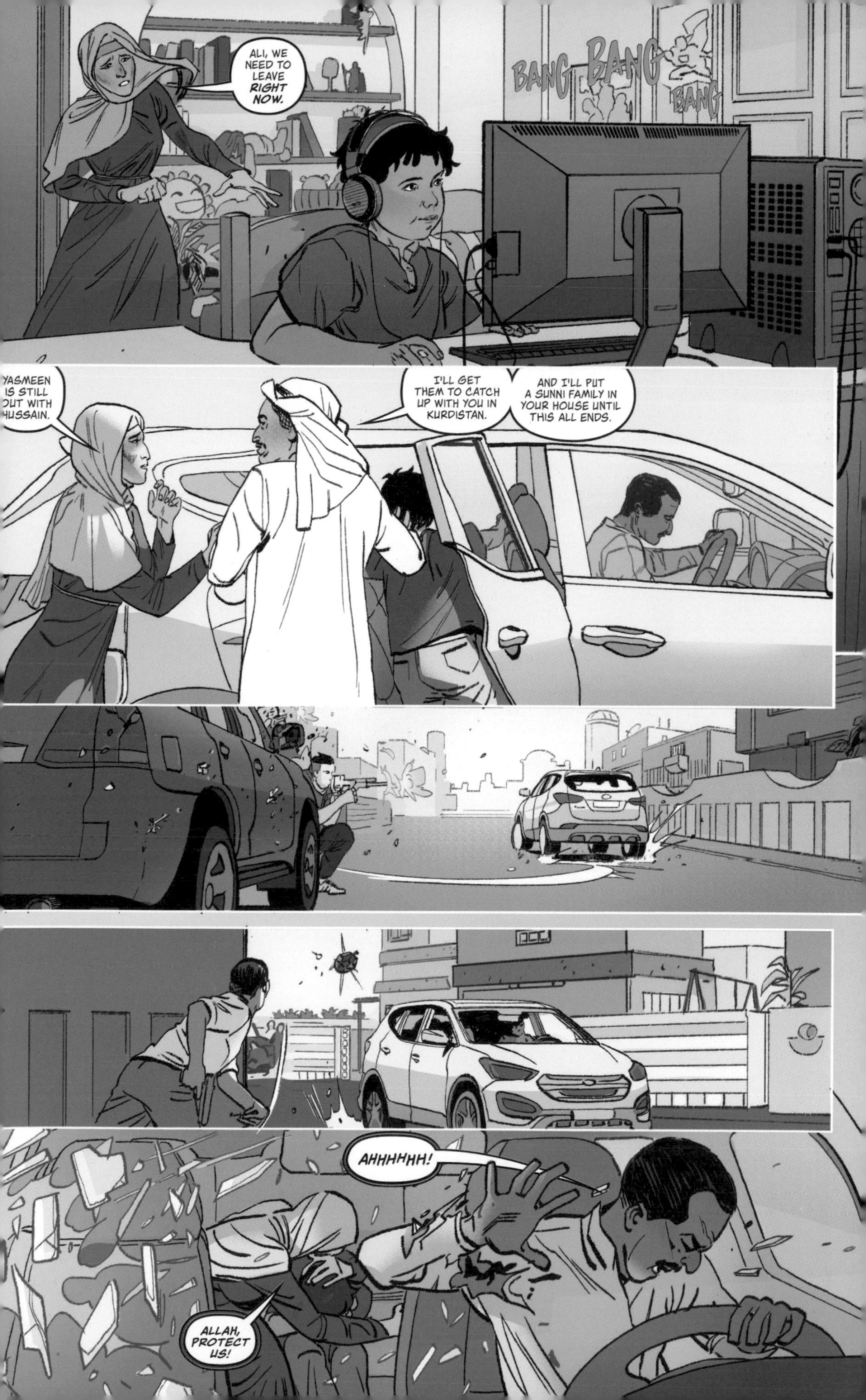
ALI, WE NEED TO LEAVE RIGHT NOW.
BANG BANG BANG
YASMEEN IS STILL OUT WITH HUSSAIN.
I'LL GET THEM TO CATCH UP WITH YOU IN KURDISTAN.
AND I'LL PUT A SUNNI FAMILY IN YOUR HOUSE UNTIL THIS ALL ENDS.
AHHHHHH!
ALLAH, PROTECT US!

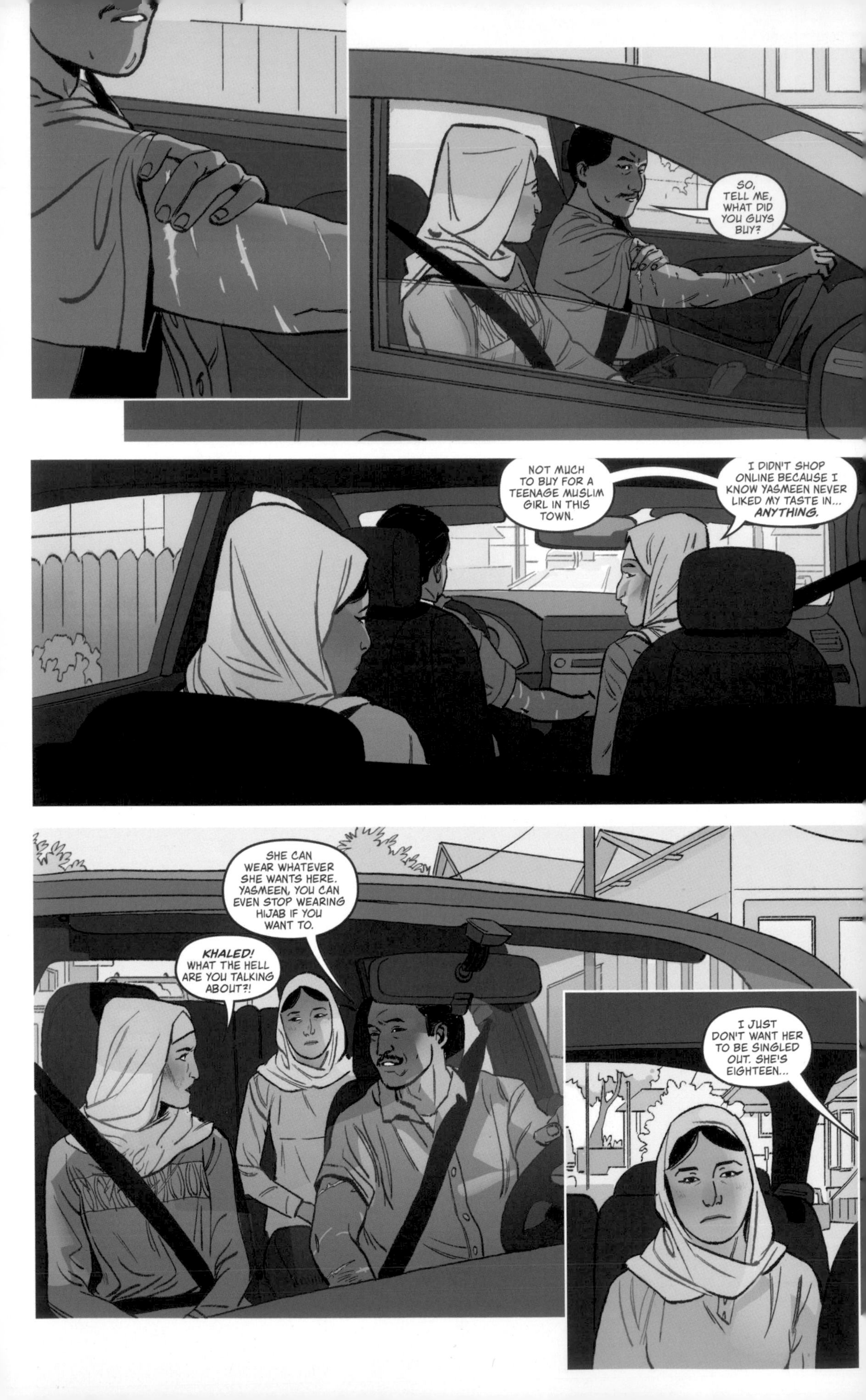
SO, TELL ME, WHAT DID YOU GUYS BUY?
NOT MUCH TO BUY FOR A TEENAGE MUSLIM GIRL IN THIS TOWN.
I DIDN'T SHOP ONLINE BECAUSE I KNOW YASMEEN NEVER LIKED MY TASTE IN... ANYTHING.
SHE CAN WEAR WHATEVER SHE WANTS HERE. YASMEEN, YOU CAN EVEN STOP WEARING HIJAB IF YOU WANT TO.
KHALED! WHAT THE HELL ARE YOU TALKING ABOUT?!
I JUST DON'T WANT HER TO BE SINGLED OUT. SHE'S EIGHTEEN...

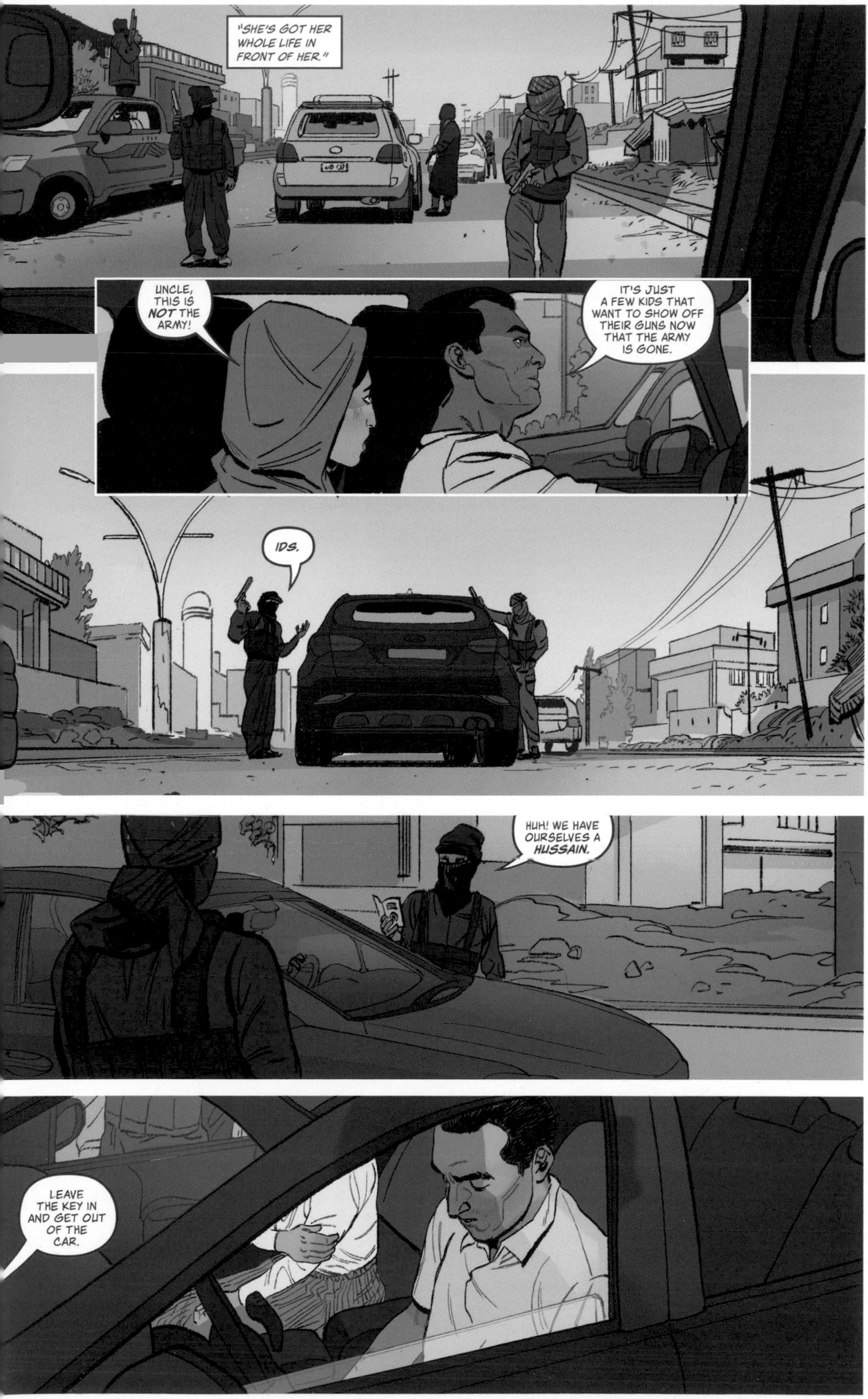
"SHE'S GOT HER WHOLE LIFE IN FRONT OF HER."
UNCLE, THIS IS NOT THE ARMY!
IT'S JUST A FEW KIDS THAT WANT TO SHOW OFF THEIR GUNS NOW THAT THE ARMY IS GONE.
IDS.
HUH! WE HAVE OURSELVES A HUSSAIN.
LEAVE THE KEY IN AND GET OUT OF THE CAR.

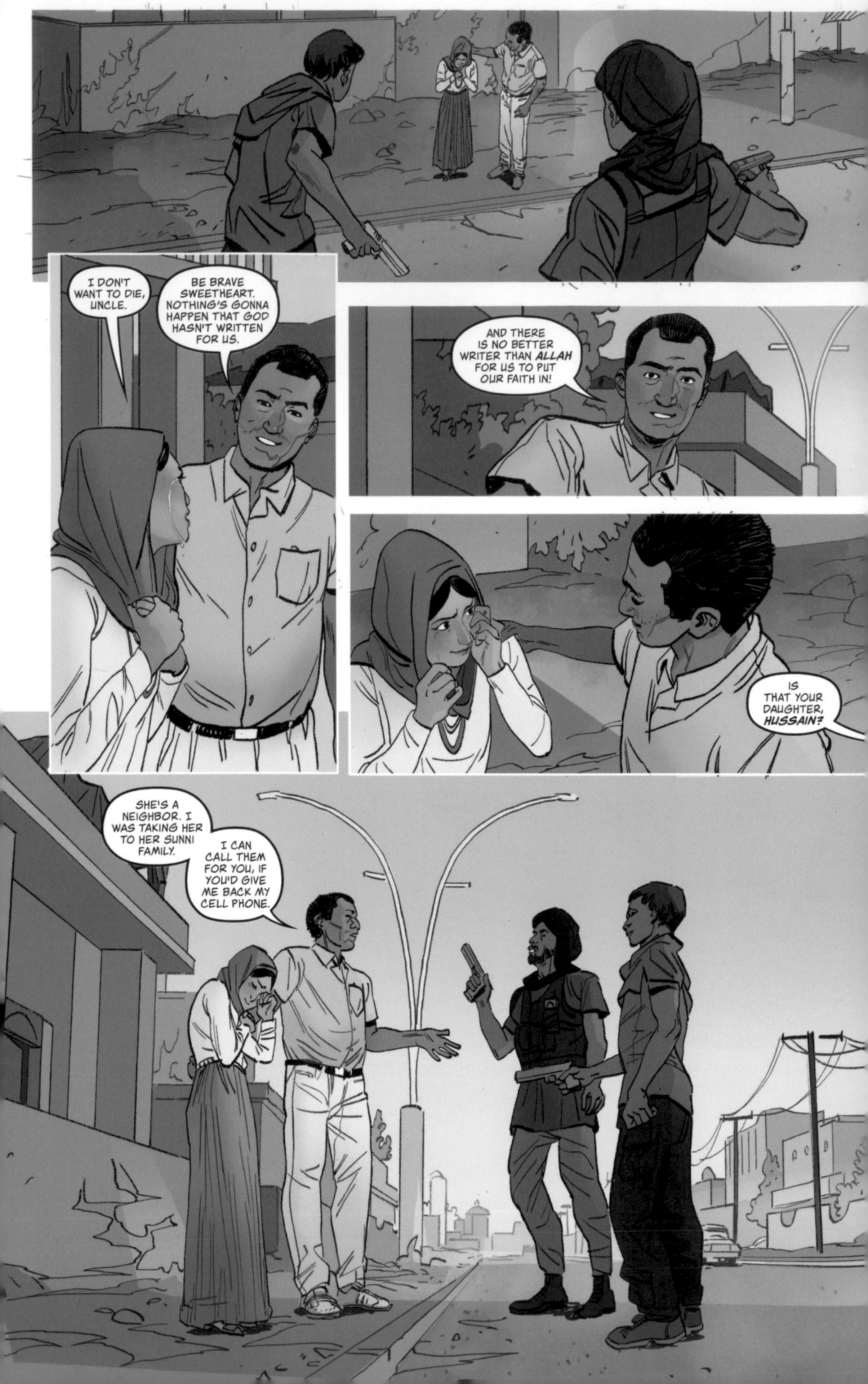
I DON'T WANT TO DIE, UNCLE.
BE BRAVE SWEETHEART. NOTHING'S GONNA HAPPEN THAT GOD HASN'T WRITTEN FOR US.
AND THERE IS NO BETTER WRITER THAN ALLAH FOR US TO PUT OUR FAITH IN!
IS THAT YOUR DAUGHTER, HUSSAIN?
SHE'S A NEIGHBOR. I WAS TAKING HER TO HER SUNNI FAMILY.
I CAN CALL THEM FOR YOU, IF YOU'D GIVE ME BACK MY CELL PHONE.

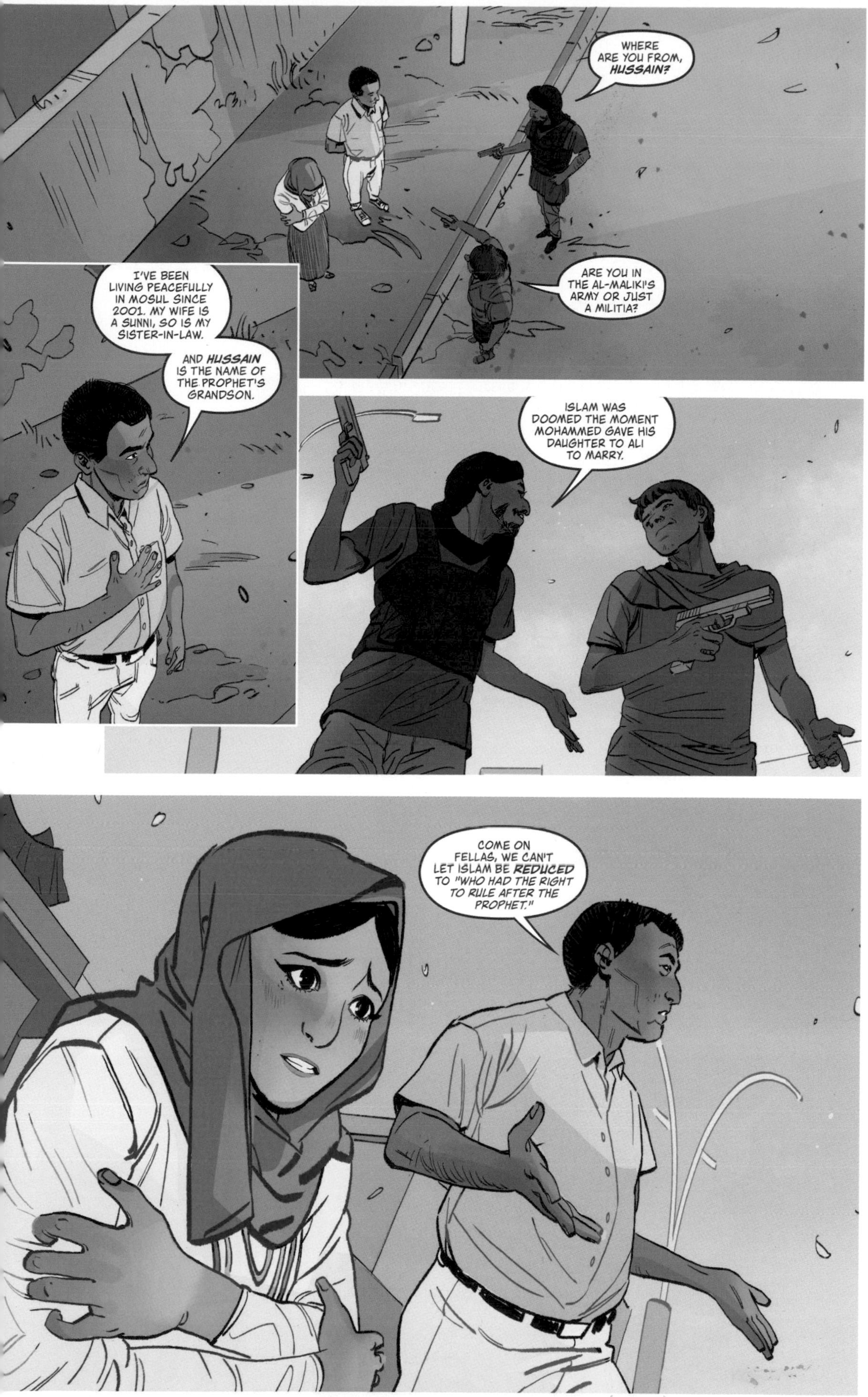
WHERE ARE YOU FROM, *HUSSAIN?*
ARE YOU IN THE AL-MALIKI'S ARMY OR JUST A MILITIA?
I'VE BEEN LIVING PEACEFULLY IN MOSUL SINCE 2001. MY WIFE IS A SUNNI, SO IS MY SISTER-IN-LAW.
AND *HUSSAIN* IS THE NAME OF THE PROPHET'S GRANDSON.
ISLAM WAS DOOMED THE MOMENT MOHAMMED GAVE HIS DAUGHTER TO ALI TO MARRY.
COME ON FELLAS, WE CAN'T LET ISLAM BE *REDUCED* TO "WHO HAD THE RIGHT TO RULE AFTER THE PROPHET."

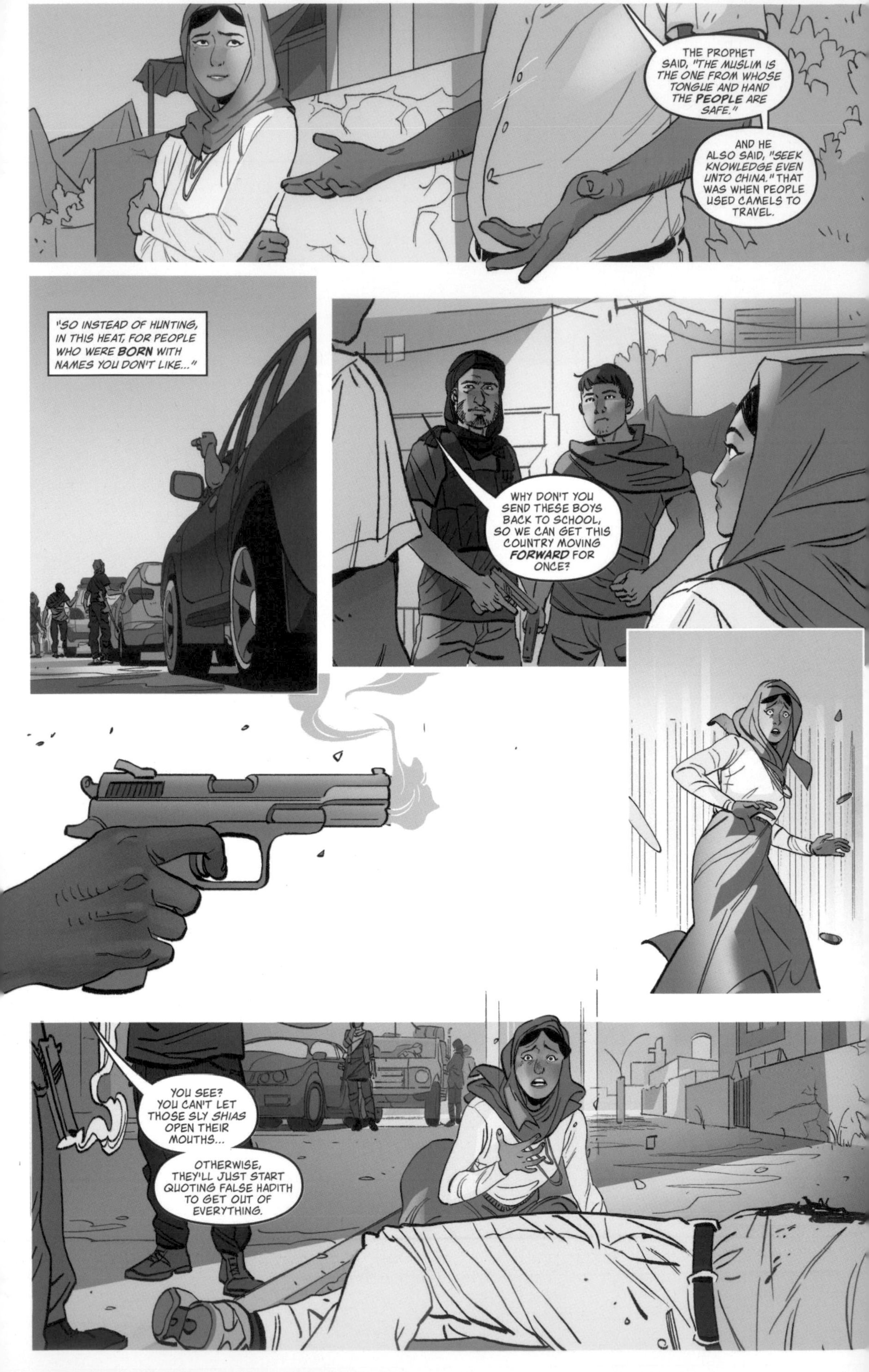
THE PROPHET SAID, "THE MUSLIM IS THE ONE FROM WHOSE TONGUE AND HAND THE PEOPLE ARE SAFE."
AND HE ALSO SAID, "SEEK KNOWLEDGE EVEN UNTO CHINA." THAT WAS WHEN PEOPLE USED CAMELS TO TRAVEL.
"SO INSTEAD OF HUNTING, IN THIS HEAT, FOR PEOPLE WHO WERE BORN WITH NAMES YOU DON'T LIKE..."
WHY DON'T YOU SEND THESE BOYS BACK TO SCHOOL, SO WE CAN GET THIS COUNTRY MOVING FORWARD FOR ONCE?
YOU SEE? YOU CAN'T LET THOSE SLY SHIAS OPEN THEIR MOUTHS...
OTHERWISE, THEY'LL JUST START QUOTING FALSE HADITH TO GET OUT OF EVERYTHING.

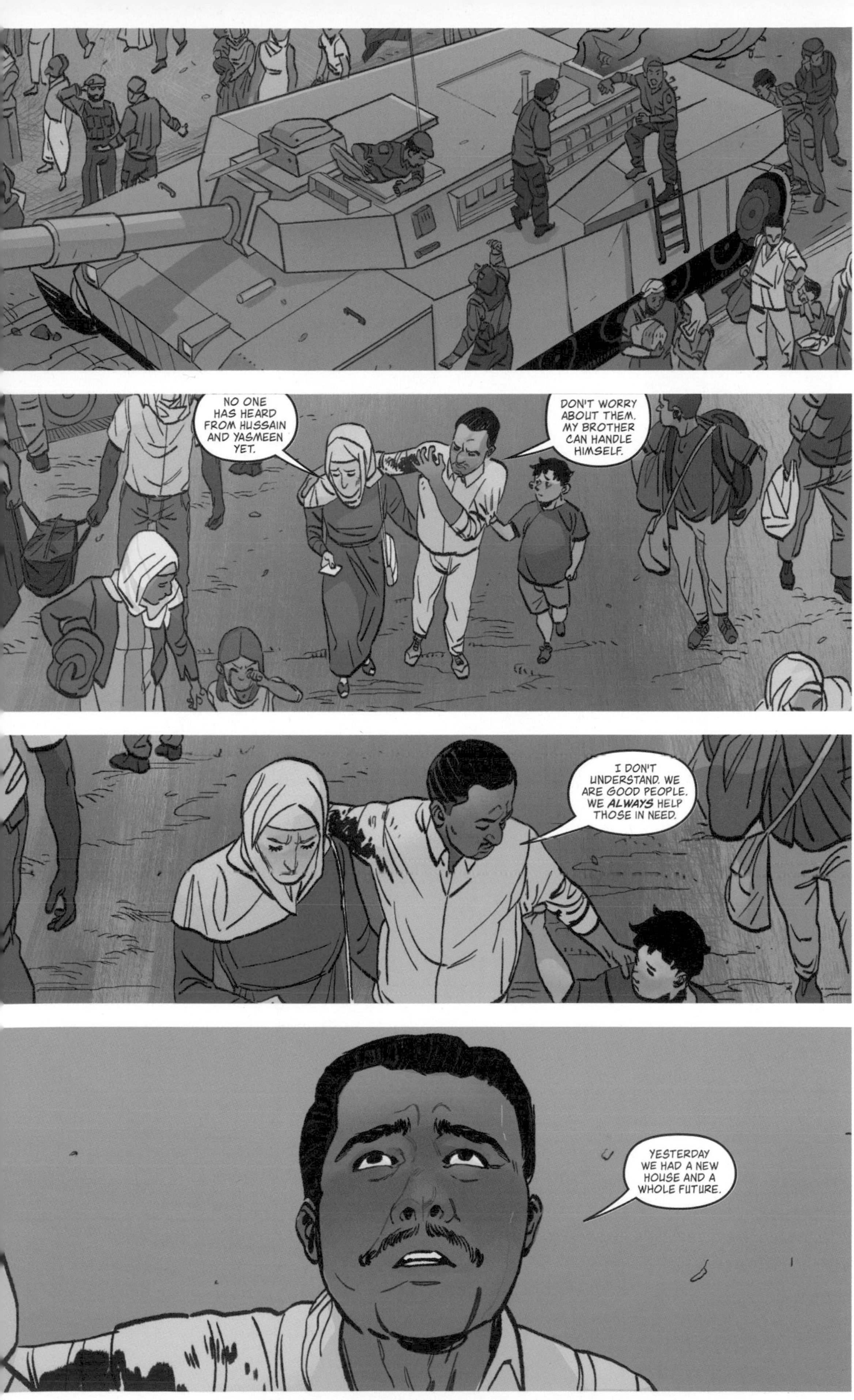
NO ONE HAS HEARD FROM HUSSAIN AND YASMEEN YET.
DON'T WORRY ABOUT THEM. MY BROTHER CAN HANDLE HIMSELF.
I DON'T UNDERSTAND. WE ARE GOOD PEOPLE. WE *ALWAYS* HELP THOSE IN NEED.
YESTERDAY WE HAD A NEW HOUSE AND A WHOLE FUTURE.

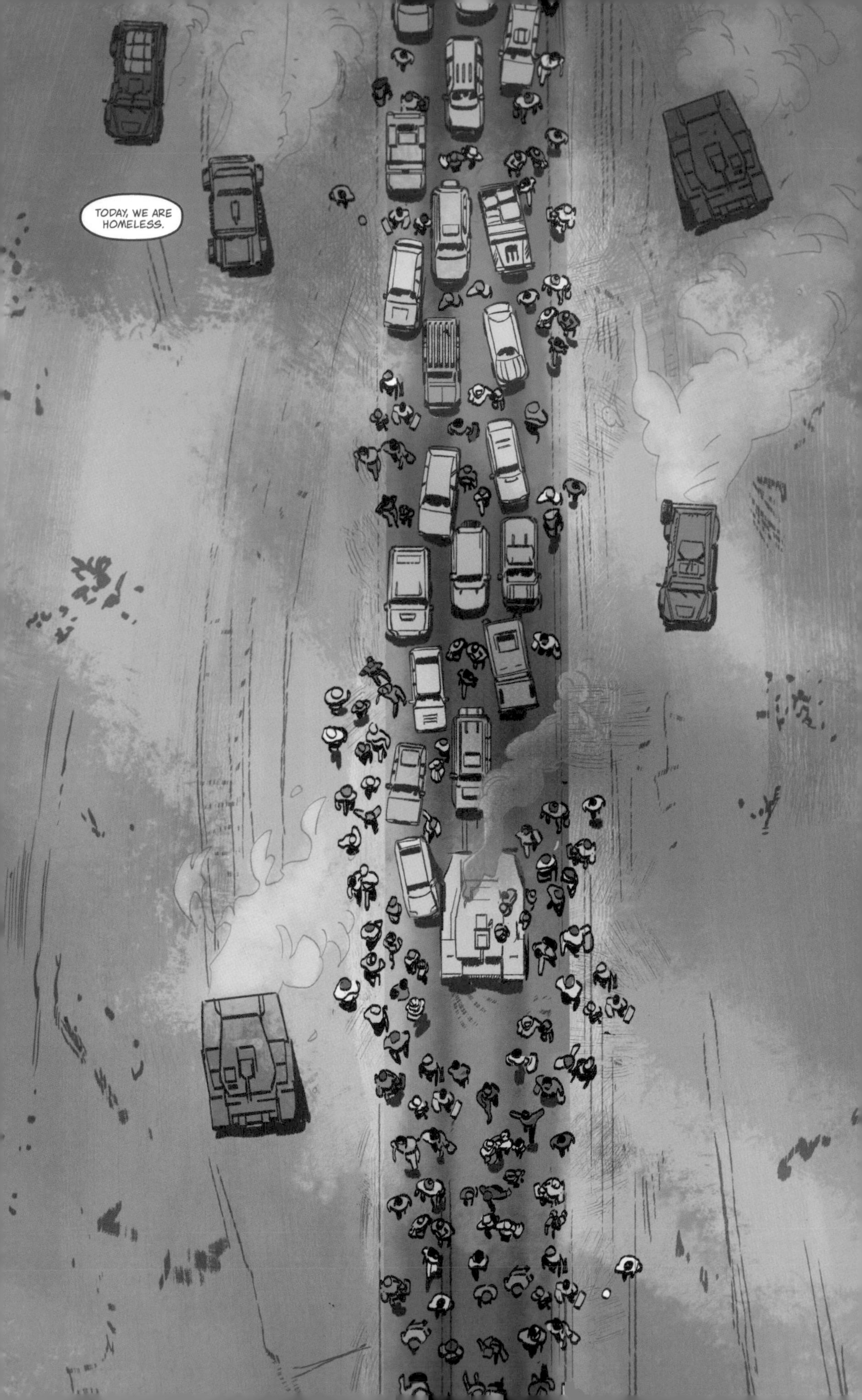
TODAY, WE ARE HOMELESS.

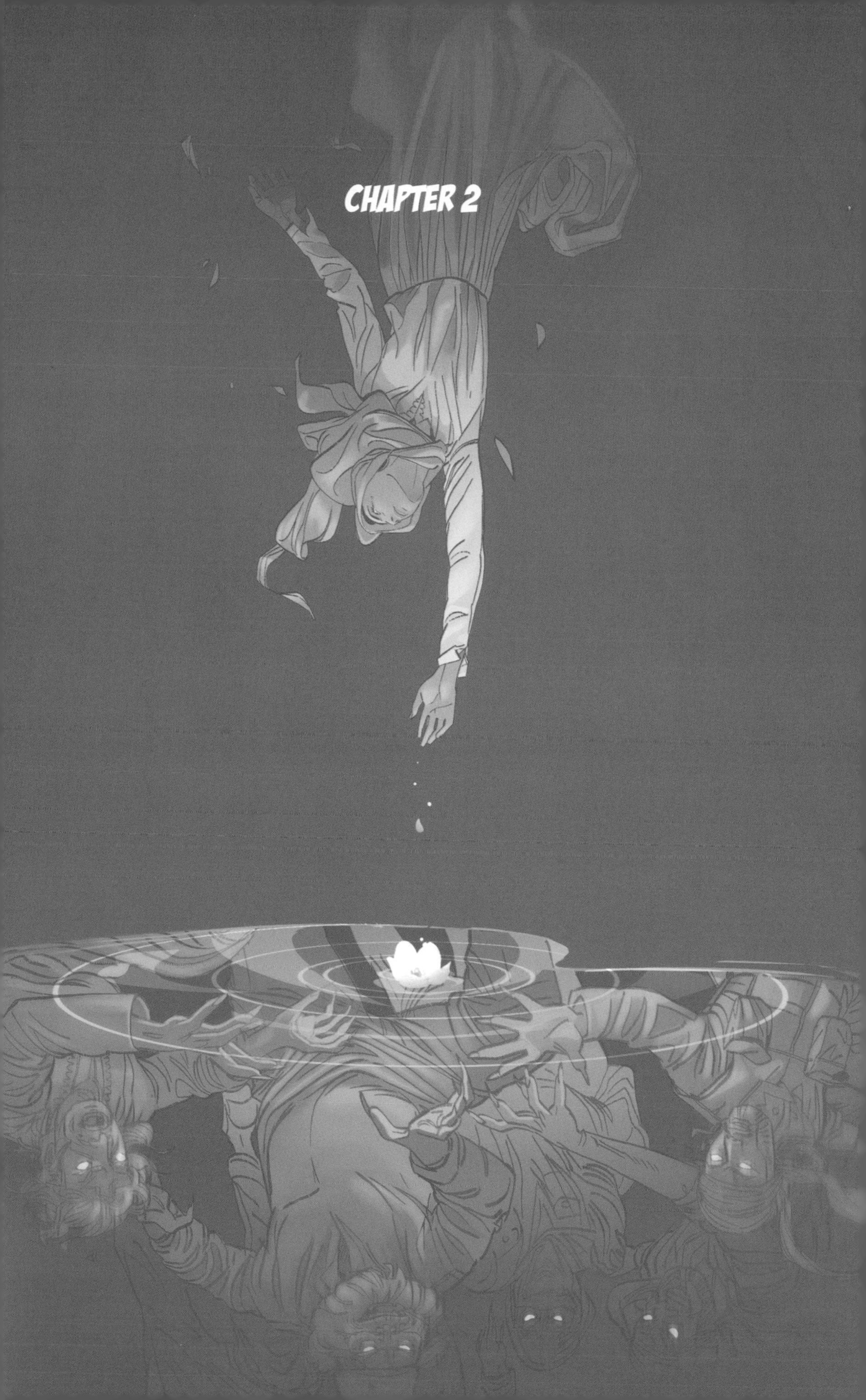
CHAPTER 2

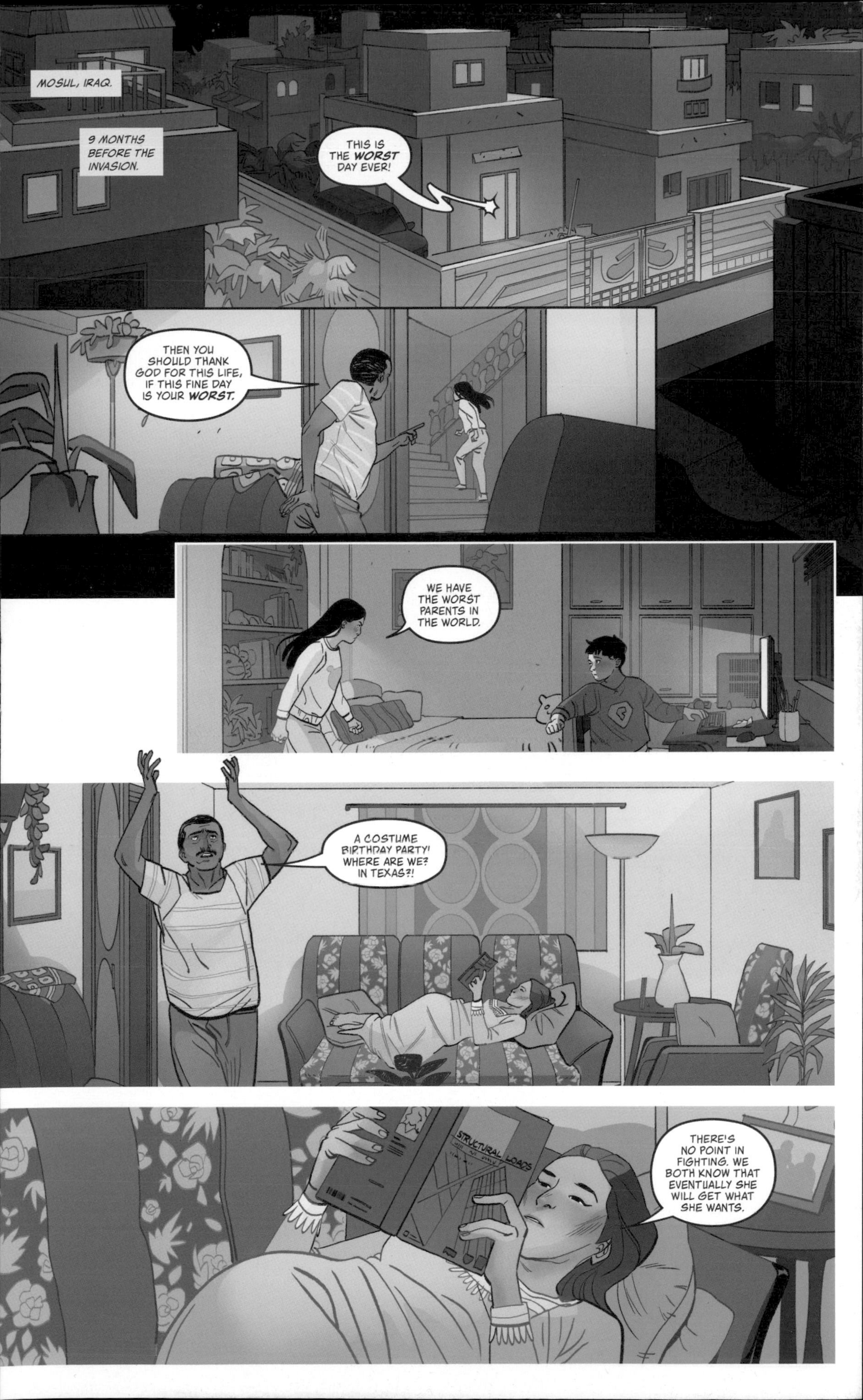
MOSUL, IRAQ.
9 MONTHS BEFORE THE INVASION.
THIS IS THE WORST DAY EVER!
THEN YOU SHOULD THANK GOD FOR THIS LIFE, IF THIS FINE DAY IS YOUR WORST.
WE HAVE THE WORST PARENTS IN THE WORLD.
A COSTUME BIRTHDAY PARTY! WHERE ARE WE? IN TEXAS?!
STRUCTURAL LOADS
THERE'S NO POINT IN FIGHTING. WE BOTH KNOW THAT EVENTUALLY SHE WILL GET WHAT SHE WANTS.

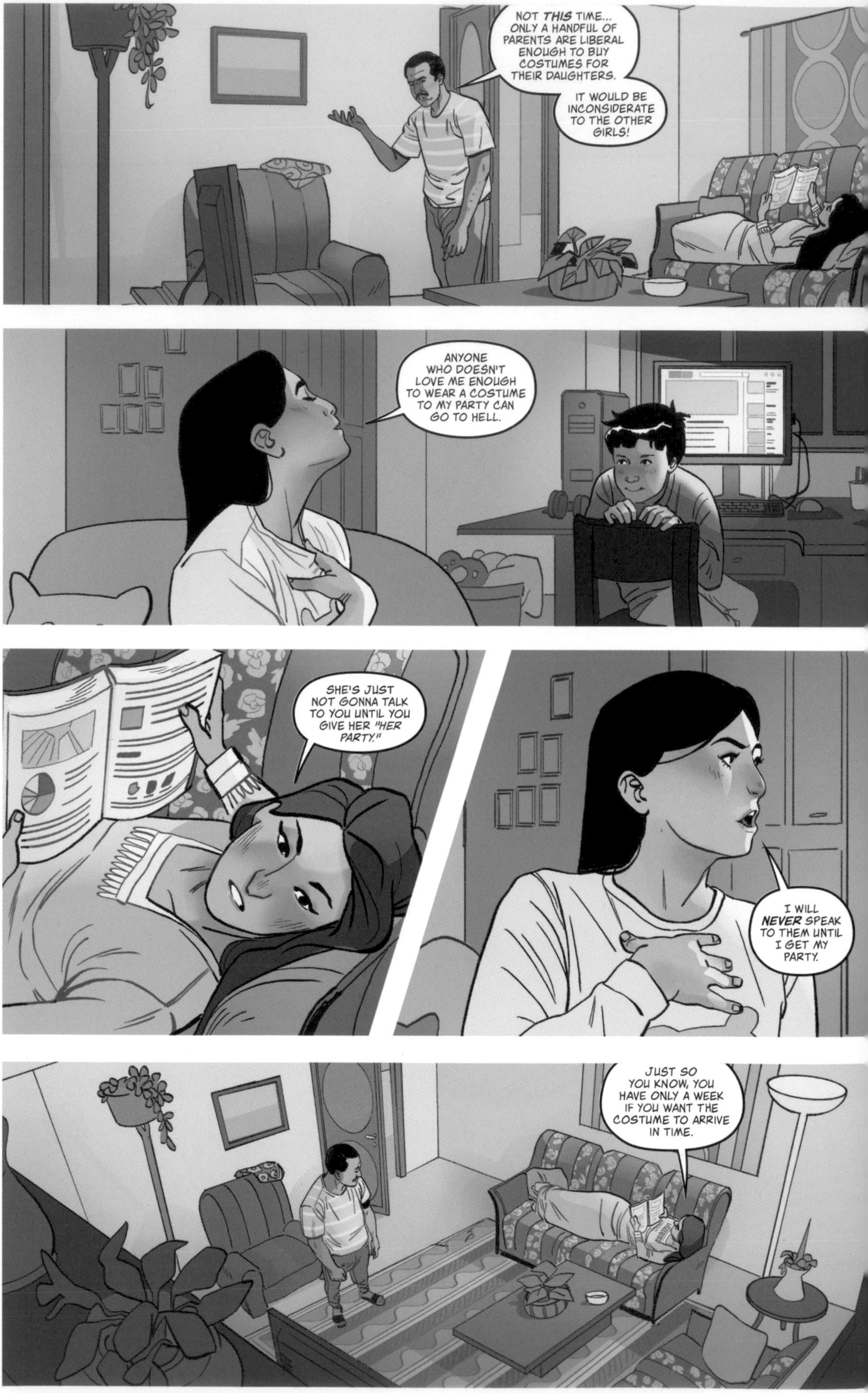
NOT *THIS* TIME... ONLY A HANDFUL OF PARENTS ARE LIBERAL ENOUGH TO BUY COSTUMES FOR THEIR DAUGHTERS.
IT WOULD BE INCONSIDERATE TO THE OTHER GIRLS!
ANYONE WHO DOESN'T LOVE ME ENOUGH TO WEAR A COSTUME TO MY PARTY CAN GO TO HELL.
SHE'S JUST NOT GONNA TALK TO YOU UNTIL YOU GIVE HER *"HER PARTY."*
I WILL *NEVER* SPEAK TO THEM UNTIL I GET MY PARTY.
JUST SO YOU KNOW, YOU HAVE ONLY A WEEK IF YOU WANT THE COSTUME TO ARRIVE IN TIME.

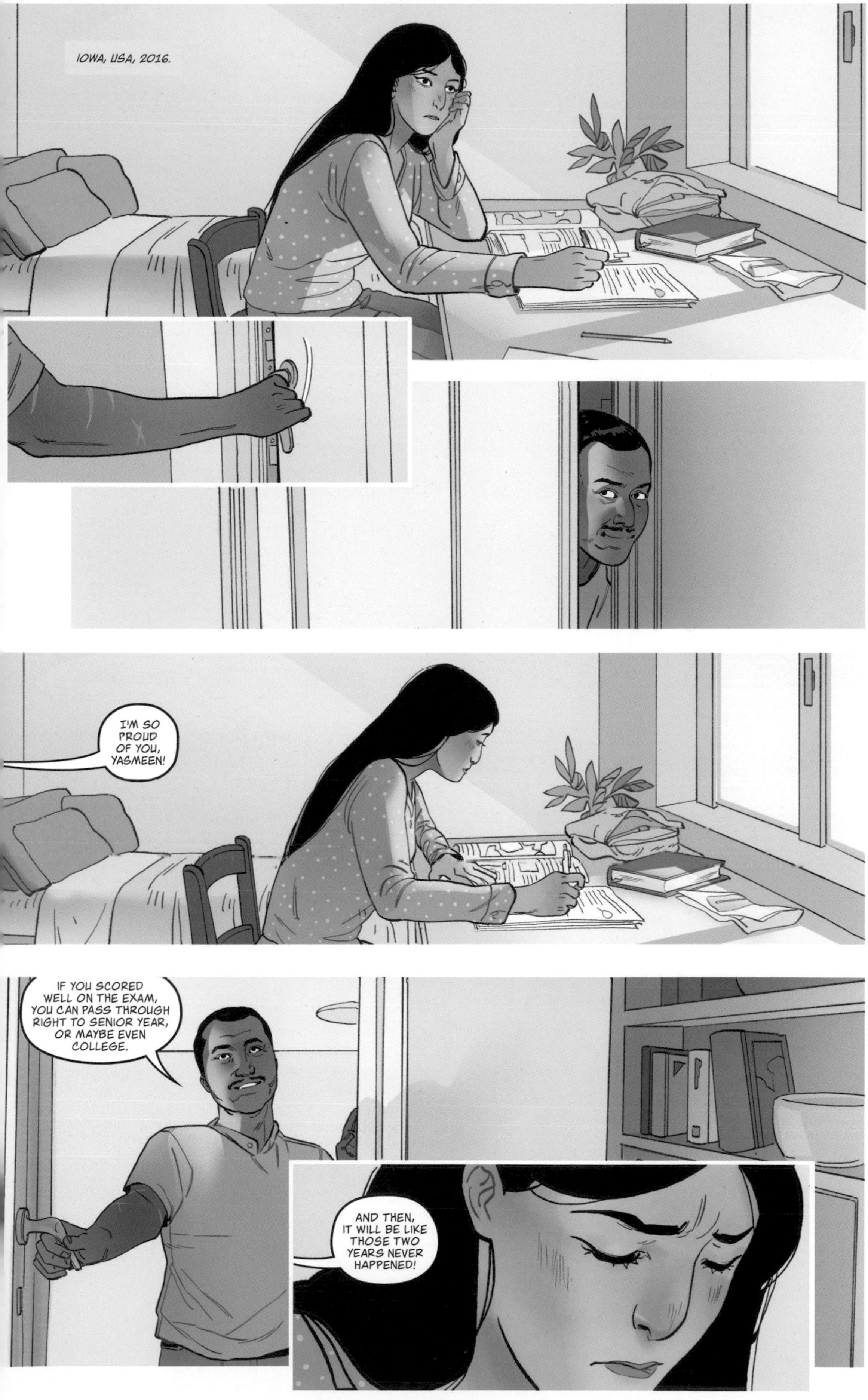
IOWA, USA, 2016.
I'M SO PROUD OF YOU, YASMEEN!
IF YOU SCORED WELL ON THE EXAM, YOU CAN PASS THROUGH RIGHT TO SENIOR YEAR, OR MAYBE EVEN COLLEGE.
AND THEN, IT WILL BE LIKE THOSE TWO YEARS NEVER HAPPENED!

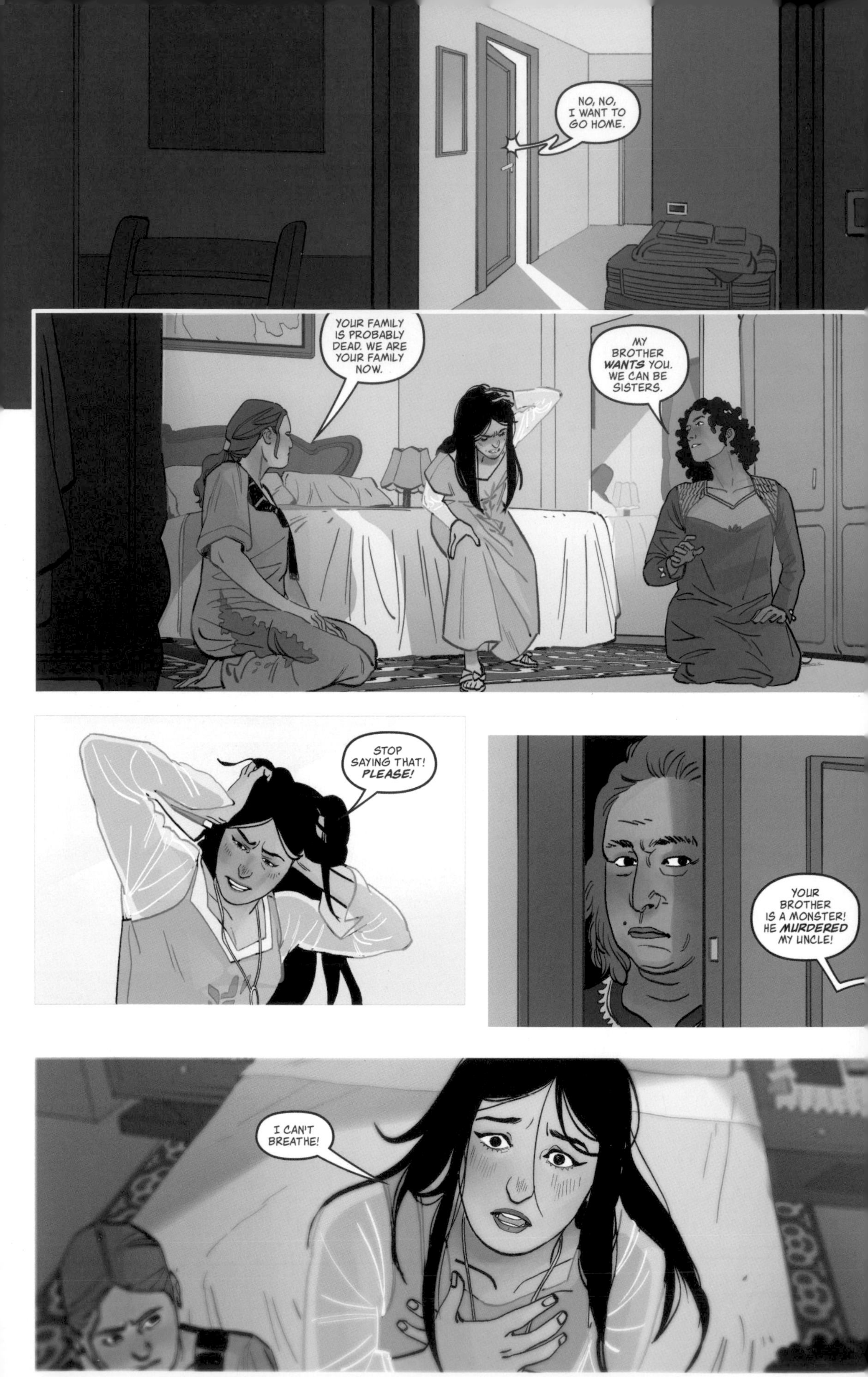
NO, NO, I WANT TO GO HOME.
YOUR FAMILY IS PROBABLY DEAD. WE ARE YOUR FAMILY NOW.
MY BROTHER WANTS YOU. WE CAN BE SISTERS.
STOP SAYING THAT! PLEASE!
YOUR BROTHER IS A MONSTER! HE MURDERED MY UNCLE!
I CAN'T BREATHE!

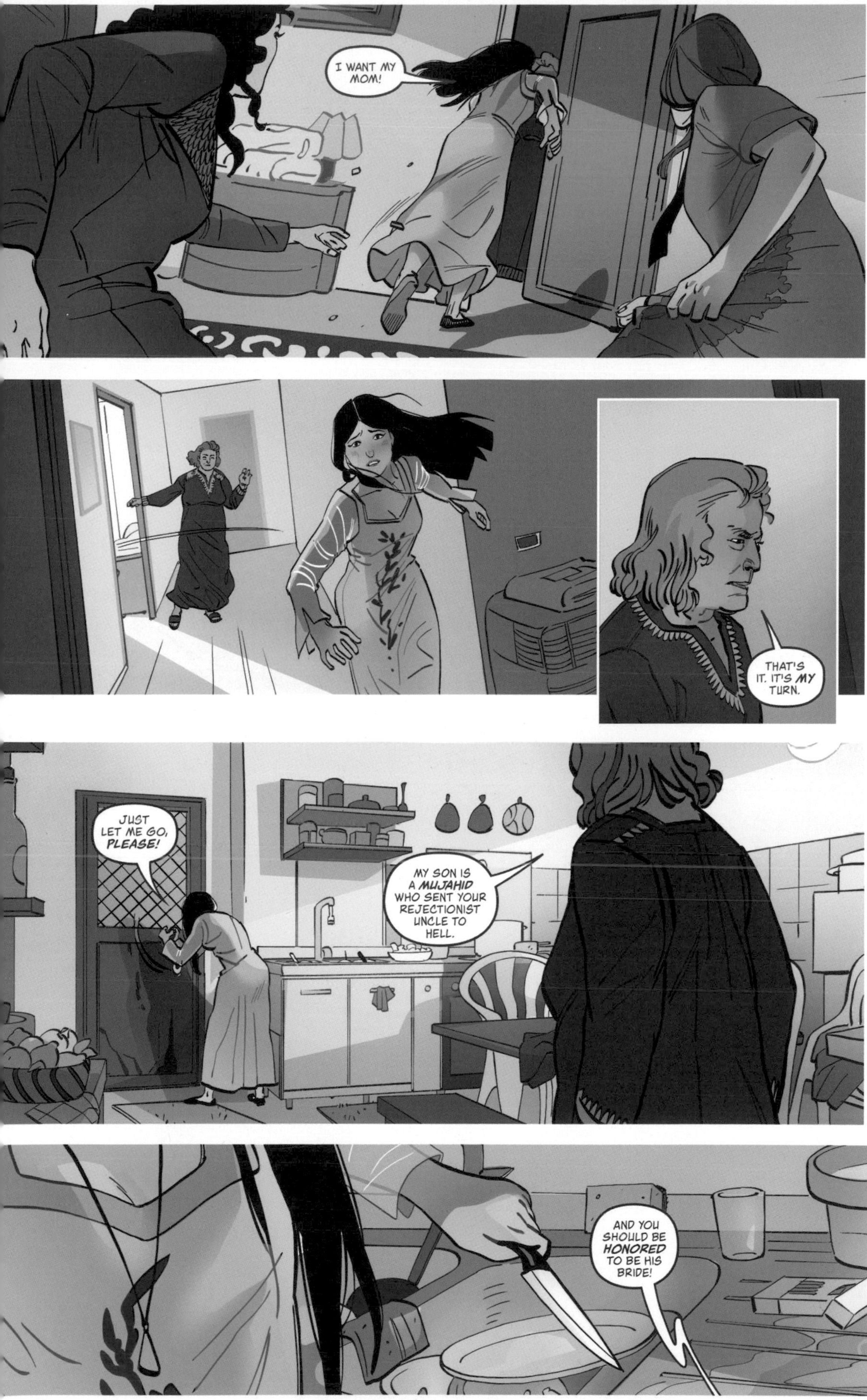
I WANT MY MOM!
THAT'S IT. IT'S MY TURN.
JUST LET ME GO, PLEASE!
MY SON IS A MUJAHID WHO SENT YOUR REJECTIONIST UNCLE TO HELL.
AND YOU SHOULD BE HONORED TO BE HIS BRIDE!

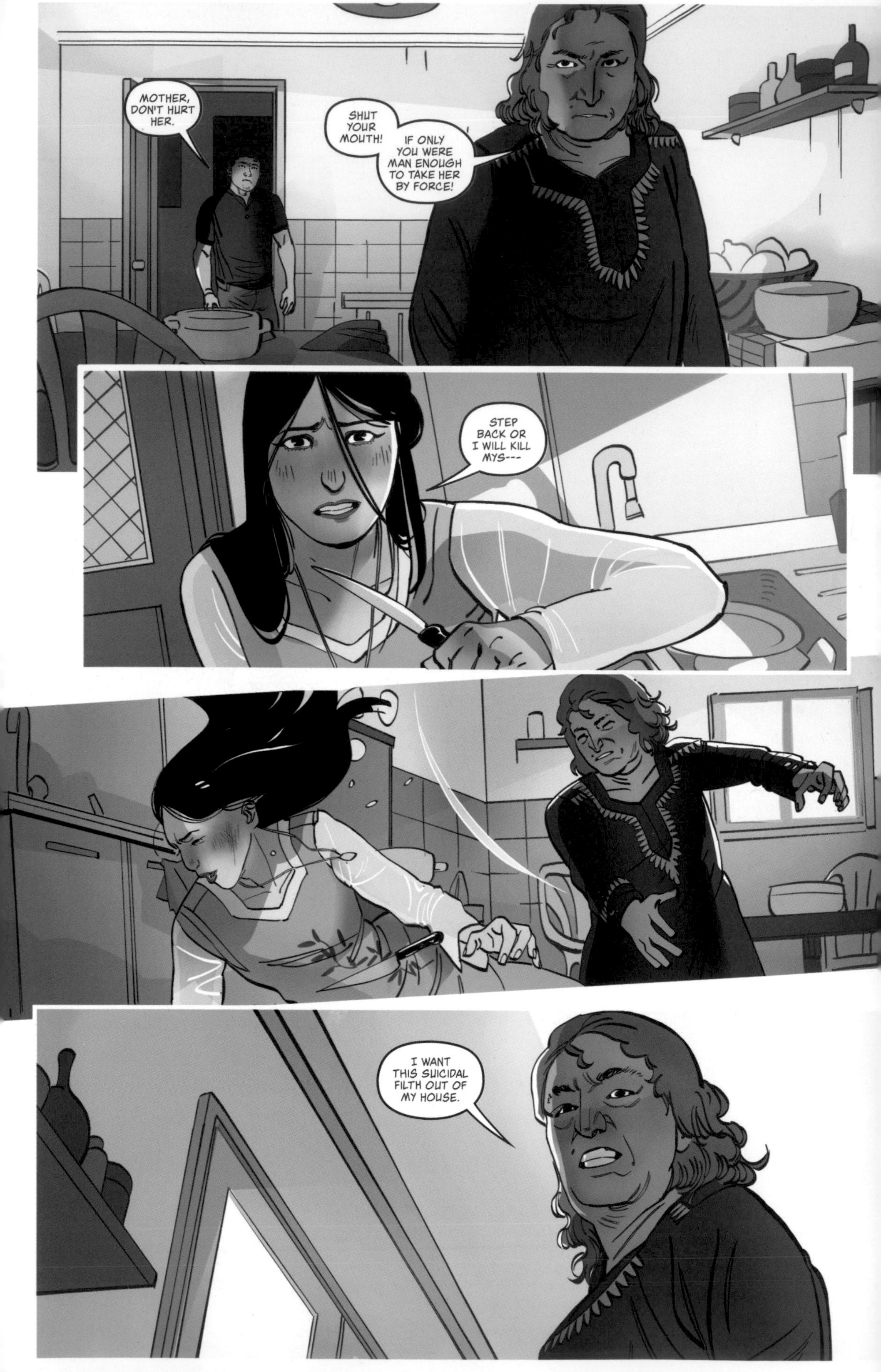
MOTHER, DON'T HURT HER.
SHUT YOUR MOUTH!
IF ONLY YOU WERE MAN ENOUGH TO TAKE HER BY FORCE!
STEP BACK OR I WILL KILL MYS---
I WANT THIS SUICIDAL FILTH OUT OF MY HOUSE.

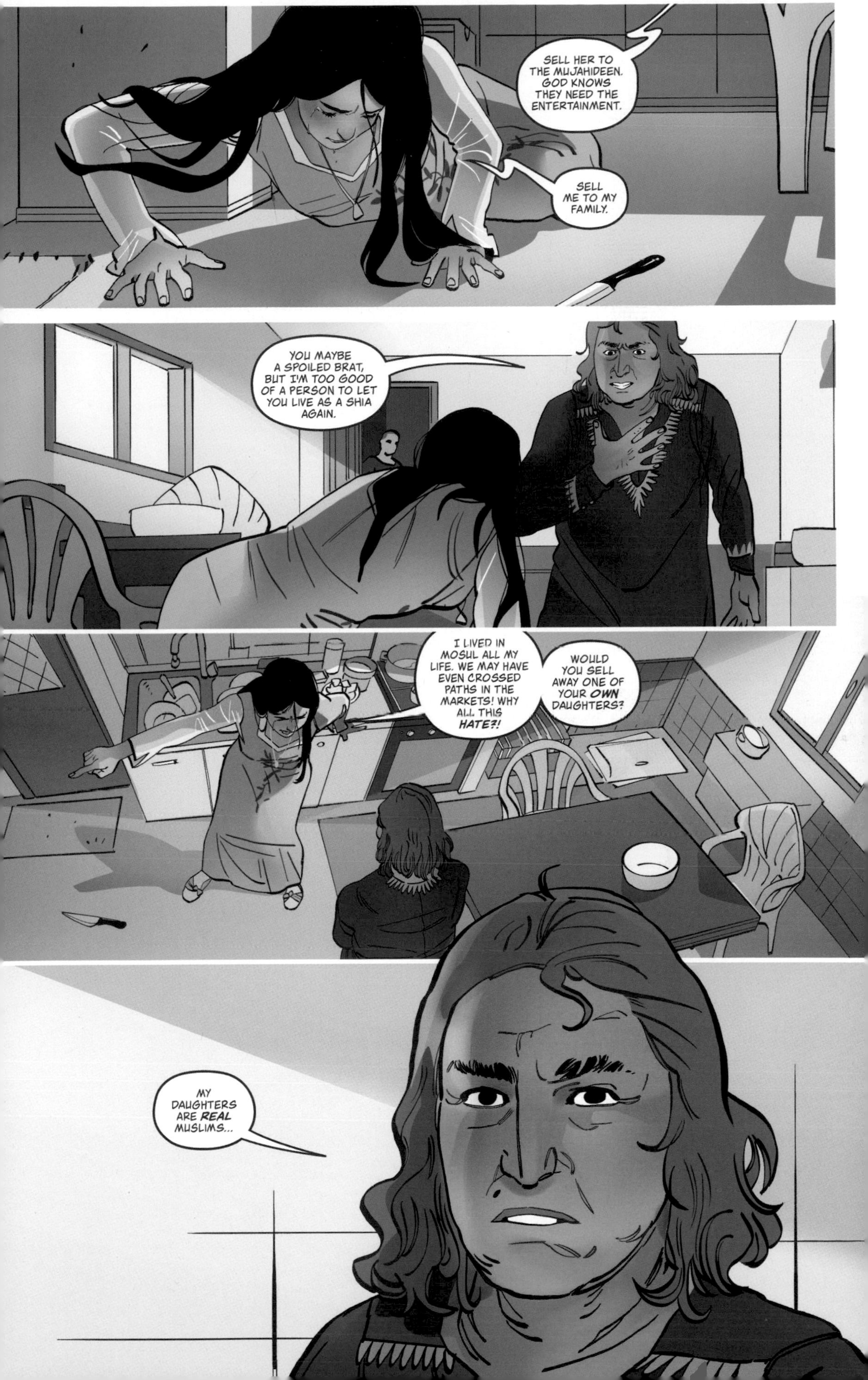
SELL HER TO THE MUJAHIDEEN. GOD KNOWS THEY NEED THE ENTERTAINMENT.
SELL ME TO MY FAMILY.
YOU MAYBE A SPOILED BRAT, BUT I'M TOO GOOD OF A PERSON TO LET YOU LIVE AS A SHIA AGAIN.
I LIVED IN MOSUL ALL MY LIFE. WE MAY HAVE EVEN CROSSED PATHS IN THE MARKETS! WHY ALL THIS HATE?!
WOULD YOU SELL AWAY ONE OF YOUR OWN DAUGHTERS?
MY DAUGHTERS ARE REAL MUSLIMS...

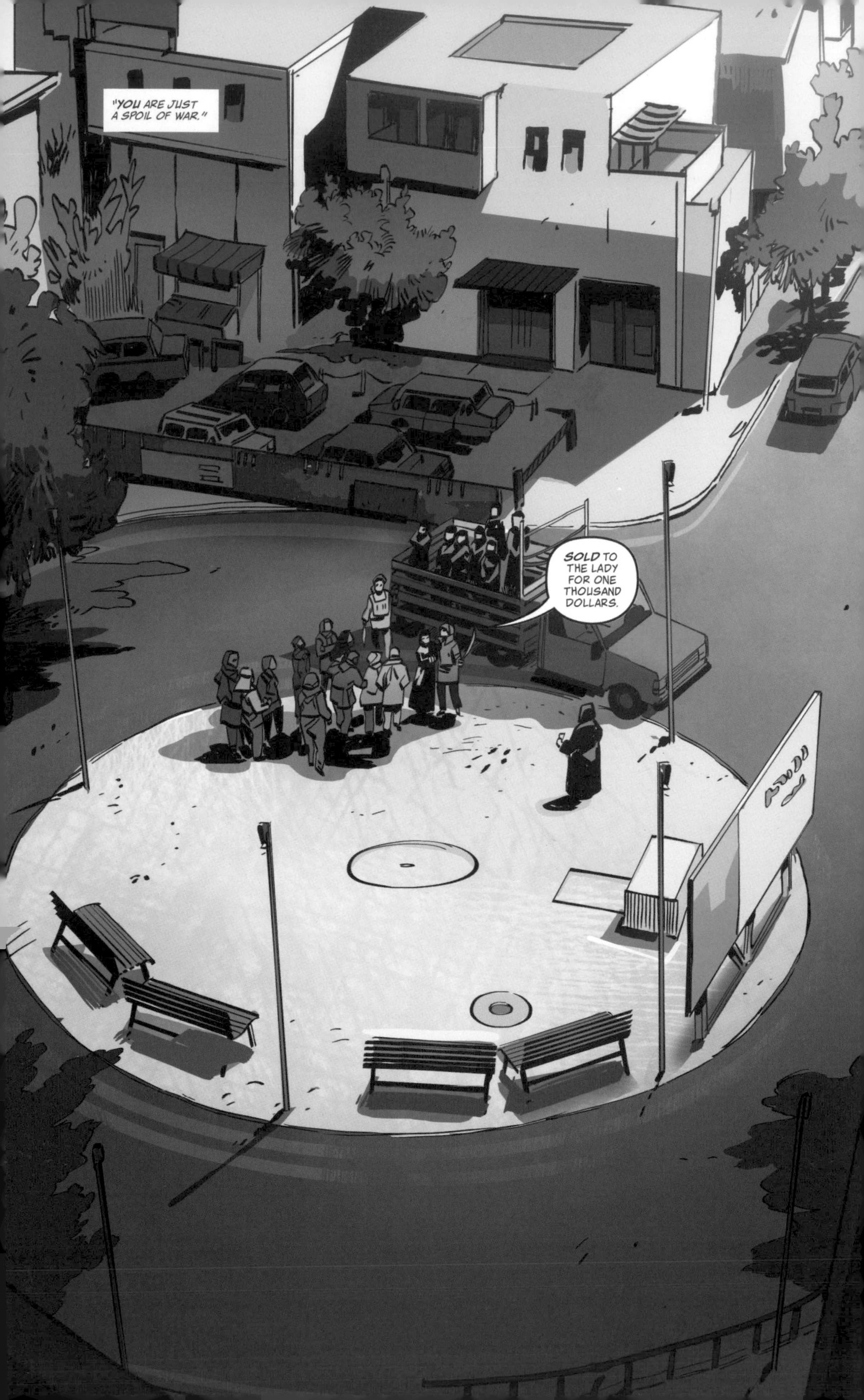
"YOU ARE JUST A SPOIL OF WAR."
SOLD TO THE LADY FOR ONE THOUSAND DOLLARS.

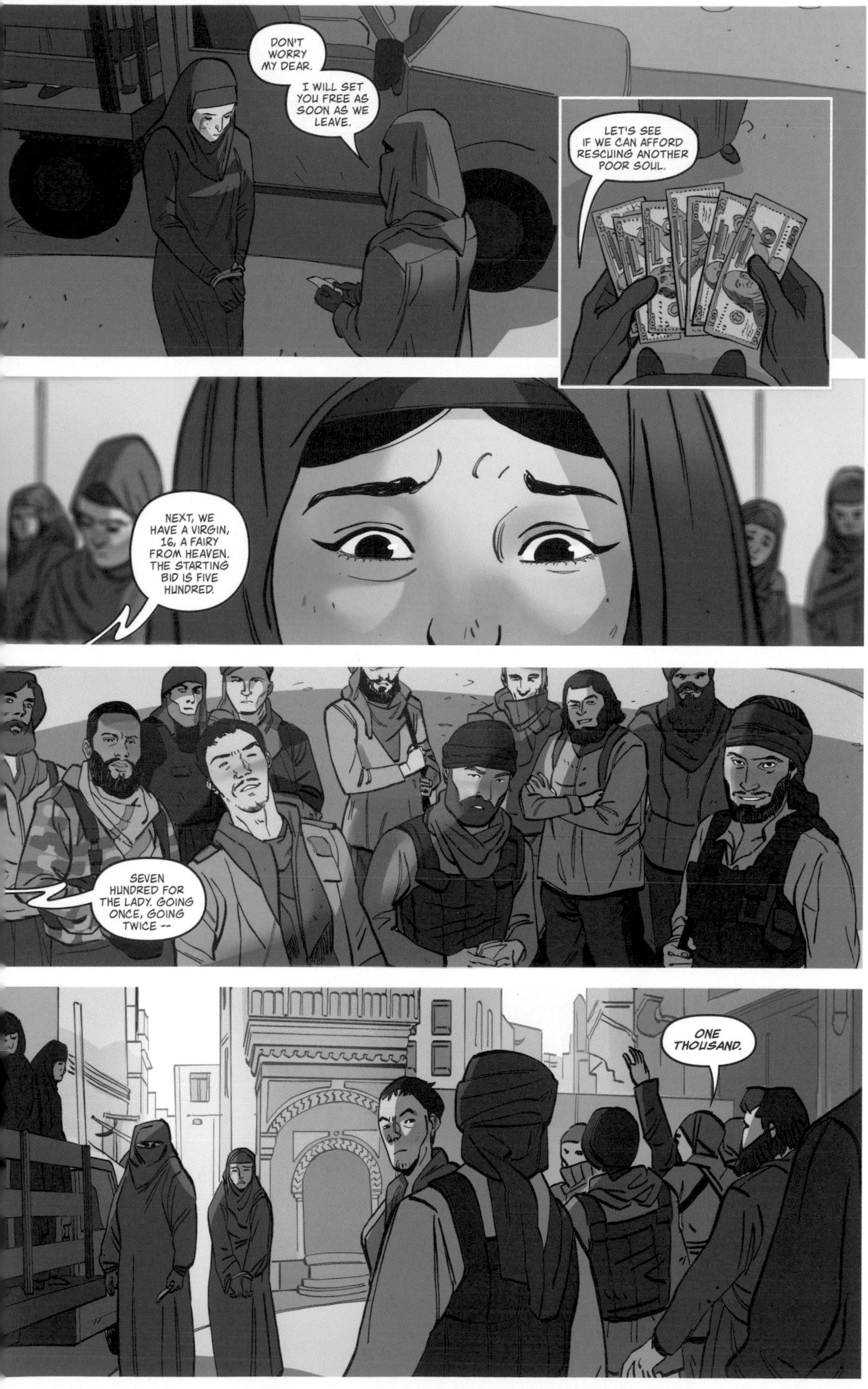
DON'T WORRY MY DEAR.
I WILL SET YOU FREE AS SOON AS WE LEAVE.
LET'S SEE IF WE CAN AFFORD RESCUING ANOTHER POOR SOUL.
NEXT, WE HAVE A VIRGIN, 16, A FAIRY FROM HEAVEN. THE STARTING BID IS FIVE HUNDRED.
SEVEN HUNDRED FOR THE LADY. GOING ONCE, GOING TWICE --
ONE THOUSAND.

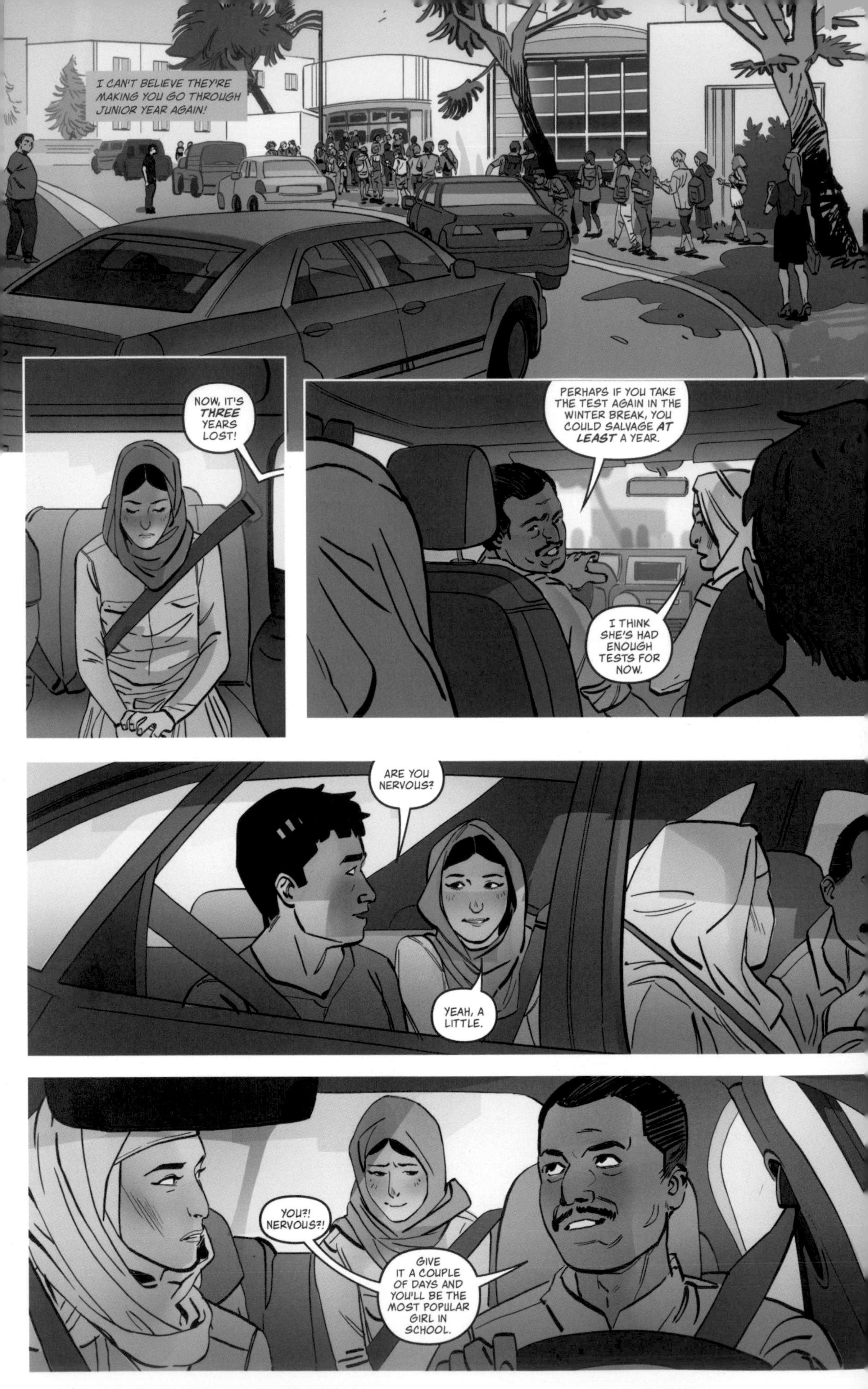
I CAN'T BELIEVE THEY'RE MAKING YOU GO THROUGH JUNIOR YEAR AGAIN!
NOW, IT'S THREE YEARS LOST!
PERHAPS IF YOU TAKE THE TEST AGAIN IN THE WINTER BREAK, YOU COULD SALVAGE AT LEAST A YEAR.
I THINK SHE'S HAD ENOUGH TESTS FOR NOW.
ARE YOU NERVOUS?
YEAH, A LITTLE.
YOU?! NERVOUS?!
GIVE IT A COUPLE OF DAYS AND YOU'LL BE THE MOST POPULAR GIRL IN SCHOOL.

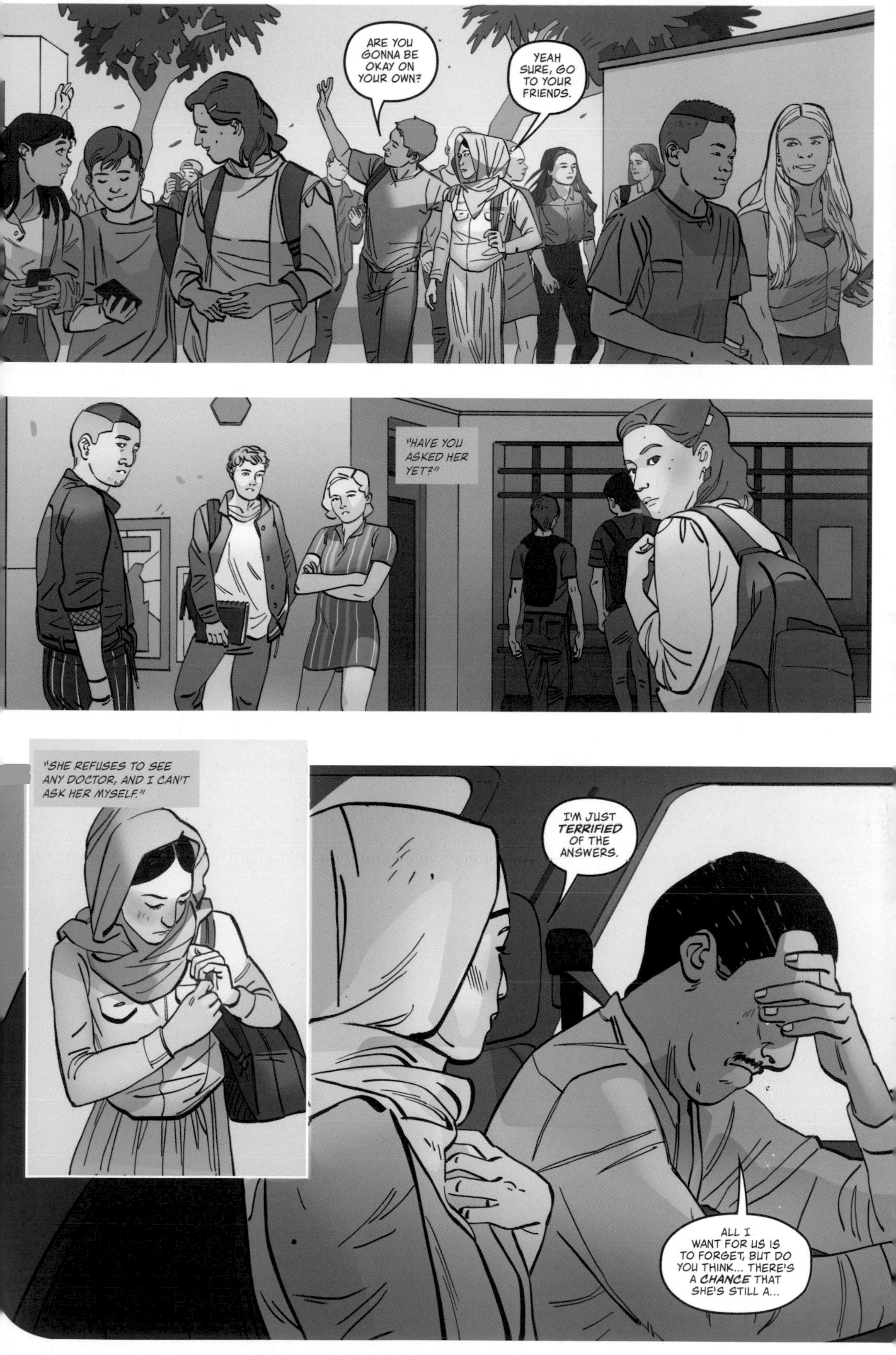
ARE YOU GONNA BE OKAY ON YOUR OWN?
YEAH SURE, GO TO YOUR FRIENDS.
"HAVE YOU ASKED HER YET?"
"SHE REFUSES TO SEE ANY DOCTOR, AND I CAN'T ASK HER MYSELF."
I'M JUST TERRIFIED OF THE ANSWERS.
ALL I WANT FOR US IS TO FORGET, BUT DO YOU THINK... THERE'S A CHANCE THAT SHE'S STILL A...

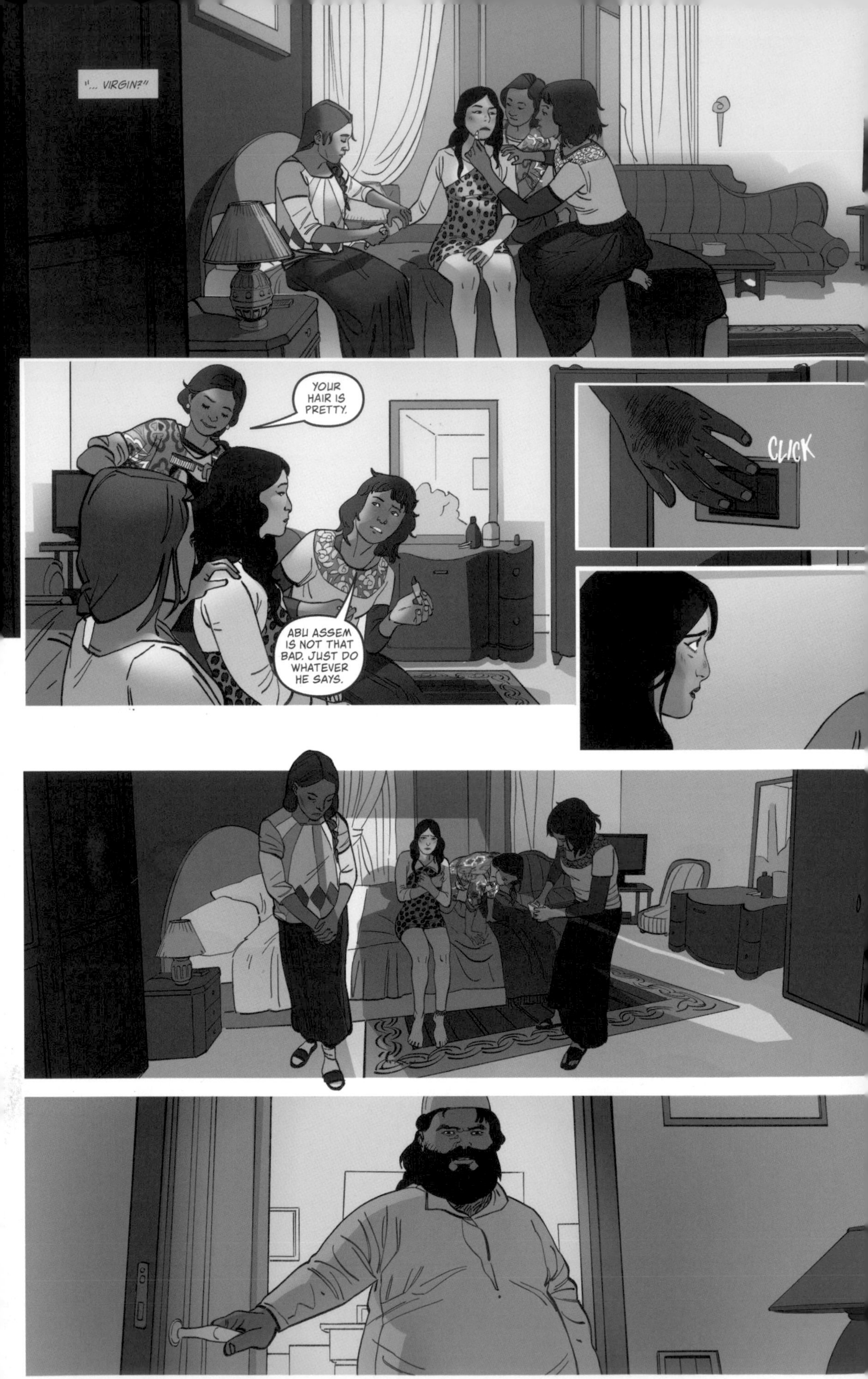
"... VIRGIN?"
YOUR HAIR IS PRETTY.
ABU ASSEM IS NOT THAT BAD. JUST DO WHATEVER HE SAYS.
CLICK

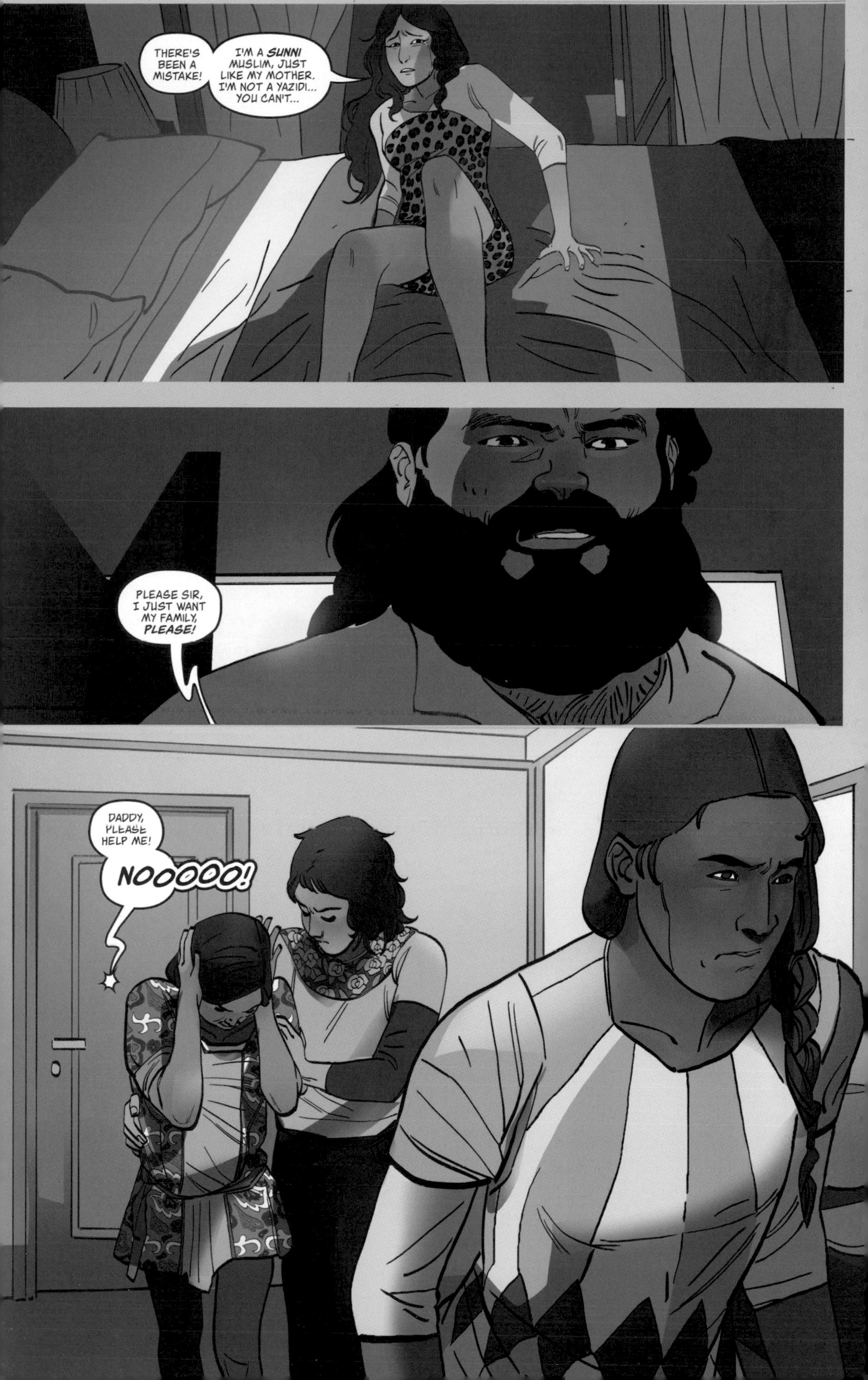
THERE'S BEEN A MISTAKE!
I'M A *SUNNI* MUSLIM, JUST LIKE MY MOTHER. I'M NOT A YAZIDI... YOU CAN'T...
PLEASE SIR, I JUST WANT MY FAMILY, ***PLEASE!***
DADDY, PLEASE HELP ME!
NOOOOO!

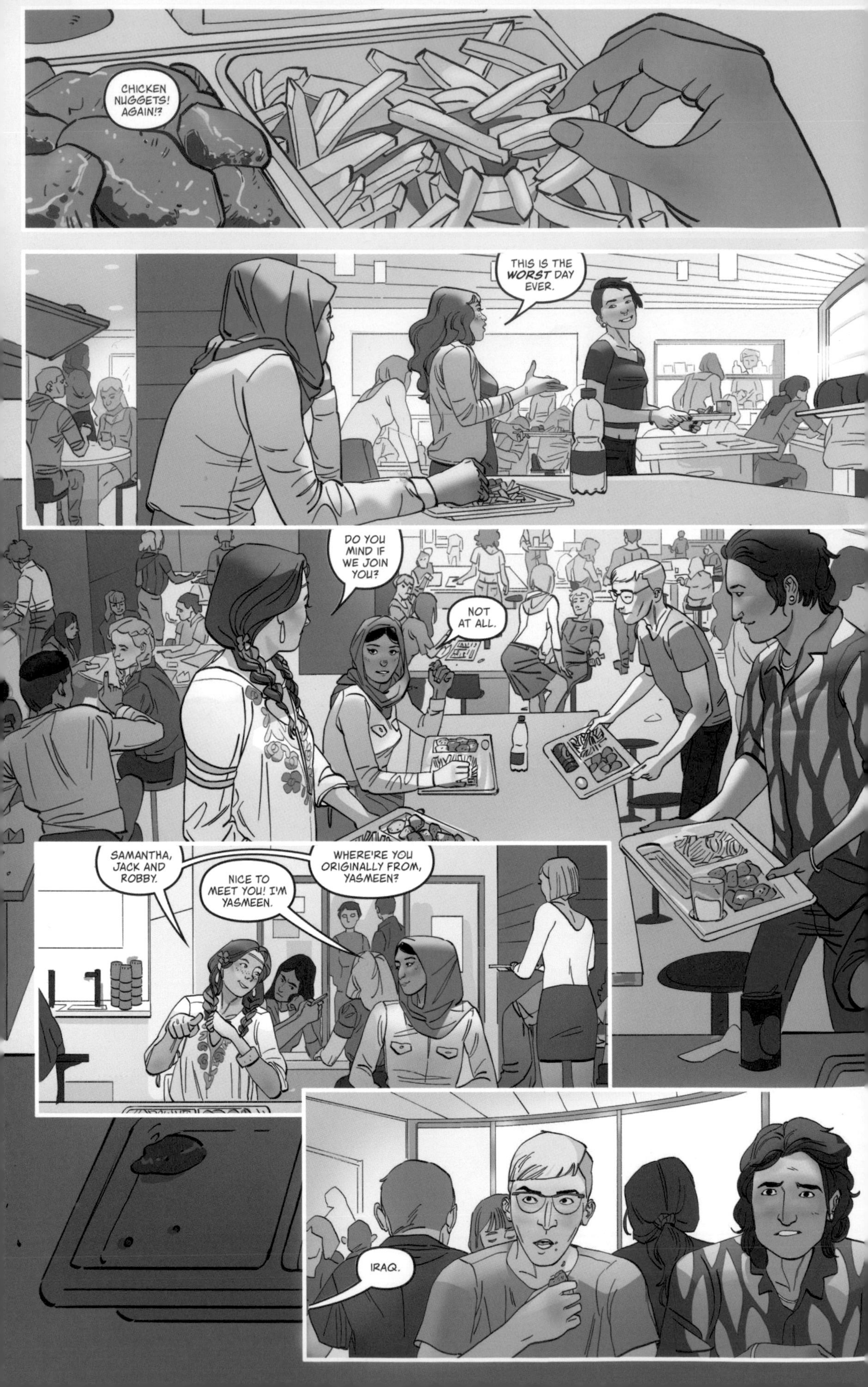
CHICKEN NUGGETS! AGAIN!?
THIS IS THE *WORST* DAY EVER.
DO YOU MIND IF WE JOIN YOU?
NOT AT ALL.
SAMANTHA, JACK AND ROBBY.
NICE TO MEET YOU! I'M YASMEEN.
WHERE'RE YOU ORIGINALLY FROM, YASMEEN?
IRAQ.

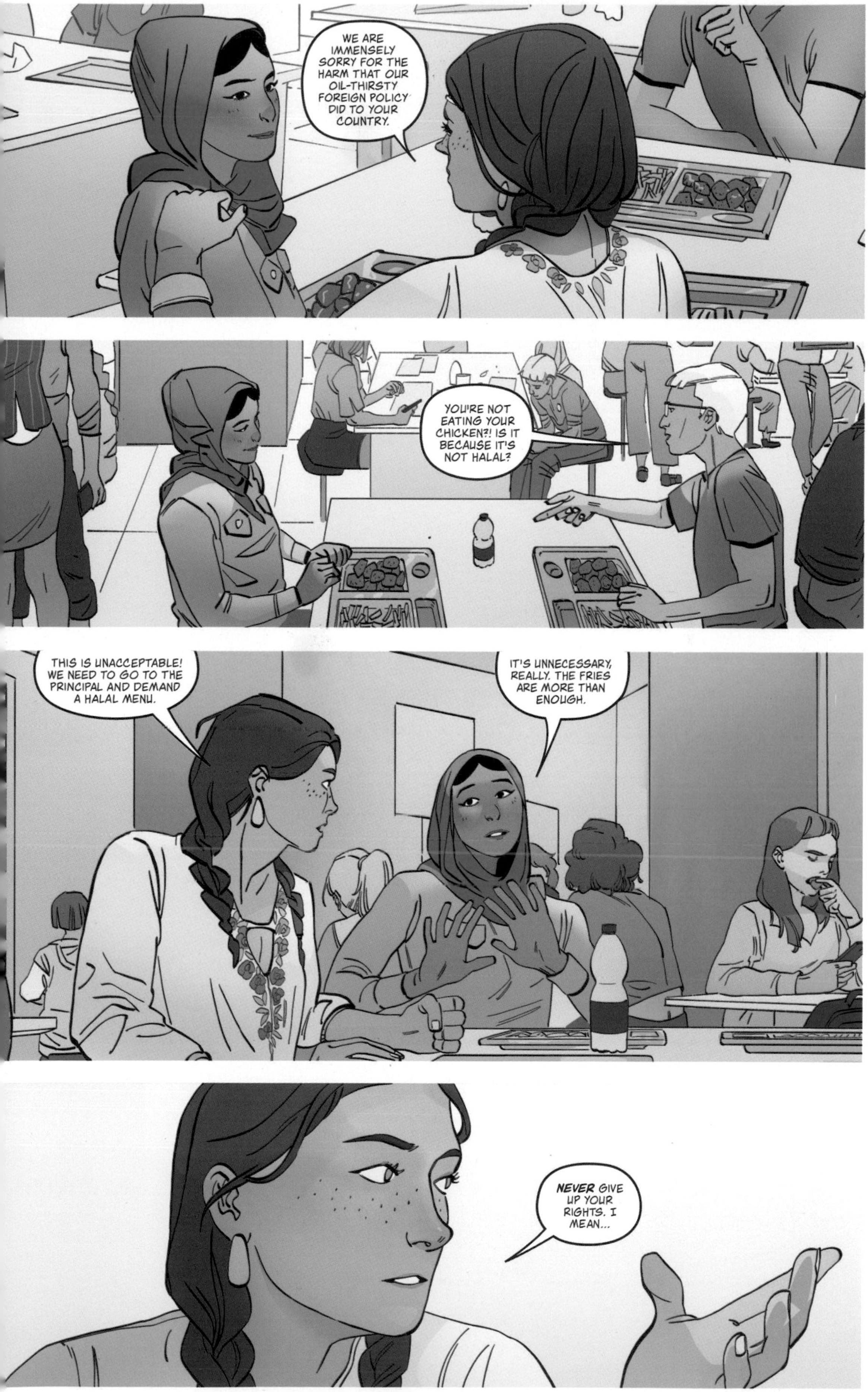

WE ARE IMMENSELY SORRY FOR THE HARM THAT OUR OIL-THIRSTY FOREIGN POLICY DID TO YOUR COUNTRY.
YOU'RE NOT EATING YOUR CHICKEN?! IS IT BECAUSE IT'S NOT HALAL?
THIS IS UNACCEPTABLE! WE NEED TO GO TO THE PRINCIPAL AND DEMAND A HALAL MENU.
IT'S UNNECESSARY, REALLY. THE FRIES ARE MORE THAN ENOUGH.
NEVER GIVE UP YOUR RIGHTS. I MEAN...

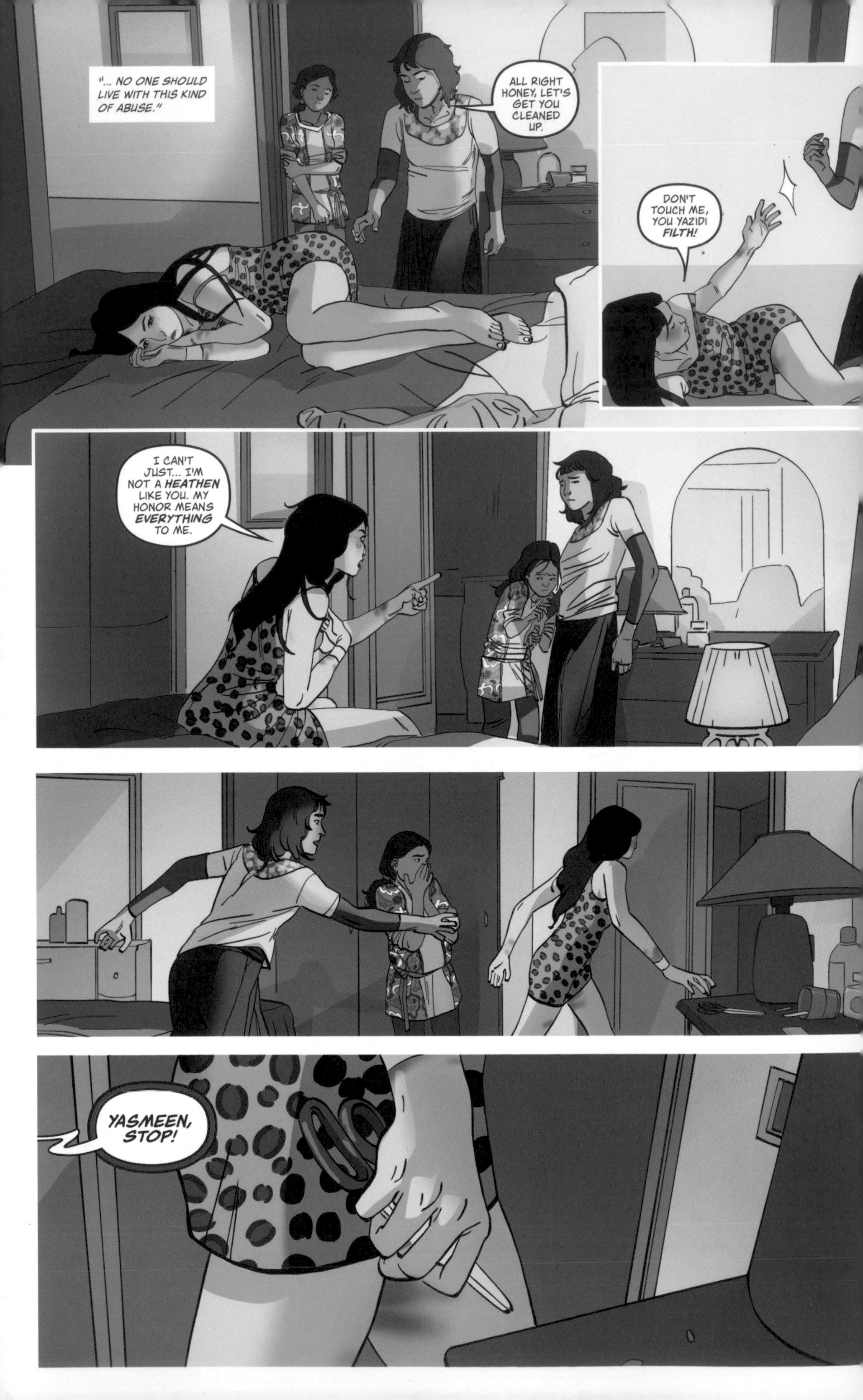
"... NO ONE SHOULD LIVE WITH THIS KIND OF ABUSE."
ALL RIGHT HONEY, LET'S GET YOU CLEANED UP.
DON'T TOUCH ME, YOU YAZIDI FILTH!
I CAN'T JUST... I'M NOT A HEATHEN LIKE YOU. MY HONOR MEANS EVERYTHING TO ME.
YASMEEN, STOP!

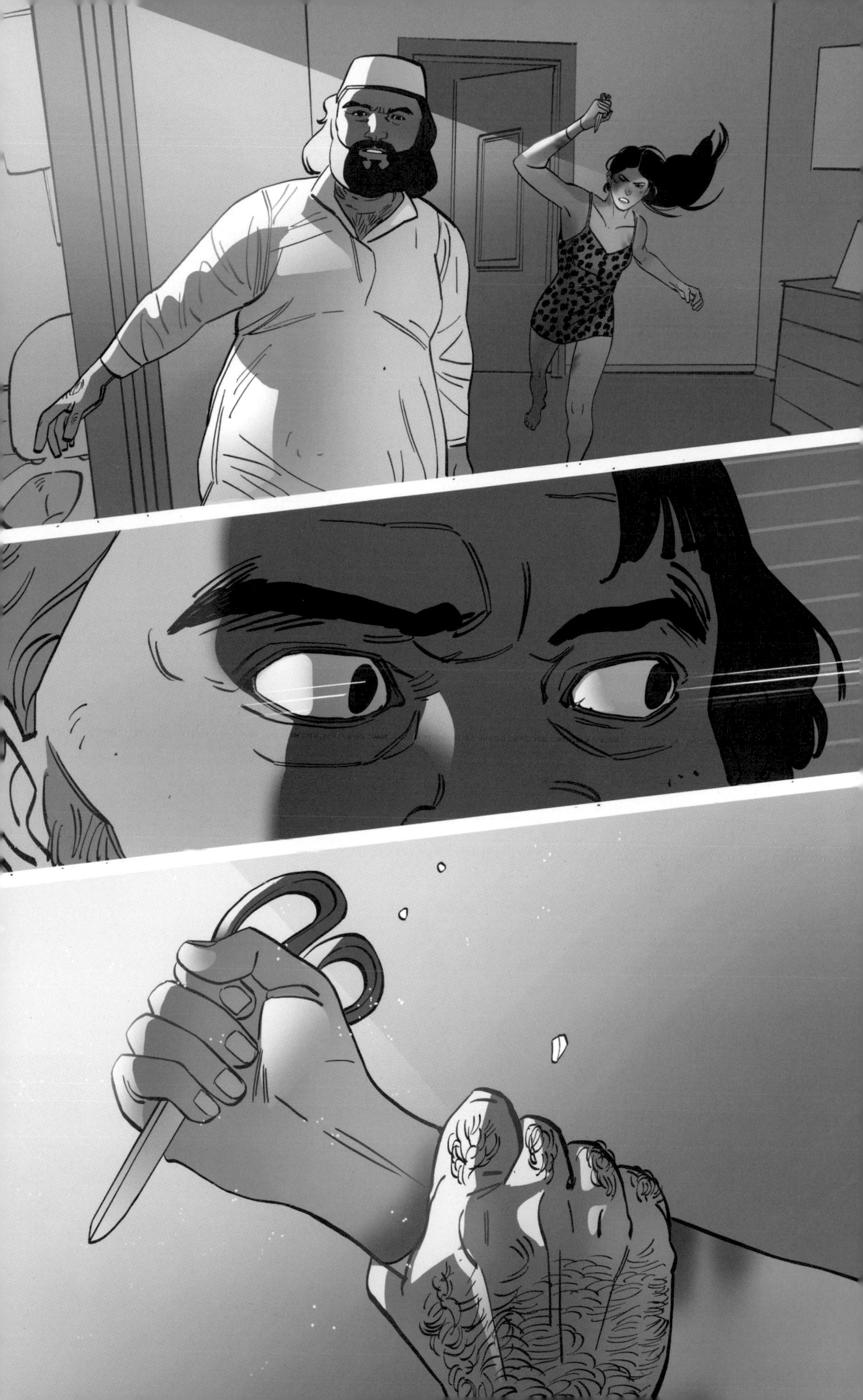

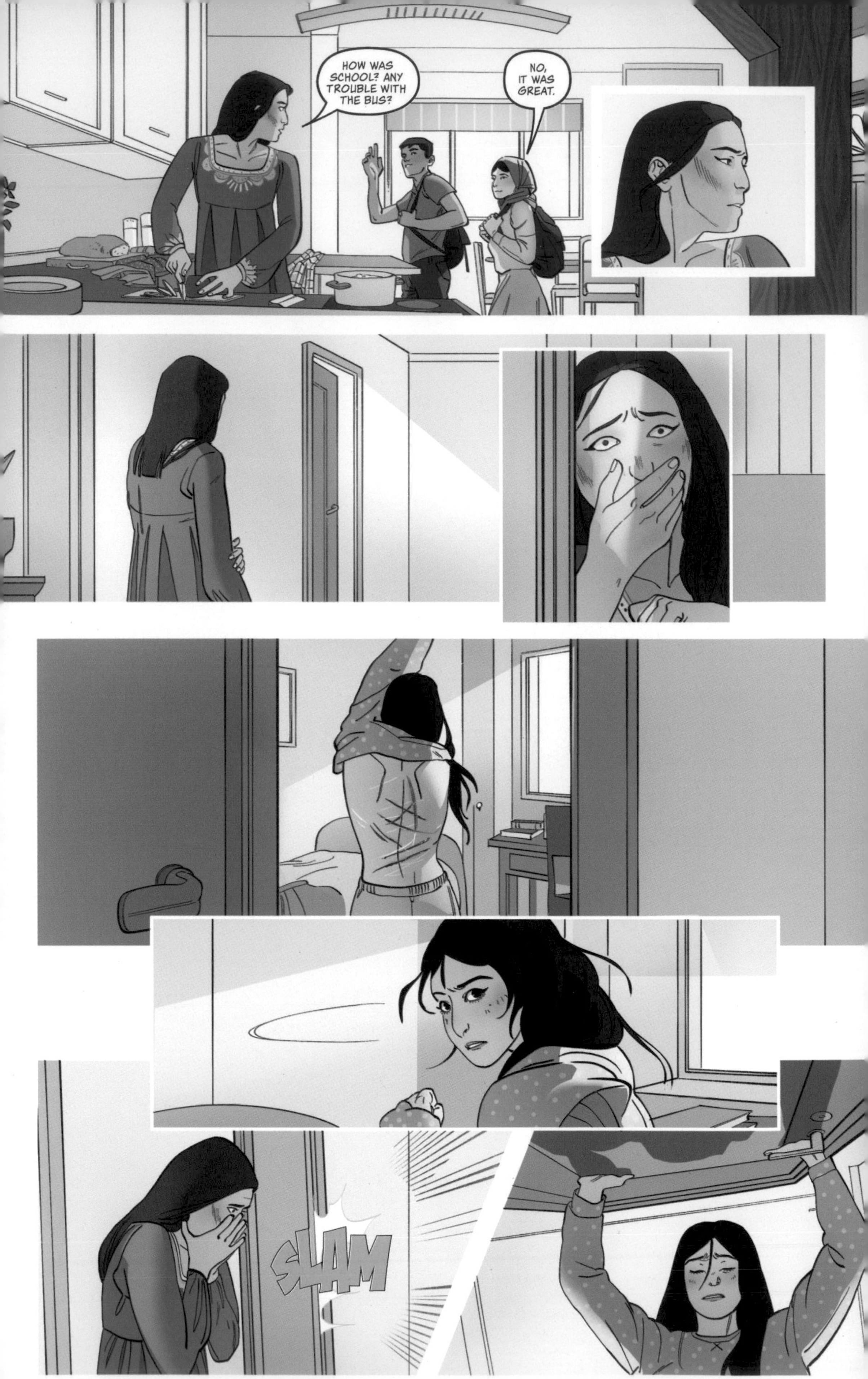
HOW WAS SCHOOL? ANY TROUBLE WITH THE BUS?
NO, IT WAS GREAT.
SLAM

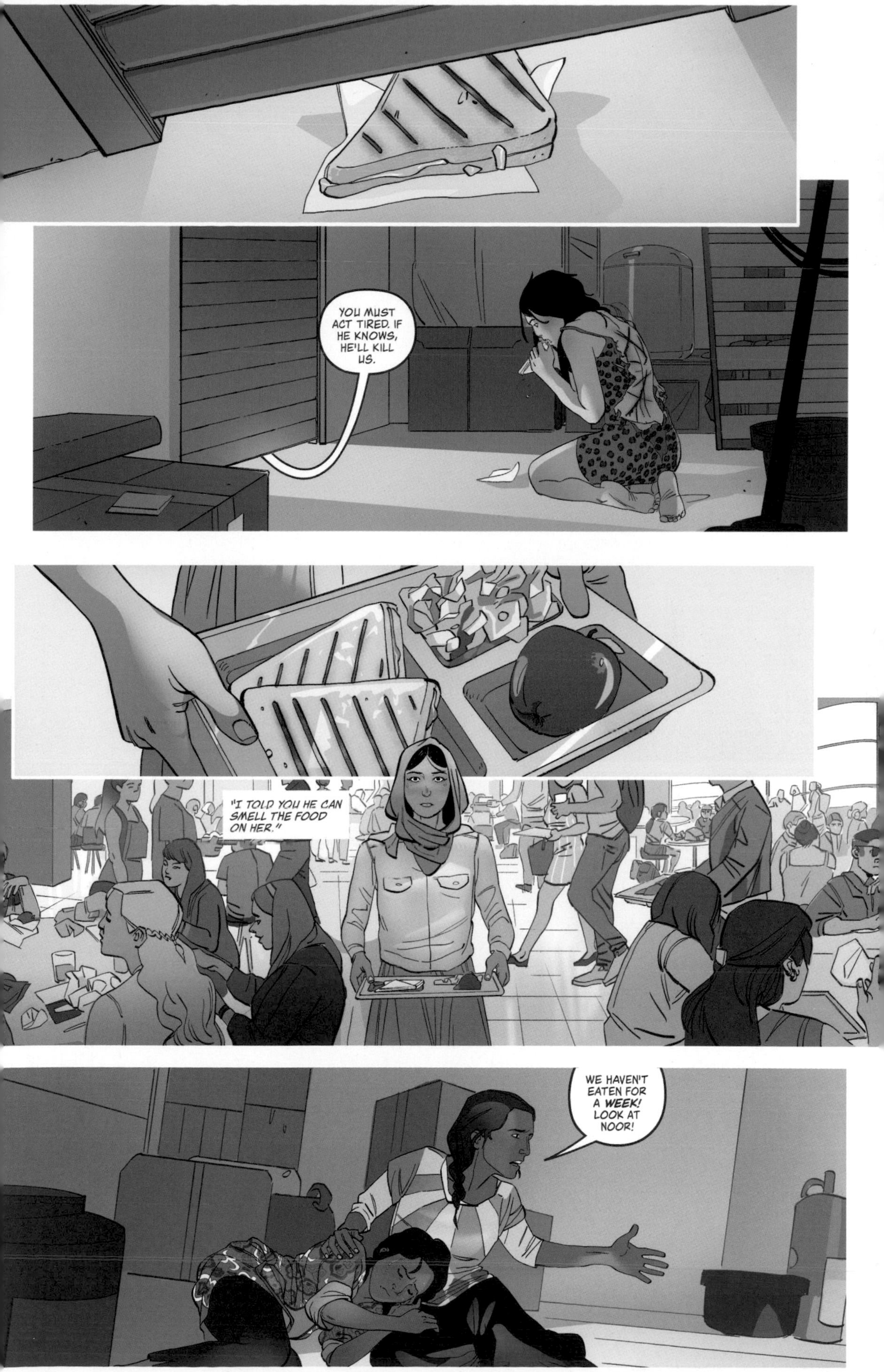
YOU MUST ACT TIRED. IF HE KNOWS, HE'LL KILL US.
"I TOLD YOU HE CAN SMELL THE FOOD ON HER."
WE HAVEN'T EATEN FOR A WEEK! LOOK AT NOOR!

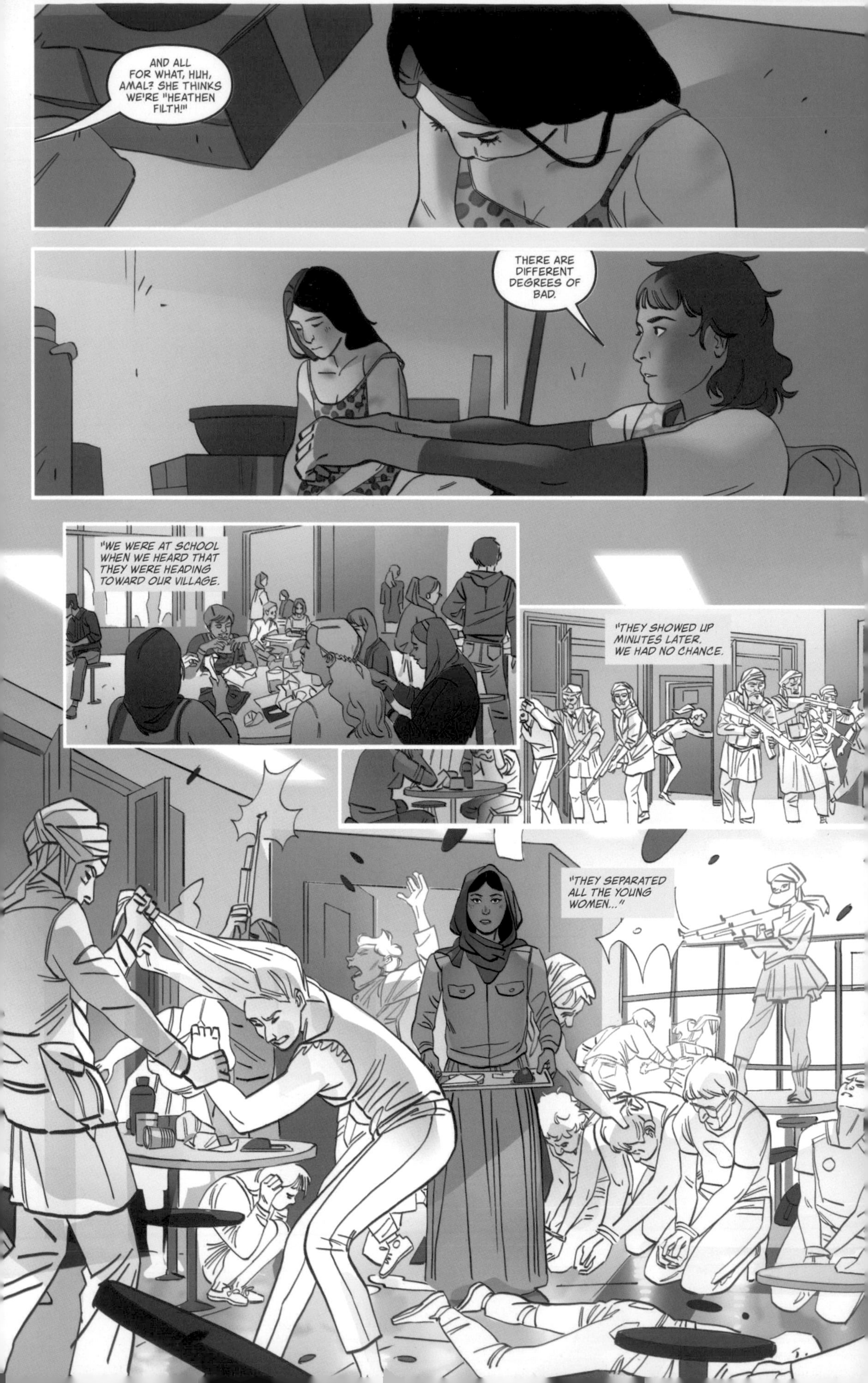
AND ALL FOR WHAT, HUH, AMAL? SHE THINKS WE'RE "HEATHEN FILTH!"
THERE ARE DIFFERENT DEGREES OF BAD.
"WE WERE AT SCHOOL WHEN WE HEARD THAT THEY WERE HEADING TOWARD OUR VILLAGE.
"THEY SHOWED UP MINUTES LATER. WE HAD NO CHANCE.
"THEY SEPARATED ALL THE YOUNG WOMEN..."

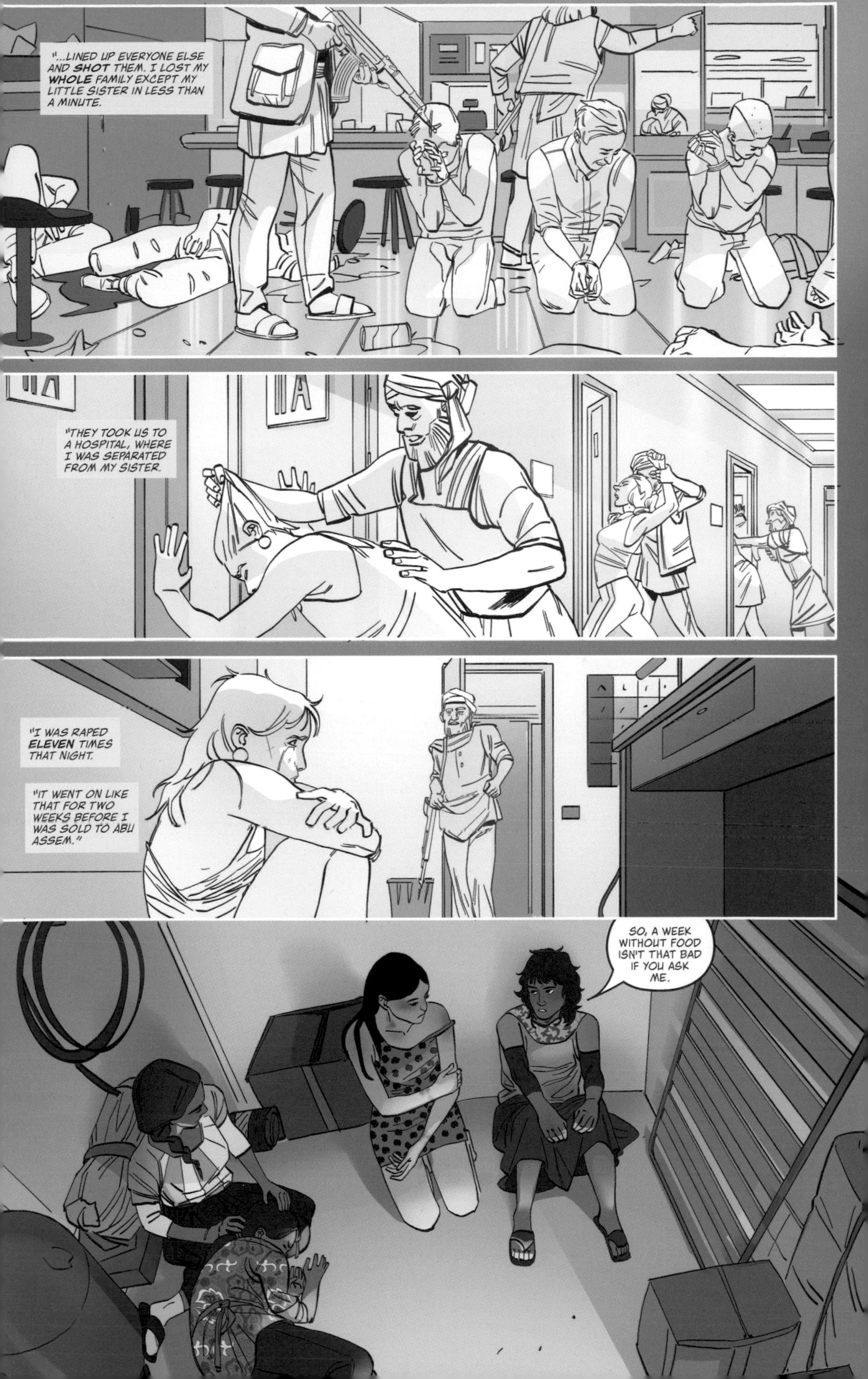
"...LINED UP EVERYONE ELSE AND SHOT THEM. I LOST MY WHOLE FAMILY EXCEPT MY LITTLE SISTER IN LESS THAN A MINUTE.
"THEY TOOK US TO A HOSPITAL, WHERE I WAS SEPARATED FROM MY SISTER.
"I WAS RAPED ELEVEN TIMES THAT NIGHT.
"IT WENT ON LIKE THAT FOR TWO WEEKS BEFORE I WAS SOLD TO ABU ASSEM."
SO, A WEEK WITHOUT FOOD ISN'T THAT BAD IF YOU ASK ME.

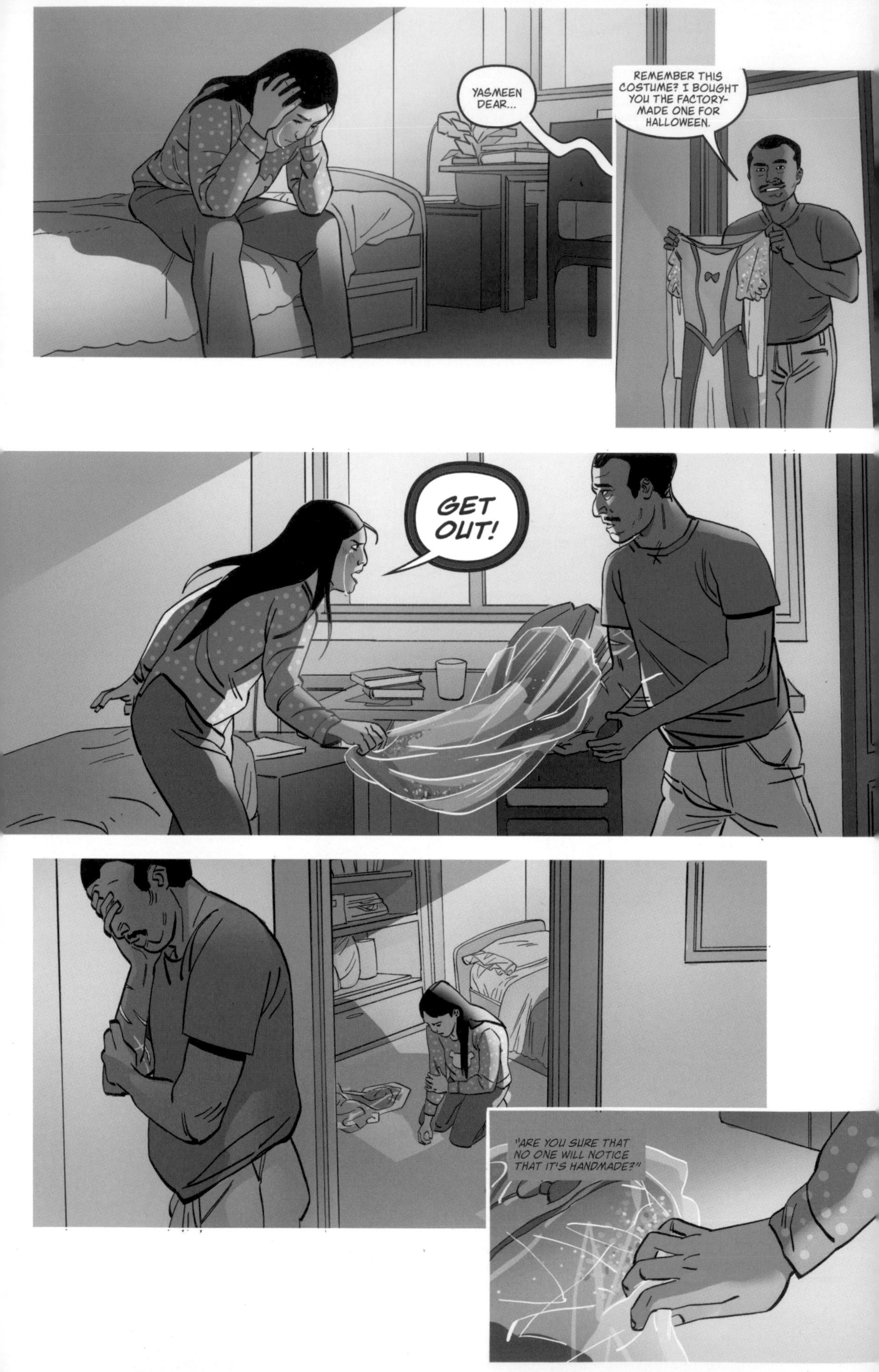
YASMEEN DEAR...
REMEMBER THIS COSTUME? I BOUGHT YOU THE FACTORY-MADE ONE FOR HALLOWEEN.
GET OUT!
"ARE YOU SURE THAT NO ONE WILL NOTICE THAT IT'S HANDMADE?"

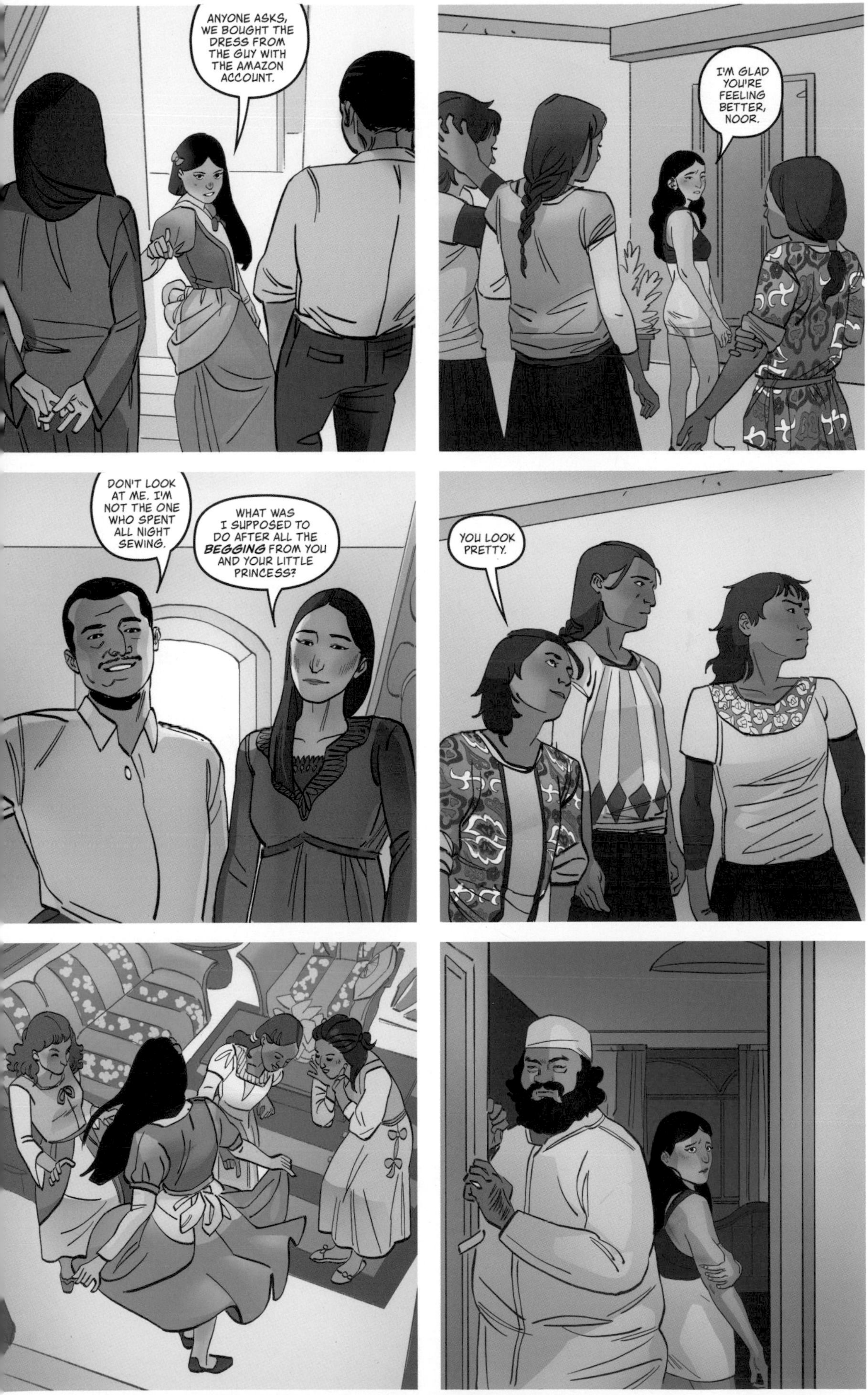
ANYONE ASKS, WE BOUGHT THE DRESS FROM THE GUY WITH THE AMAZON ACCOUNT.
I'M GLAD YOU'RE FEELING BETTER, NOOR.
DON'T LOOK AT ME. I'M NOT THE ONE WHO SPENT ALL NIGHT SEWING.
WHAT WAS I SUPPOSED TO DO AFTER ALL THE BEGGING FROM YOU AND YOUR LITTLE PRINCESS?
YOU LOOK PRETTY.

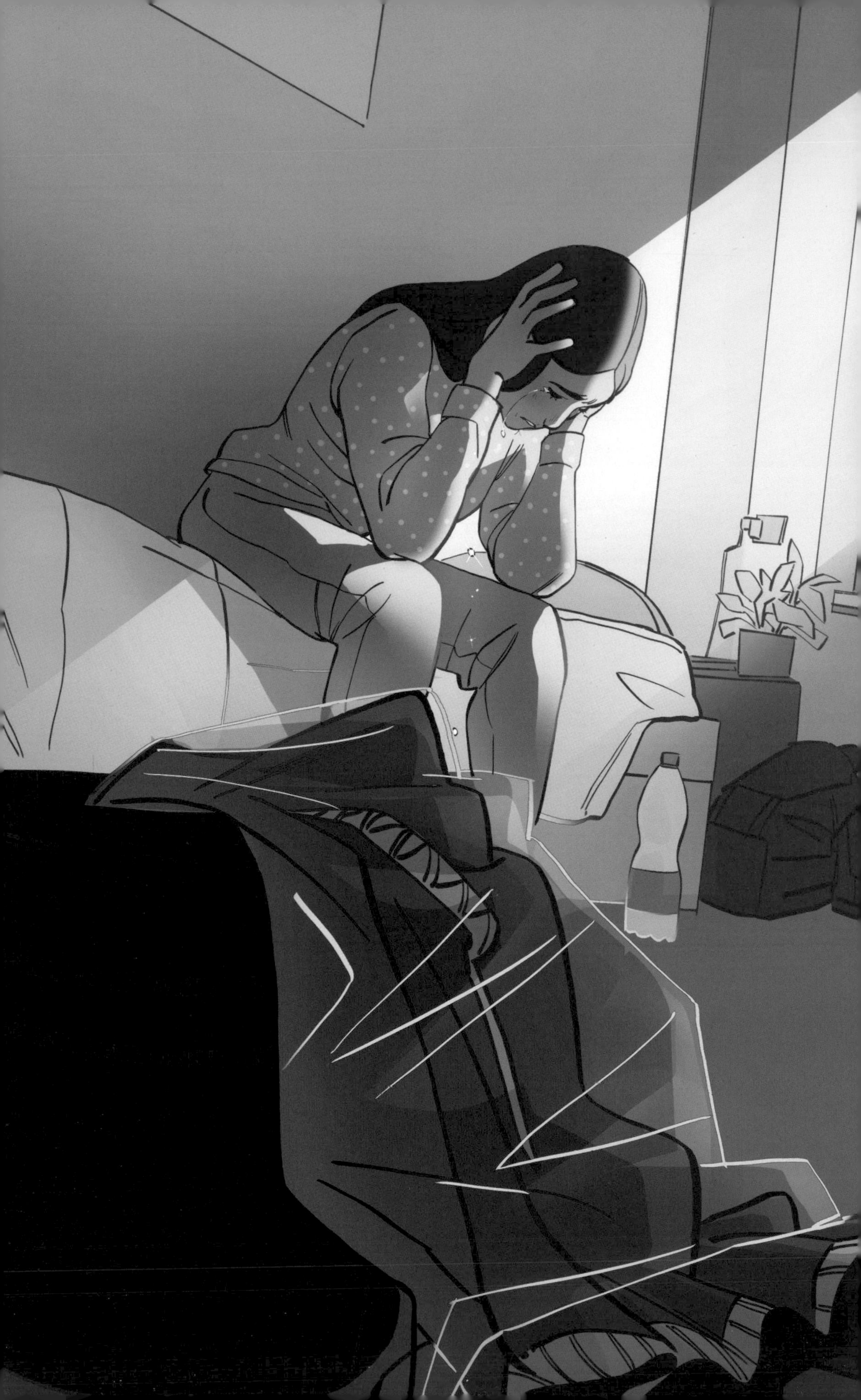

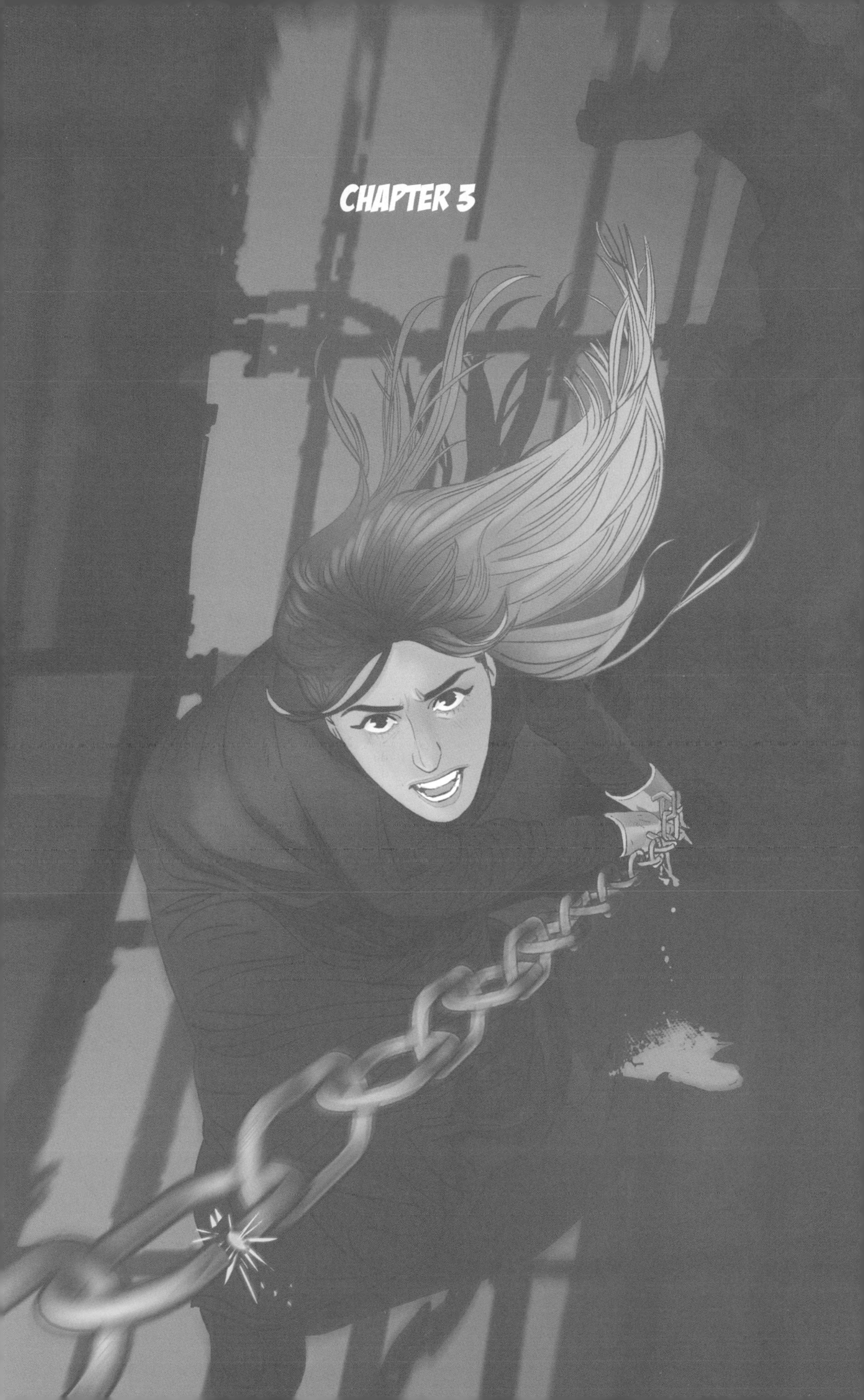
CHAPTER 3

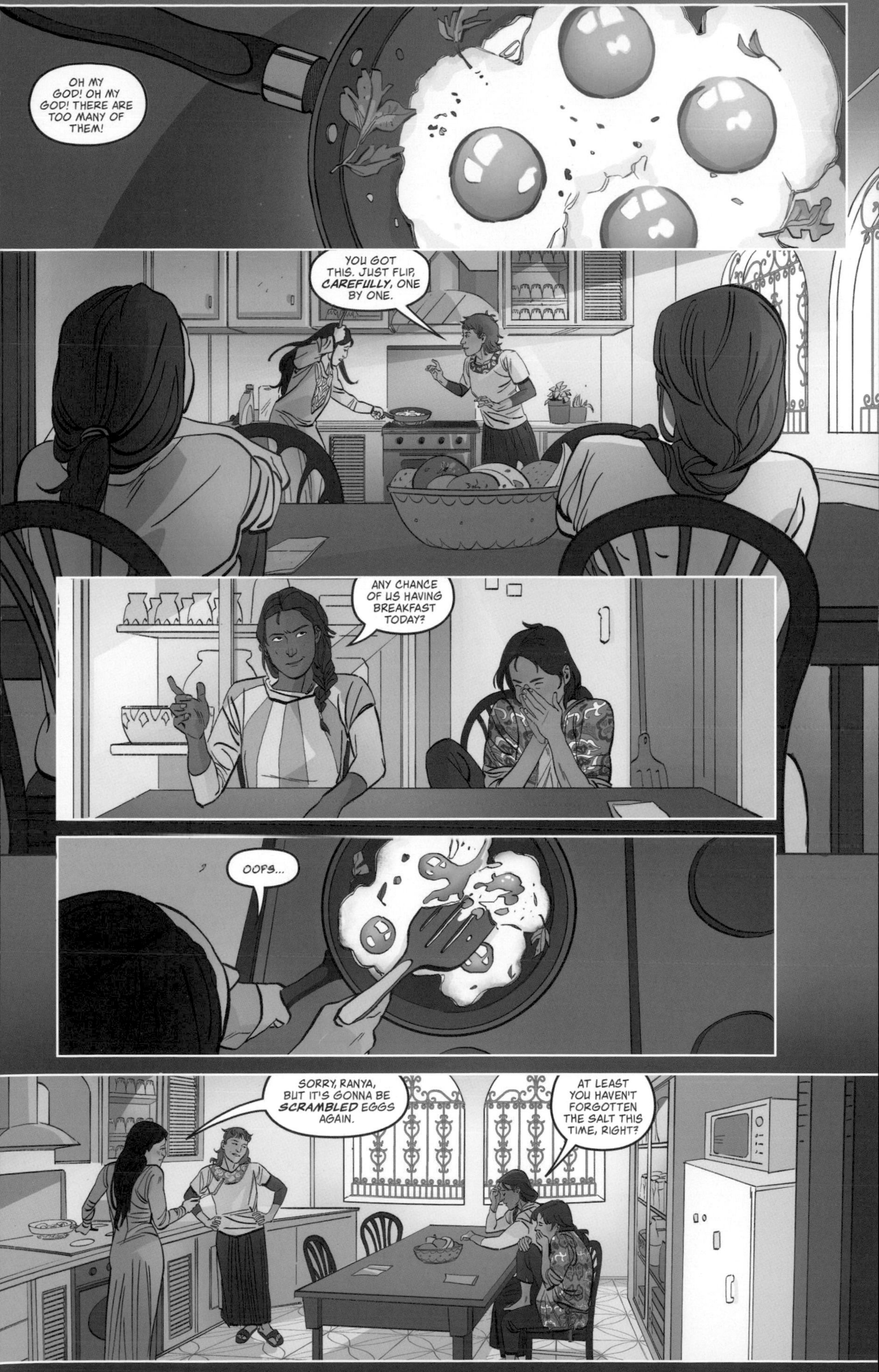
OH MY GOD! OH MY GOD! THERE ARE TOO MANY OF THEM!
YOU GOT THIS. JUST FLIP, CAREFULLY, ONE BY ONE.
ANY CHANCE OF US HAVING BREAKFAST TODAY?
OOPS...
SORRY, RANYA, BUT IT'S GONNA BE SCRAMBLED EGGS AGAIN.
AT LEAST YOU HAVEN'T FORGOTTEN THE SALT THIS TIME, RIGHT?

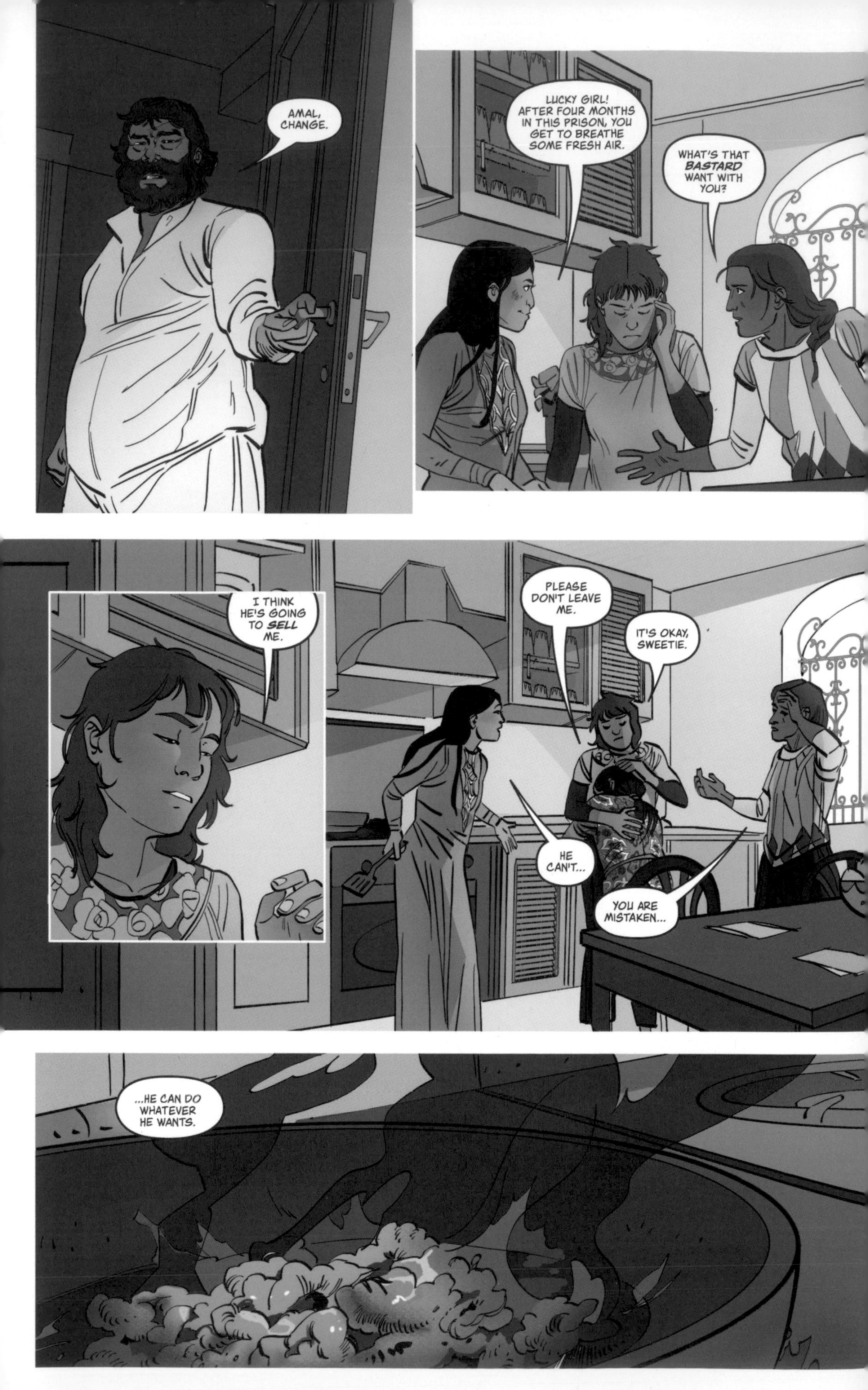
AMAL, CHANGE.
LUCKY GIRL! AFTER FOUR MONTHS IN THIS PRISON, YOU GET TO BREATHE SOME FRESH AIR.
WHAT'S THAT BASTARD WANT WITH YOU?
I THINK HE'S GOING TO SELL ME.
PLEASE DON'T LEAVE ME.
IT'S OKAY, SWEETIE.
HE CAN'T...
YOU ARE MISTAKEN...
...HE CAN DO WHATEVER HE WANTS.

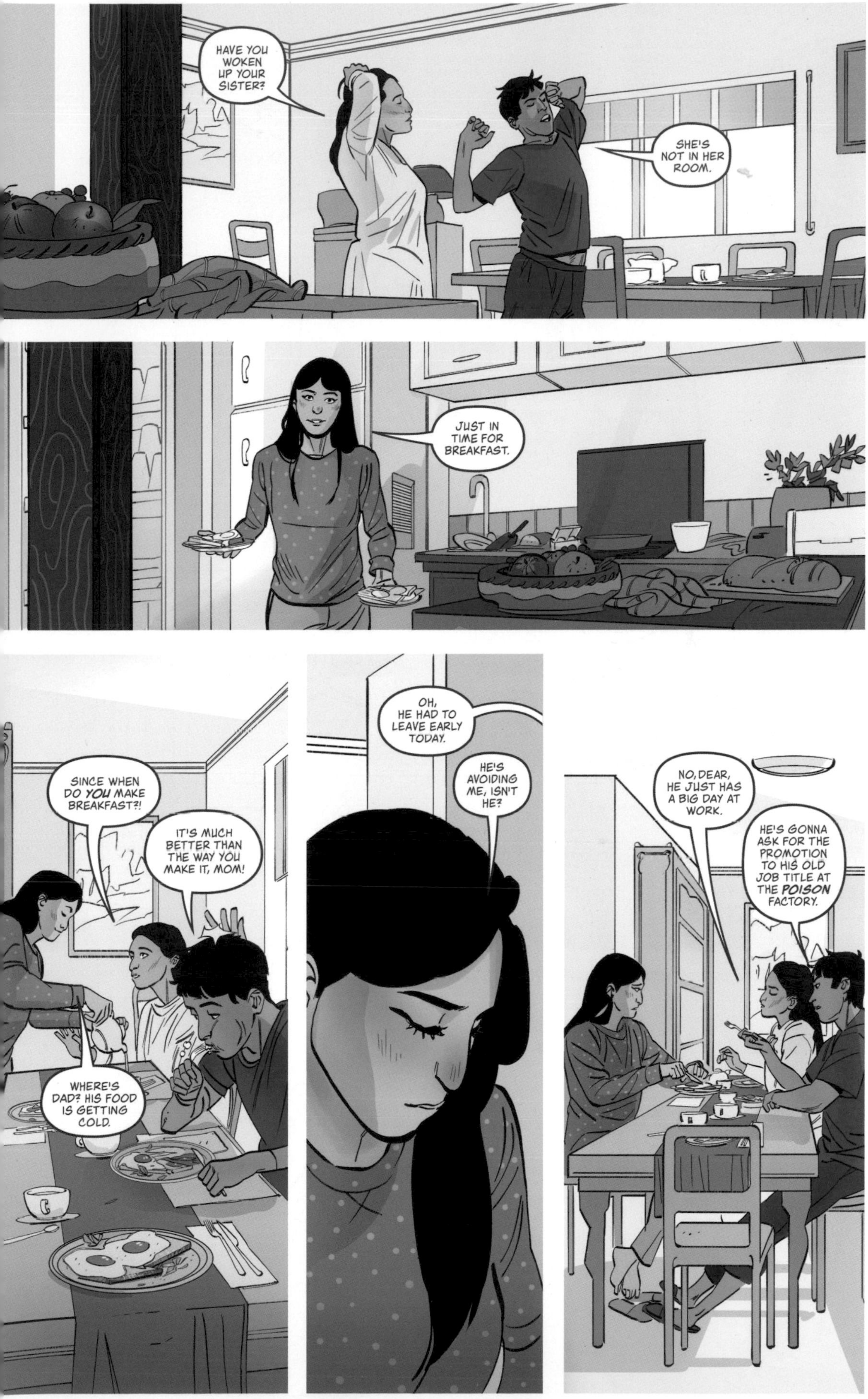
HAVE YOU WOKEN UP YOUR SISTER?
SHE'S NOT IN HER ROOM.
JUST IN TIME FOR BREAKFAST.
SINCE WHEN DO *YOU* MAKE BREAKFAST?!
IT'S MUCH BETTER THAN THE WAY YOU MAKE IT, MOM!
WHERE'S DAD? HIS FOOD IS GETTING COLD.
OH, HE HAD TO LEAVE EARLY TODAY.
HE'S AVOIDING ME, ISN'T HE?
NO, DEAR, HE JUST HAS A BIG DAY AT WORK.
HE'S GONNA ASK FOR THE PROMOTION TO HIS OLD JOB TITLE AT THE ***POISON*** FACTORY.

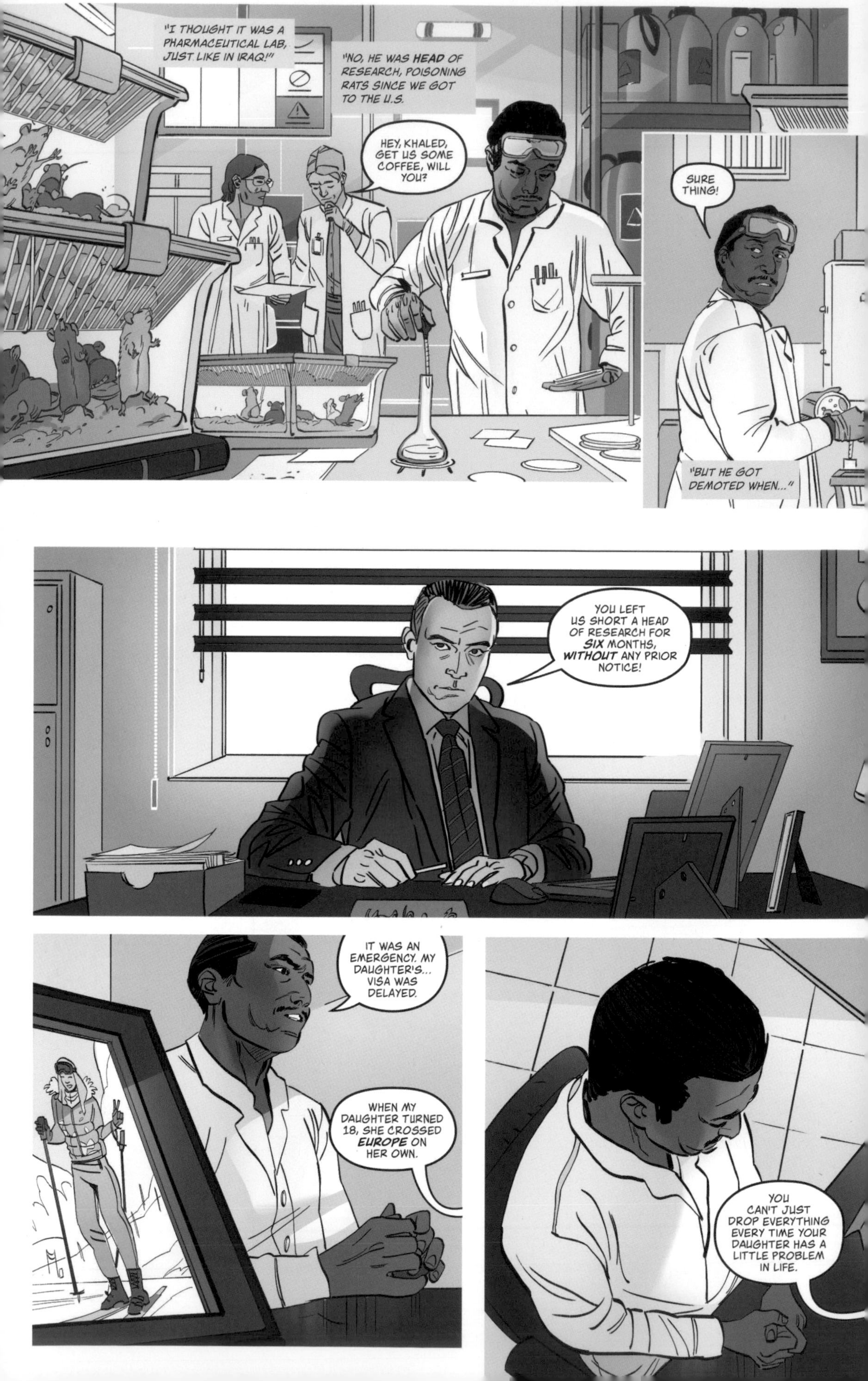
"I THOUGHT IT WAS A PHARMACEUTICAL LAB, JUST LIKE IN IRAQ!"
"NO, HE WAS HEAD OF RESEARCH, POISONING RATS SINCE WE GOT TO THE U.S.
HEY, KHALED, GET US SOME COFFEE, WILL YOU?
SURE THING!
"BUT HE GOT DEMOTED WHEN..."
YOU LEFT US SHORT A HEAD OF RESEARCH FOR SIX MONTHS, WITHOUT ANY PRIOR NOTICE!
IT WAS AN EMERGENCY. MY DAUGHTER'S... VISA WAS DELAYED.
WHEN MY DAUGHTER TURNED 18, SHE CROSSED EUROPE ON HER OWN.
YOU CAN'T JUST DROP EVERYTHING EVERY TIME YOUR DAUGHTER HAS A LITTLE PROBLEM IN LIFE.

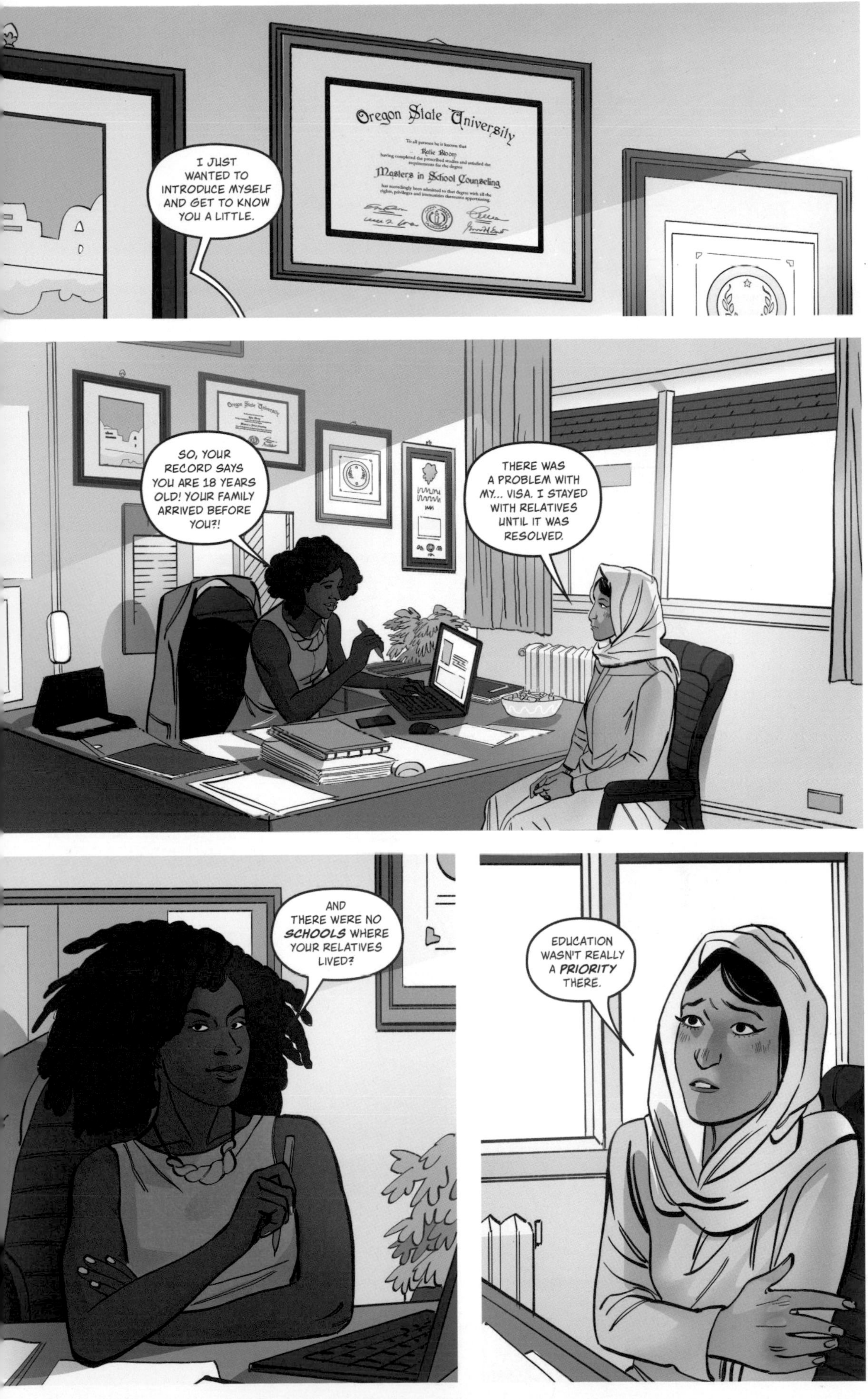
Oregon State University
Masters in School Counseling
I JUST WANTED TO INTRODUCE MYSELF AND GET TO KNOW YOU A LITTLE.
SO, YOUR RECORD SAYS YOU ARE 18 YEARS OLD! YOUR FAMILY ARRIVED BEFORE YOU?!
THERE WAS A PROBLEM WITH MY... VISA. I STAYED WITH RELATIVES UNTIL IT WAS RESOLVED.
AND THERE WERE NO *SCHOOLS* WHERE YOUR RELATIVES LIVED?
EDUCATION WASN'T REALLY A *PRIORITY* THERE.

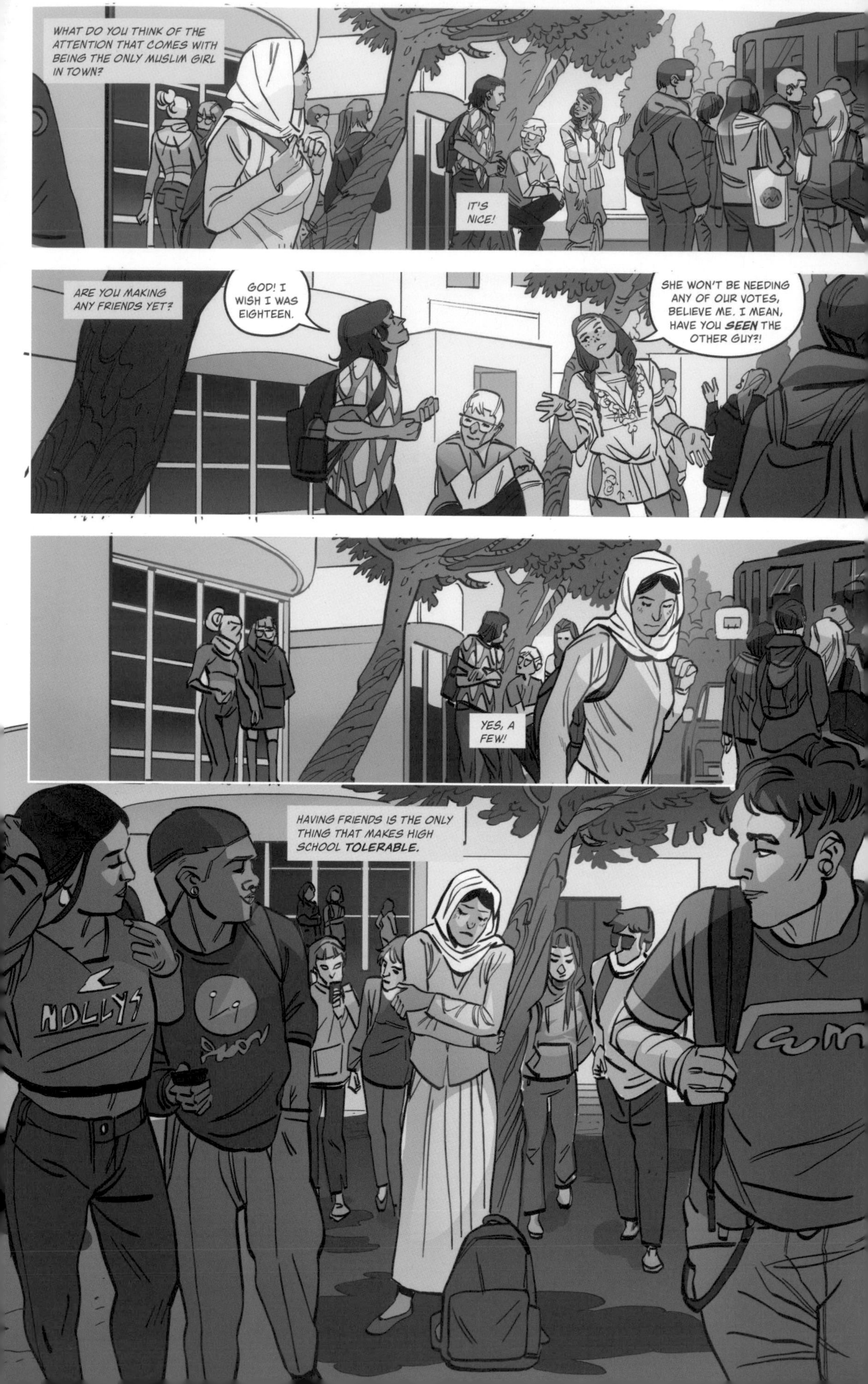
WHAT DO YOU THINK OF THE ATTENTION THAT COMES WITH BEING THE ONLY MUSLIM GIRL IN TOWN?
IT'S NICE!
ARE YOU MAKING ANY FRIENDS YET?
GOD! I WISH I WAS EIGHTEEN.
SHE WON'T BE NEEDING ANY OF OUR VOTES, BELIEVE ME. I MEAN, HAVE YOU SEEN THE OTHER GUY?!
YES, A FEW!
HAVING FRIENDS IS THE ONLY THING THAT MAKES HIGH SCHOOL TOLERABLE.
HOLLYS

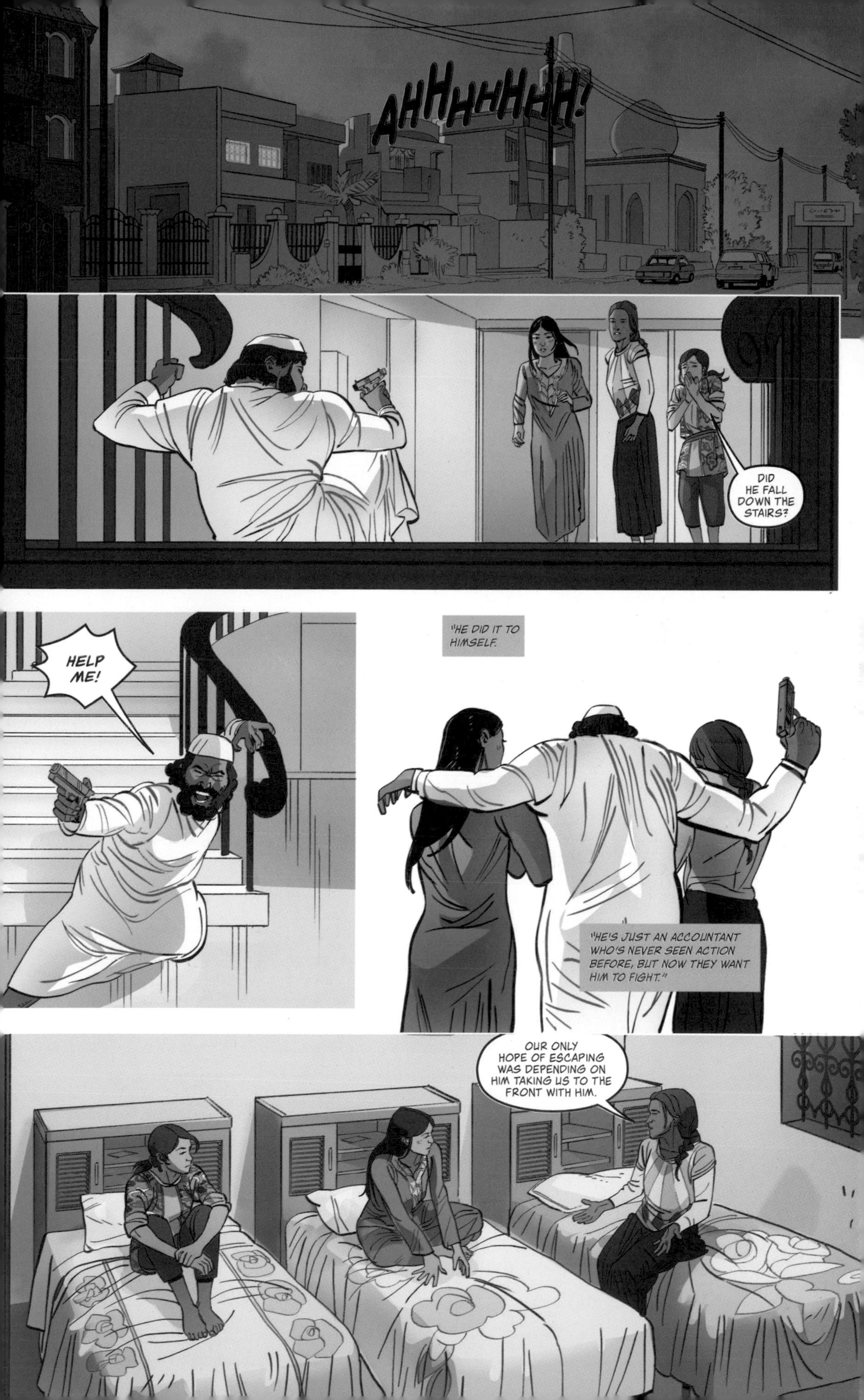
AHHHHHHH!
DID HE FALL DOWN THE STAIRS?
HELP ME!
"HE DID IT TO HIMSELF.
"HE'S JUST AN ACCOUNTANT WHO'S NEVER SEEN ACTION BEFORE, BUT NOW THEY WANT HIM TO FIGHT."
OUR ONLY HOPE OF ESCAPING WAS DEPENDING ON HIM TAKING US TO THE FRONT WITH HIM.

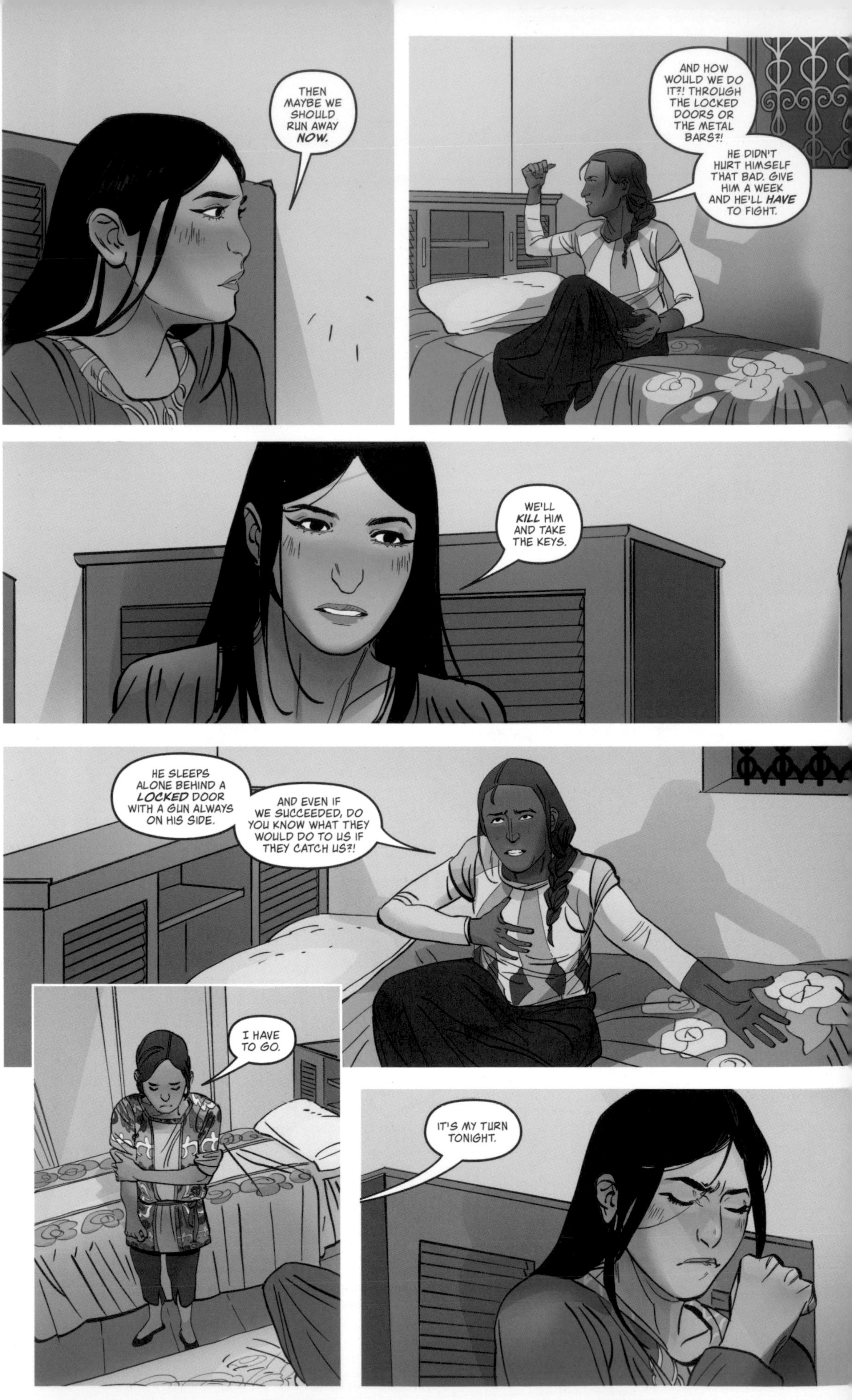
THEN MAYBE WE SHOULD RUN AWAY *NOW.*
AND HOW WOULD WE DO IT?! THROUGH THE LOCKED DOORS OR THE METAL BARS?!
HE DIDN'T HURT HIMSELF THAT BAD. GIVE HIM A WEEK AND HE'LL *HAVE* TO FIGHT.
WE'LL *KILL* HIM AND TAKE THE KEYS.
HE SLEEPS ALONE BEHIND A *LOCKED* DOOR WITH A GUN ALWAYS ON HIS SIDE.
AND EVEN IF WE SUCCEEDED, DO YOU KNOW WHAT THEY WOULD DO TO US IF THEY CATCH US?!
I HAVE TO GO.
IT'S MY TURN TONIGHT.

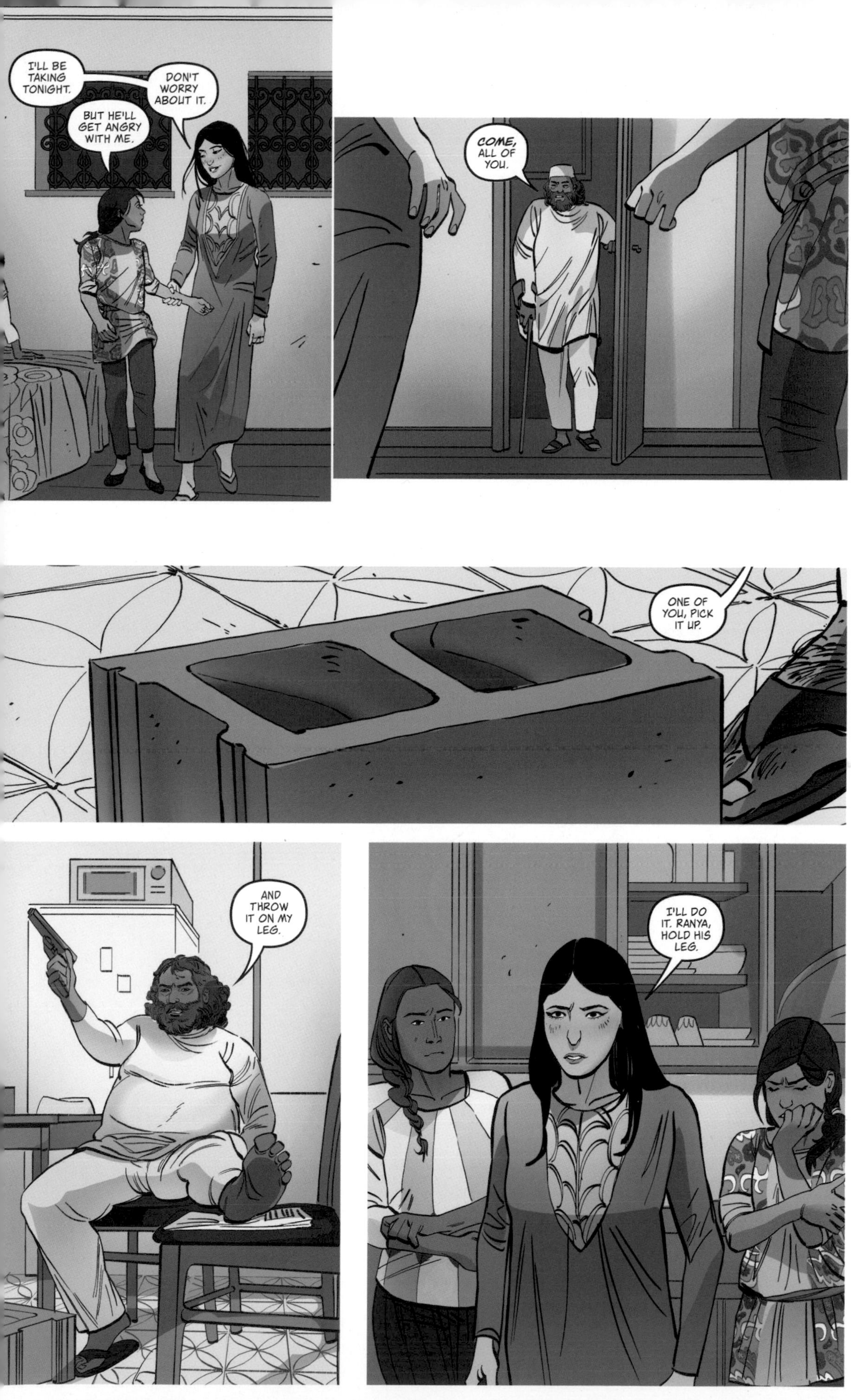
I'LL BE TAKING TONIGHT.
DON'T WORRY ABOUT IT.
BUT HE'LL GET ANGRY WITH ME.
COME, ALL OF YOU.
ONE OF YOU, PICK IT UP.
AND THROW IT ON MY LEG.
I'LL DO IT. RANYA, HOLD HIS LEG.

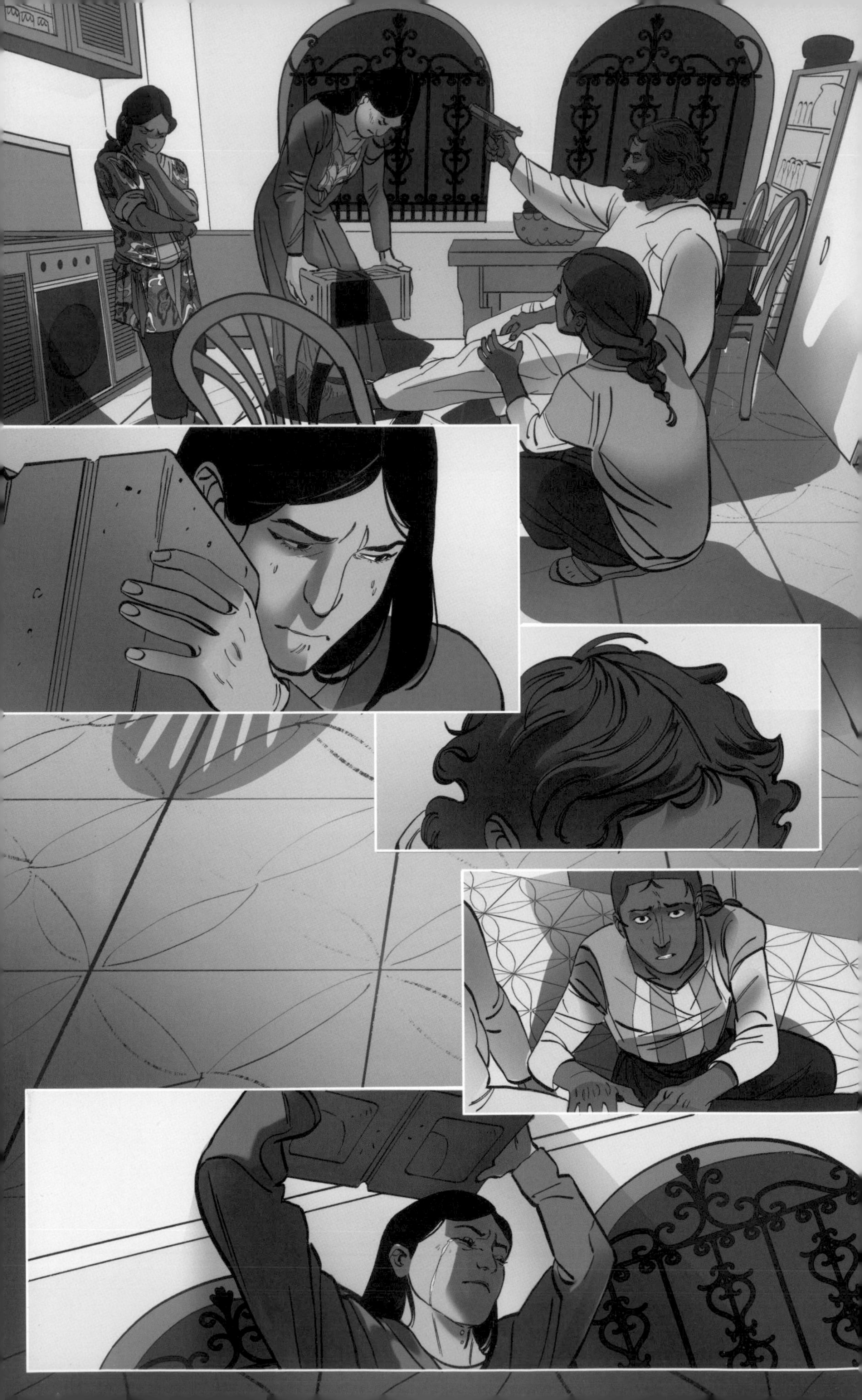

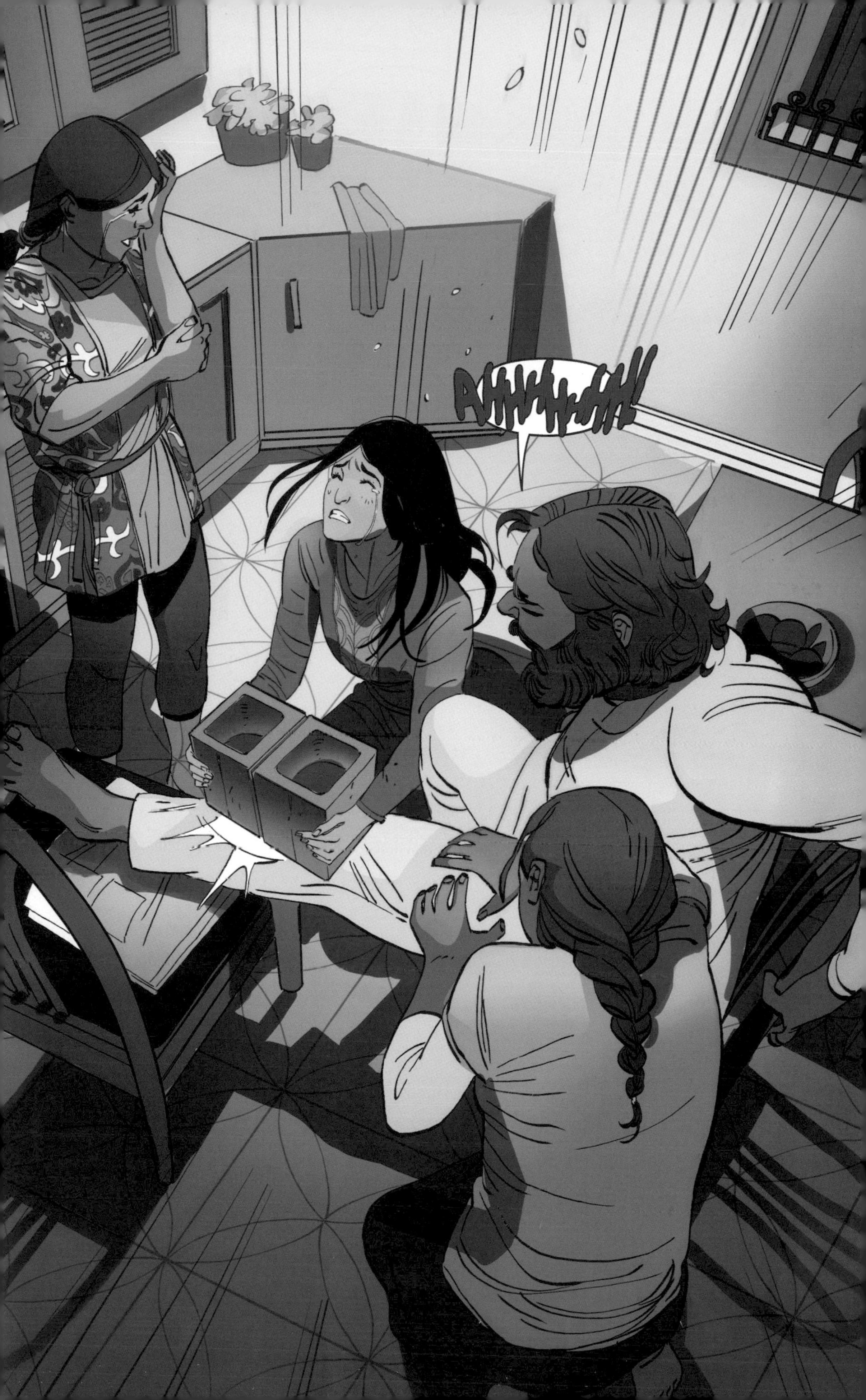
AHHHHHH!

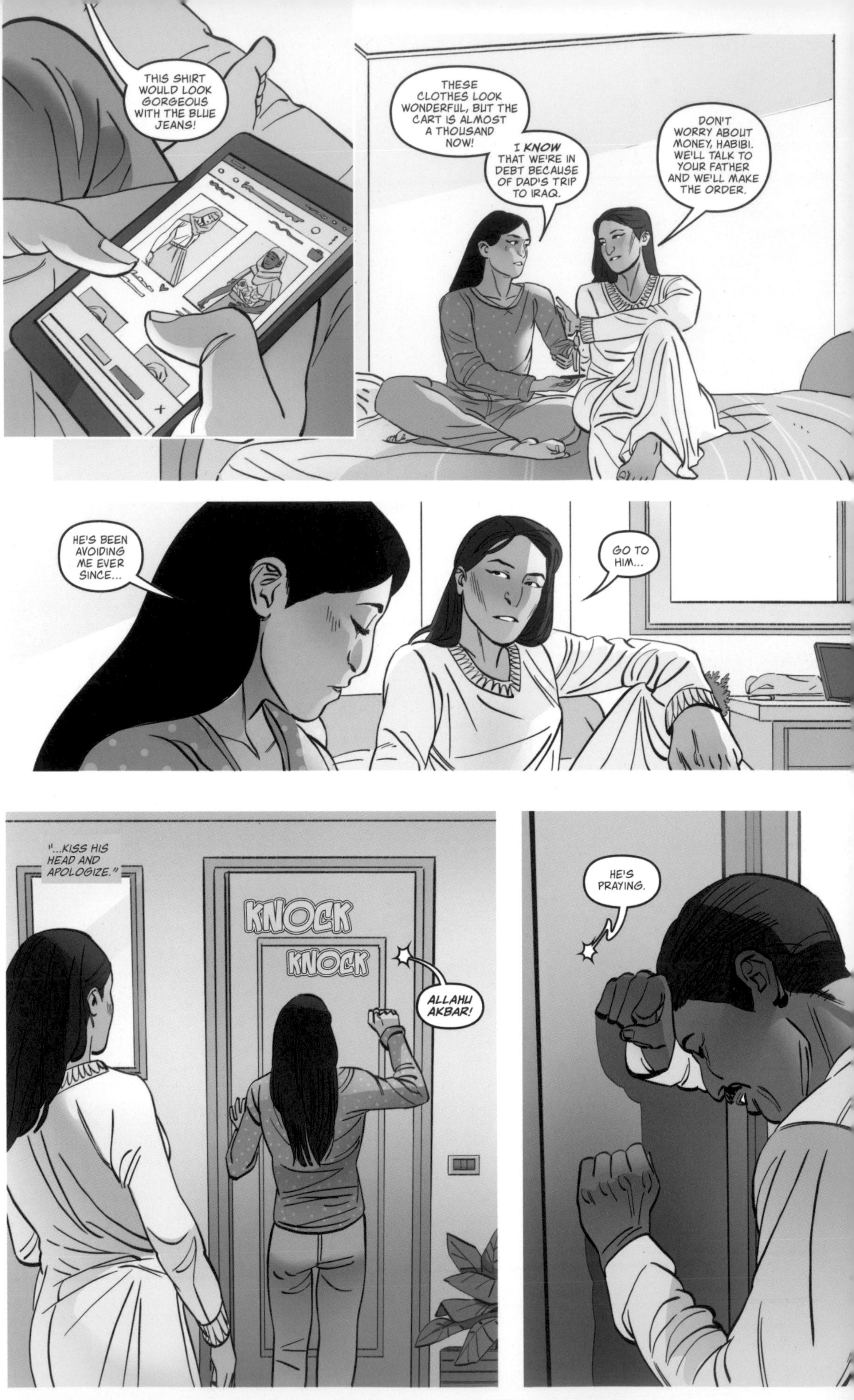
THIS SHIRT WOULD LOOK GORGEOUS WITH THE BLUE JEANS!
THESE CLOTHES LOOK WONDERFUL, BUT THE CART IS ALMOST A THOUSAND NOW!
I KNOW THAT WE'RE IN DEBT BECAUSE OF DAD'S TRIP TO IRAQ.
DON'T WORRY ABOUT MONEY, HABIBI. WE'LL TALK TO YOUR FATHER AND WE'LL MAKE THE ORDER.
HE'S BEEN AVOIDING ME EVER SINCE...
GO TO HIM...
"...KISS HIS HEAD AND APOLOGIZE."
KNOCK
KNOCK
ALLAHU AKBAR!
HE'S PRAYING.

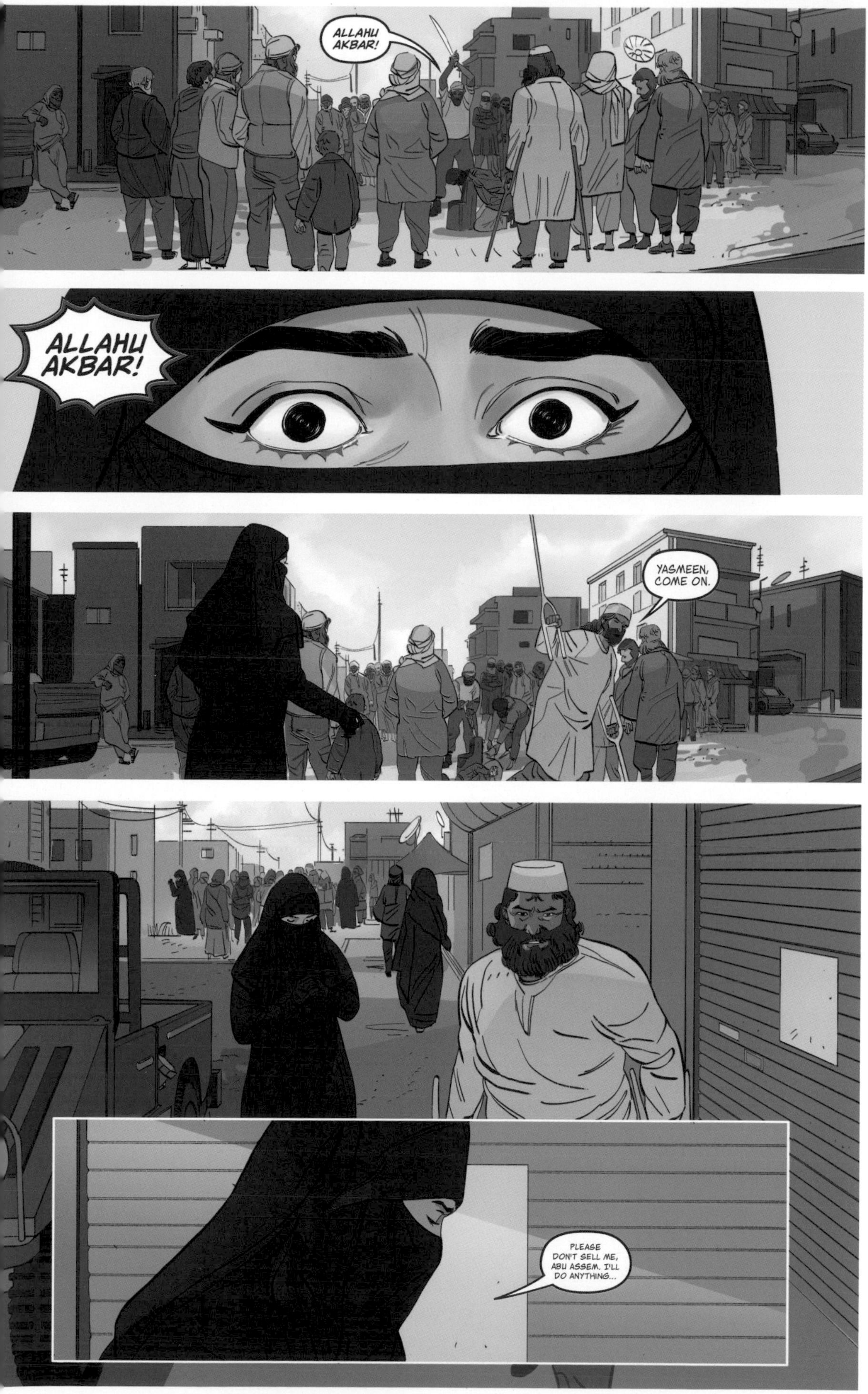
ALLAHU AKBAR!
ALLAHU AKBAR!
YASMEEN, COME ON.
PLEASE DON'T SELL ME, ABU ASSEM. I'LL DO ANYTHING...

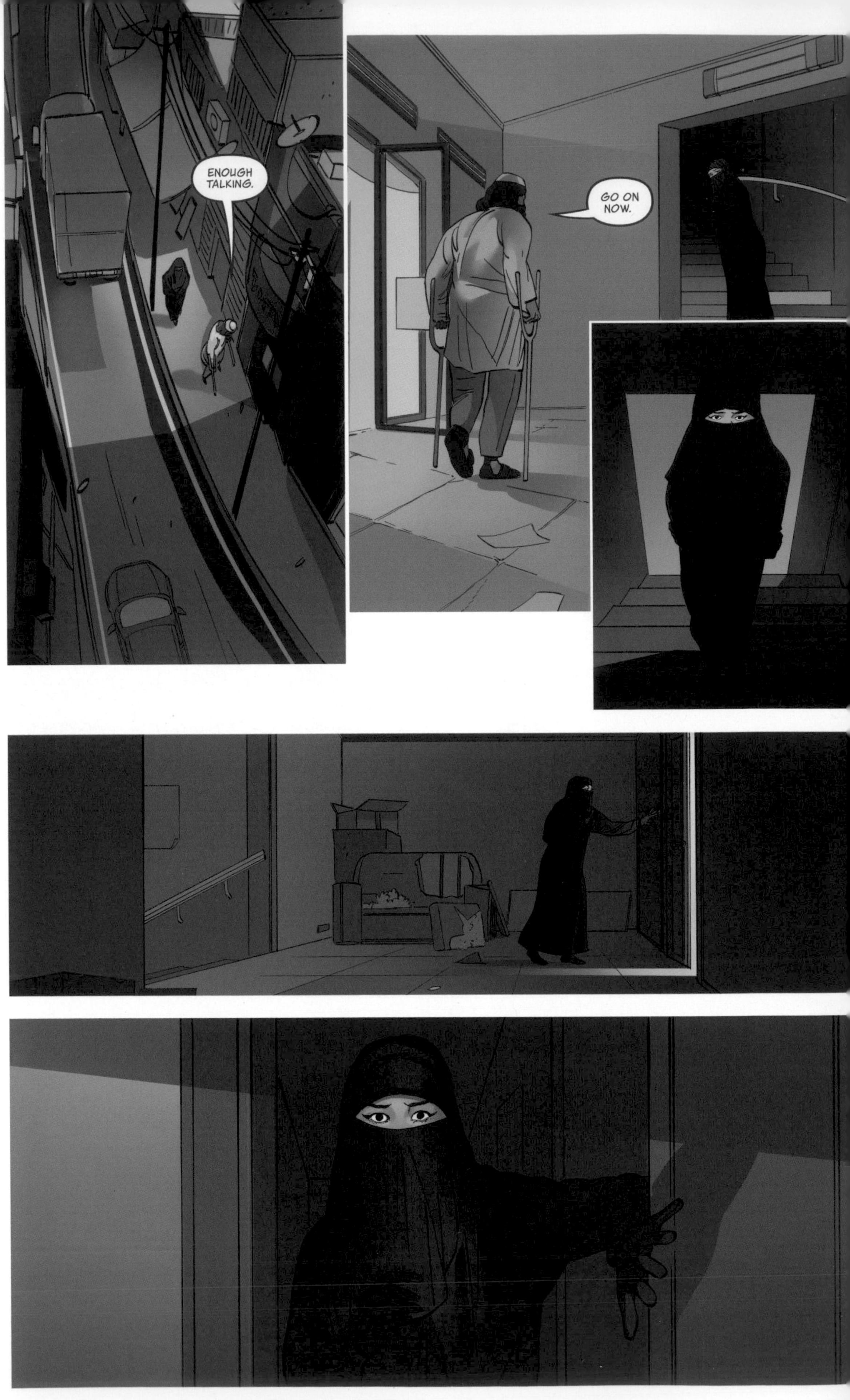
ENOUGH TALKING.
GO ON NOW.

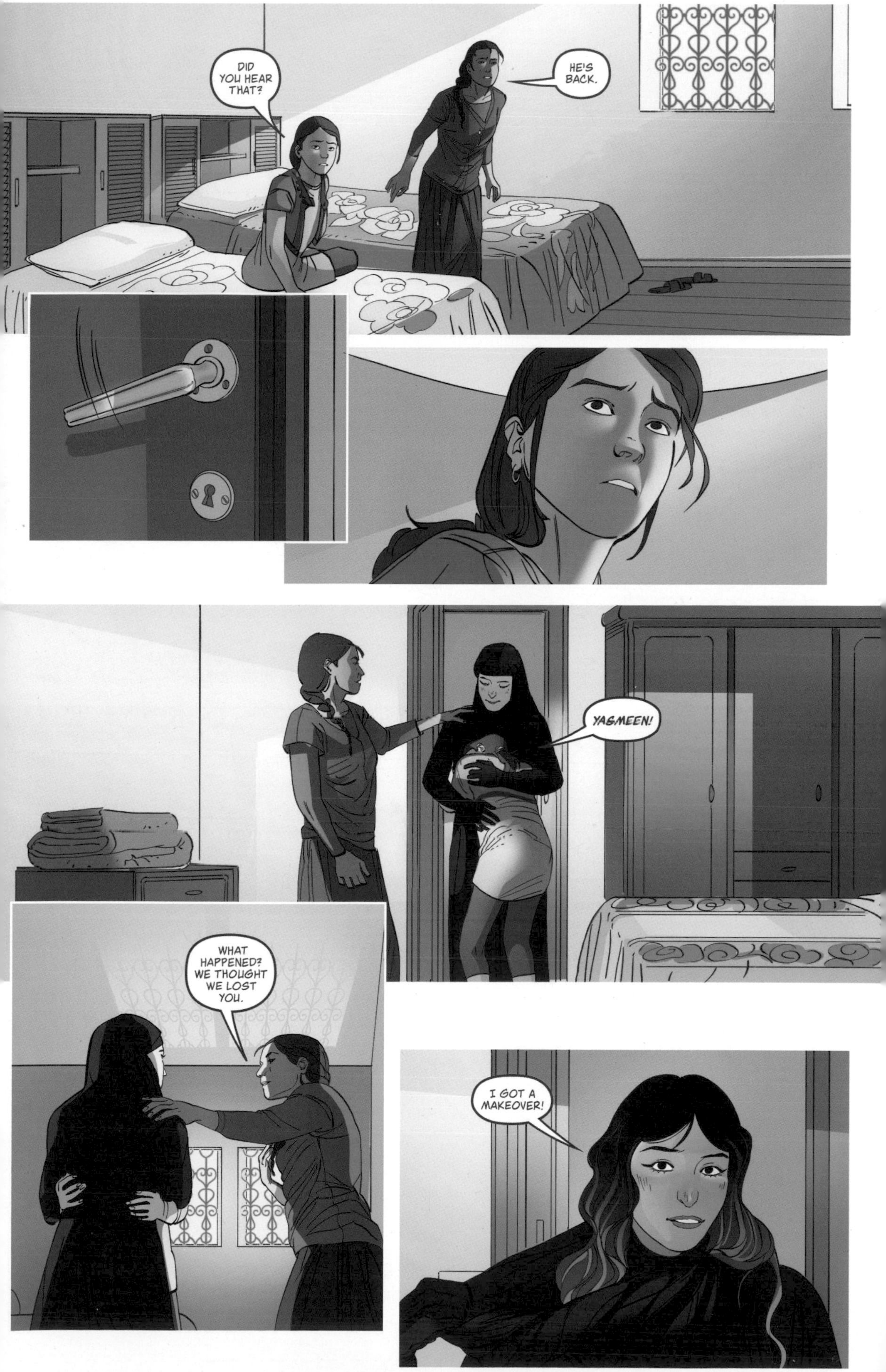
DID YOU HEAR THAT?
HE'S BACK.
YASMEEN!
WHAT HAPPENED? WE THOUGHT WE LOST YOU.
I GOT A MAKEOVER!

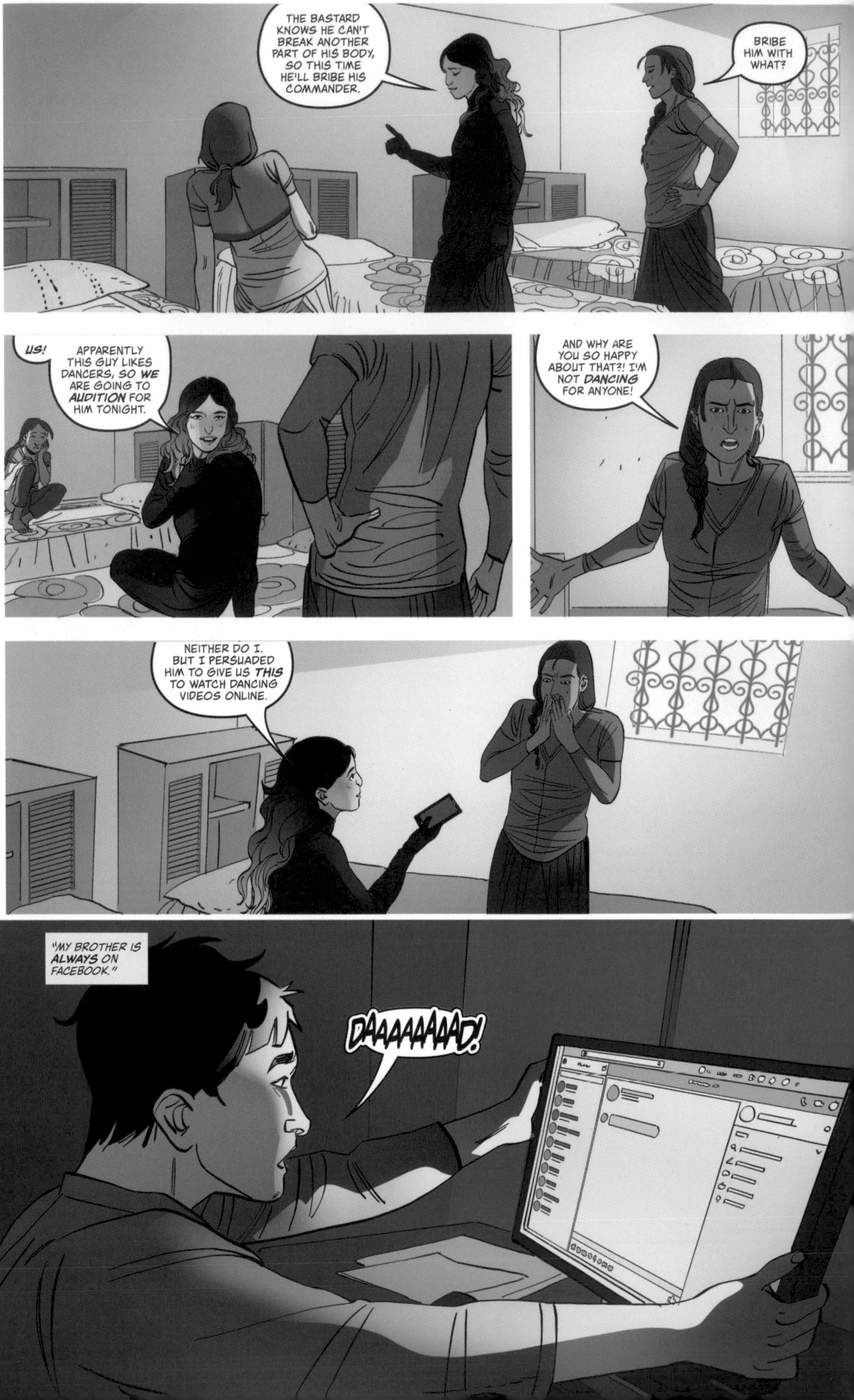
THE BASTARD KNOWS HE CAN'T BREAK ANOTHER PART OF HIS BODY, SO THIS TIME HE'LL BRIBE HIS COMMANDER.
BRIBE HIM WITH WHAT?
US!
APPARENTLY THIS GUY LIKES DANCERS, SO WE ARE GOING TO AUDITION FOR HIM TONIGHT.
AND WHY ARE YOU SO HAPPY ABOUT THAT?! I'M NOT DANCING FOR ANYONE!
NEITHER DO I. BUT I PERSUADED HIM TO GIVE US THIS TO WATCH DANCING VIDEOS ONLINE.
"MY BROTHER IS ALWAYS ON FACEBOOK."
DAAAAAAAAD!

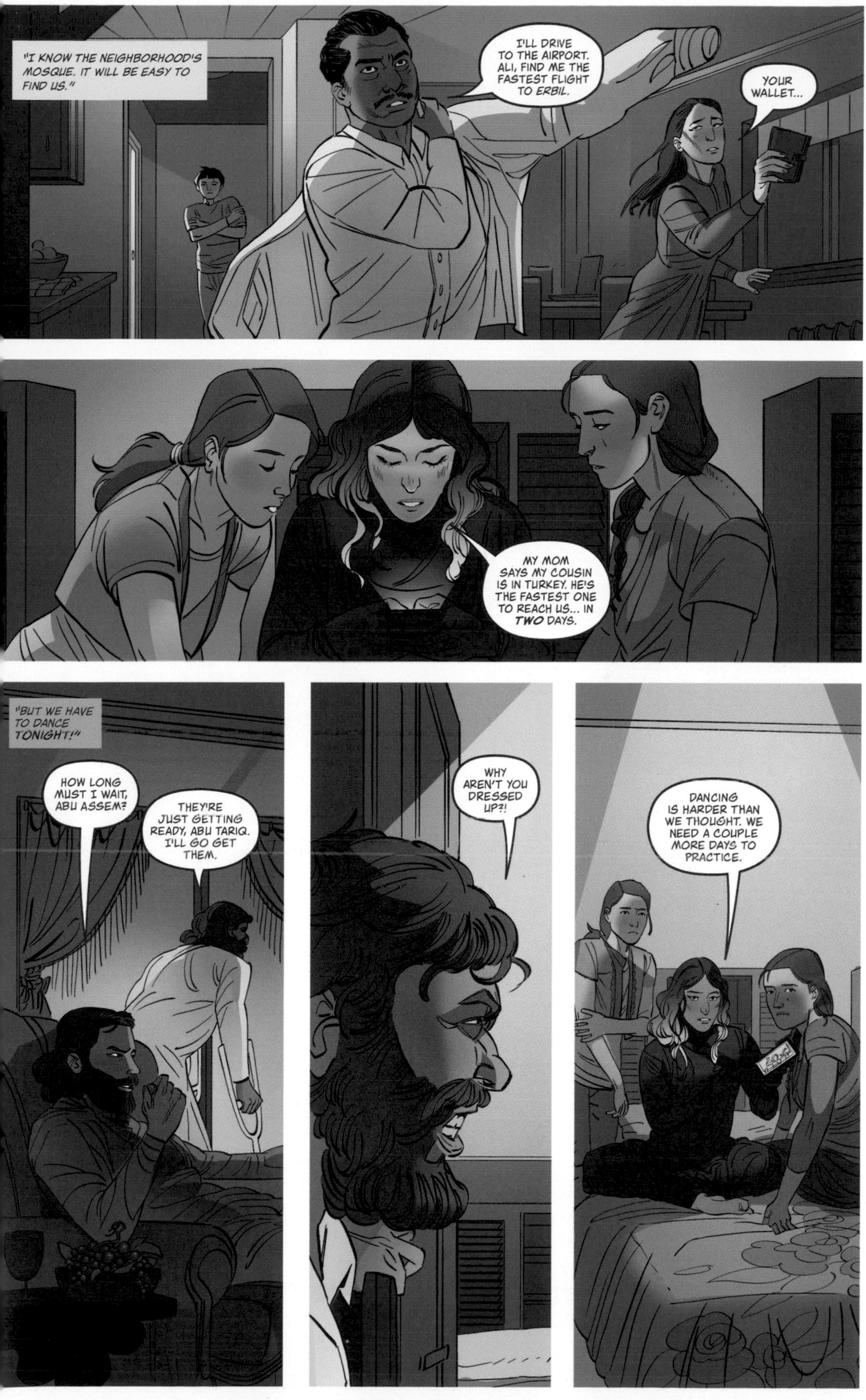
"I KNOW THE NEIGHBORHOOD'S MOSQUE. IT WILL BE EASY TO FIND US."
I'LL DRIVE TO THE AIRPORT. ALI, FIND ME THE FASTEST FLIGHT TO ERBIL.
YOUR WALLET...
MY MOM SAYS MY COUSIN IS IN TURKEY. HE'S THE FASTEST ONE TO REACH US... IN **TWO** DAYS.
"BUT WE HAVE TO DANCE **TONIGHT!**"
HOW LONG MUST I WAIT, ABU ASSEM?
THEY'RE JUST GETTING READY, ABU TARIQ. I'LL GO GET THEM.
WHY AREN'T YOU DRESSED UP?!
DANCING IS HARDER THAN WE THOUGHT. WE NEED A COUPLE MORE DAYS TO PRACTICE.

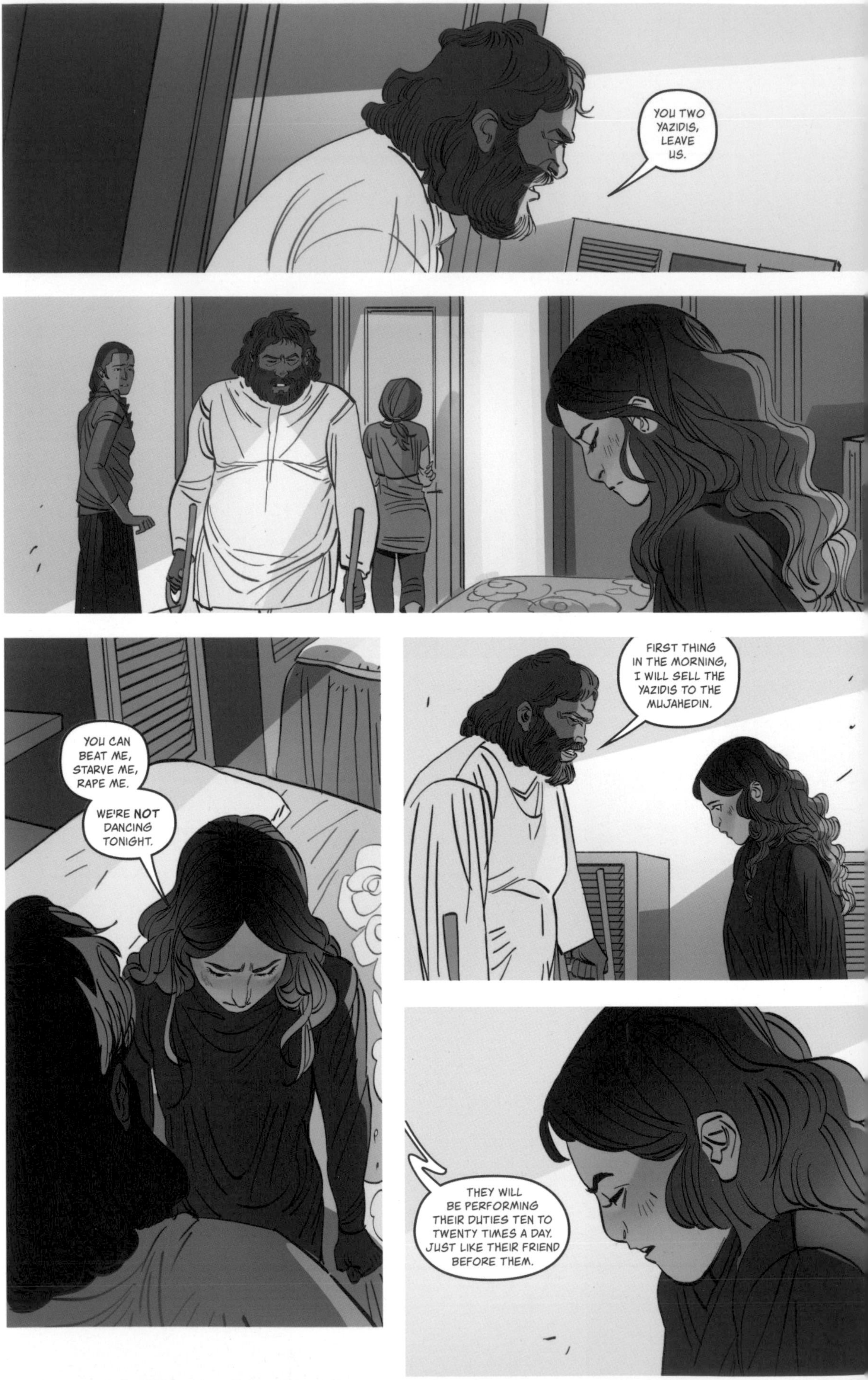
YOU TWO YAZIDIS, LEAVE US.
YOU CAN BEAT ME, STARVE ME, RAPE ME.
WE'RE **NOT** DANCING TONIGHT.
FIRST THING IN THE MORNING, I WILL SELL THE YAZIDIS TO THE MUJAHEDIN.
THEY WILL BE PERFORMING THEIR DUTIES TEN TO TWENTY TIMES A DAY. JUST LIKE THEIR FRIEND BEFORE THEM.

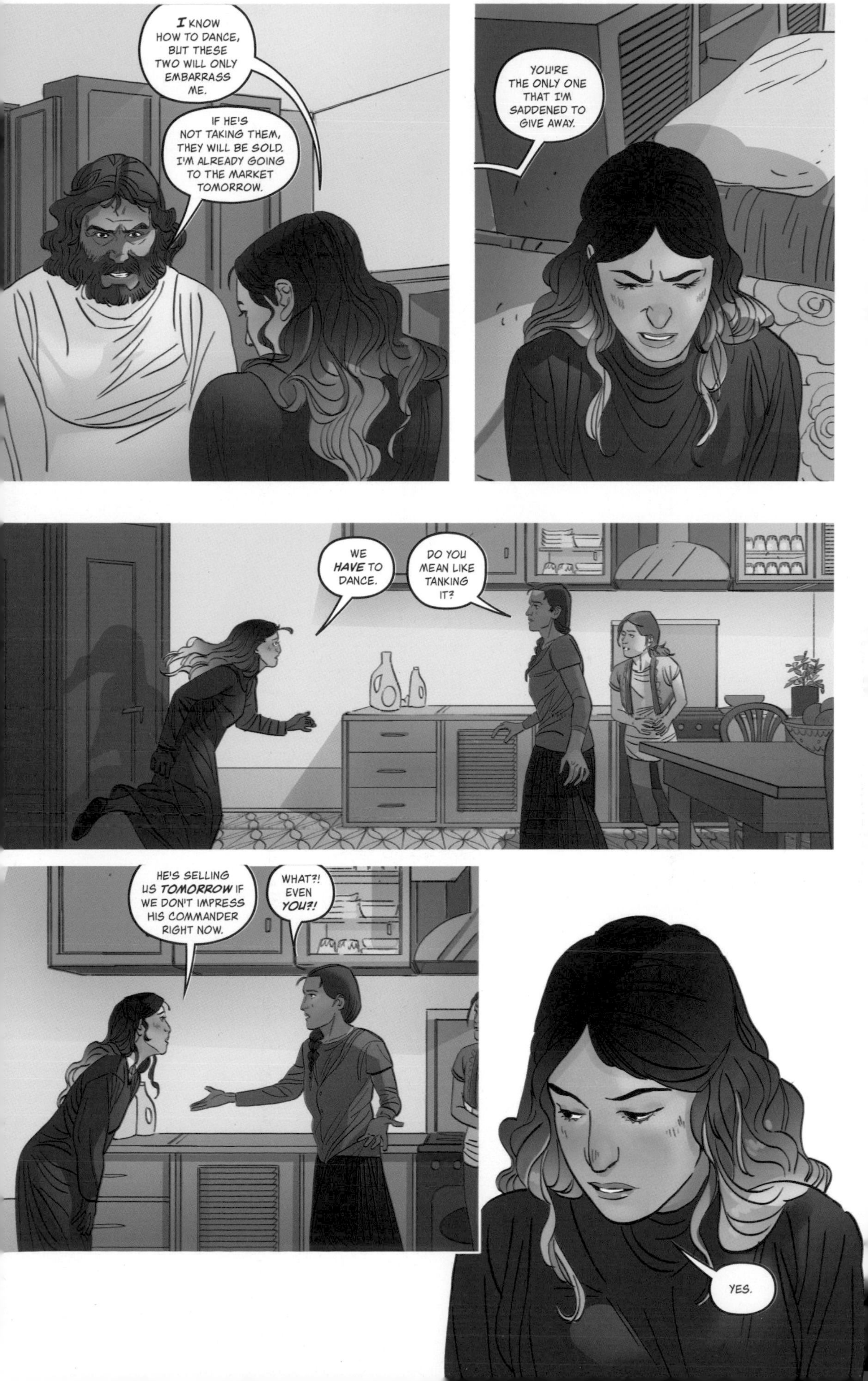
I KNOW HOW TO DANCE, BUT THESE TWO WILL ONLY EMBARRASS ME.
IF HE'S NOT TAKING THEM, THEY WILL BE SOLD. I'M ALREADY GOING TO THE MARKET TOMORROW.
YOU'RE THE ONLY ONE THAT I'M SADDENED TO GIVE AWAY.
WE HAVE TO DANCE.
DO YOU MEAN LIKE TANKING IT?
HE'S SELLING US TOMORROW IF WE DON'T IMPRESS HIS COMMANDER RIGHT NOW.
WHAT?! EVEN YOU?!
YES.

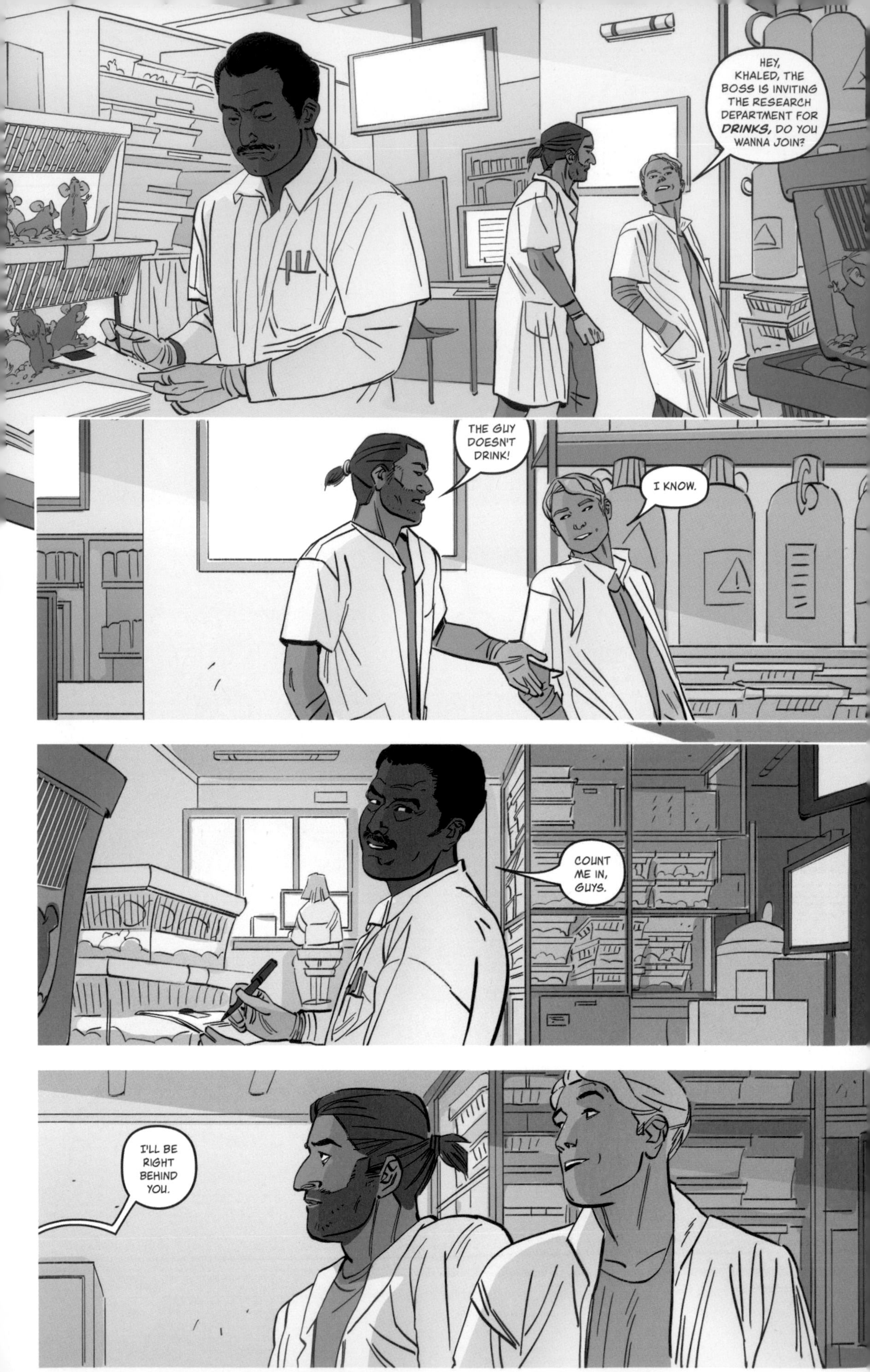
HEY, KHALED, THE BOSS IS INVITING THE RESEARCH DEPARTMENT FOR DRINKS, DO YOU WANNA JOIN?
THE GUY DOESN'T DRINK!
I KNOW.
COUNT ME IN, GUYS.
I'LL BE RIGHT BEHIND YOU.

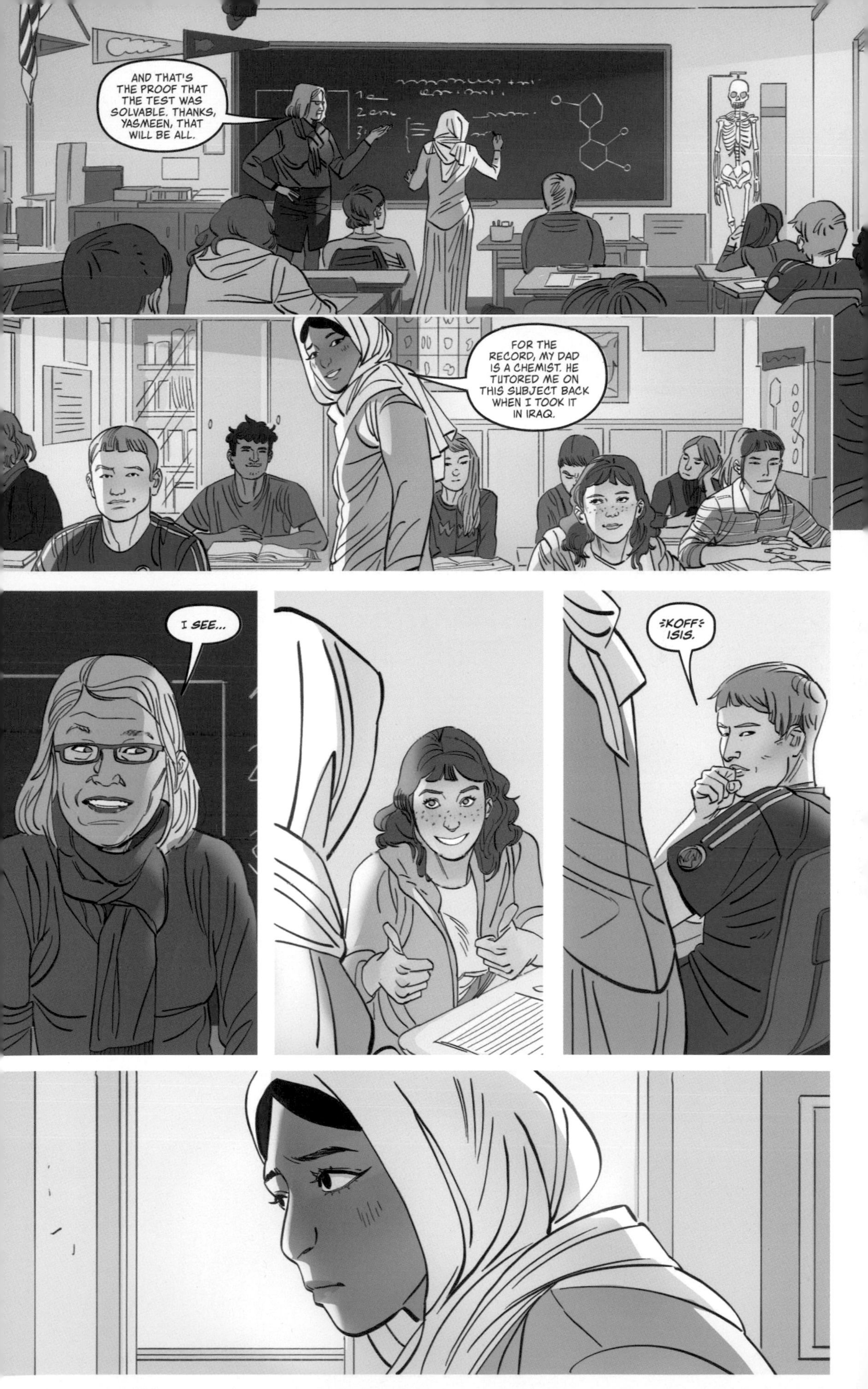
AND THAT'S THE PROOF THAT THE TEST WAS SOLVABLE. THANKS, YASMEEN, THAT WILL BE ALL.
FOR THE RECORD, MY DAD IS A CHEMIST. HE TUTORED ME ON THIS SUBJECT BACK WHEN I TOOK IT IN IRAQ.
I SEE...
KOFF ISIS.

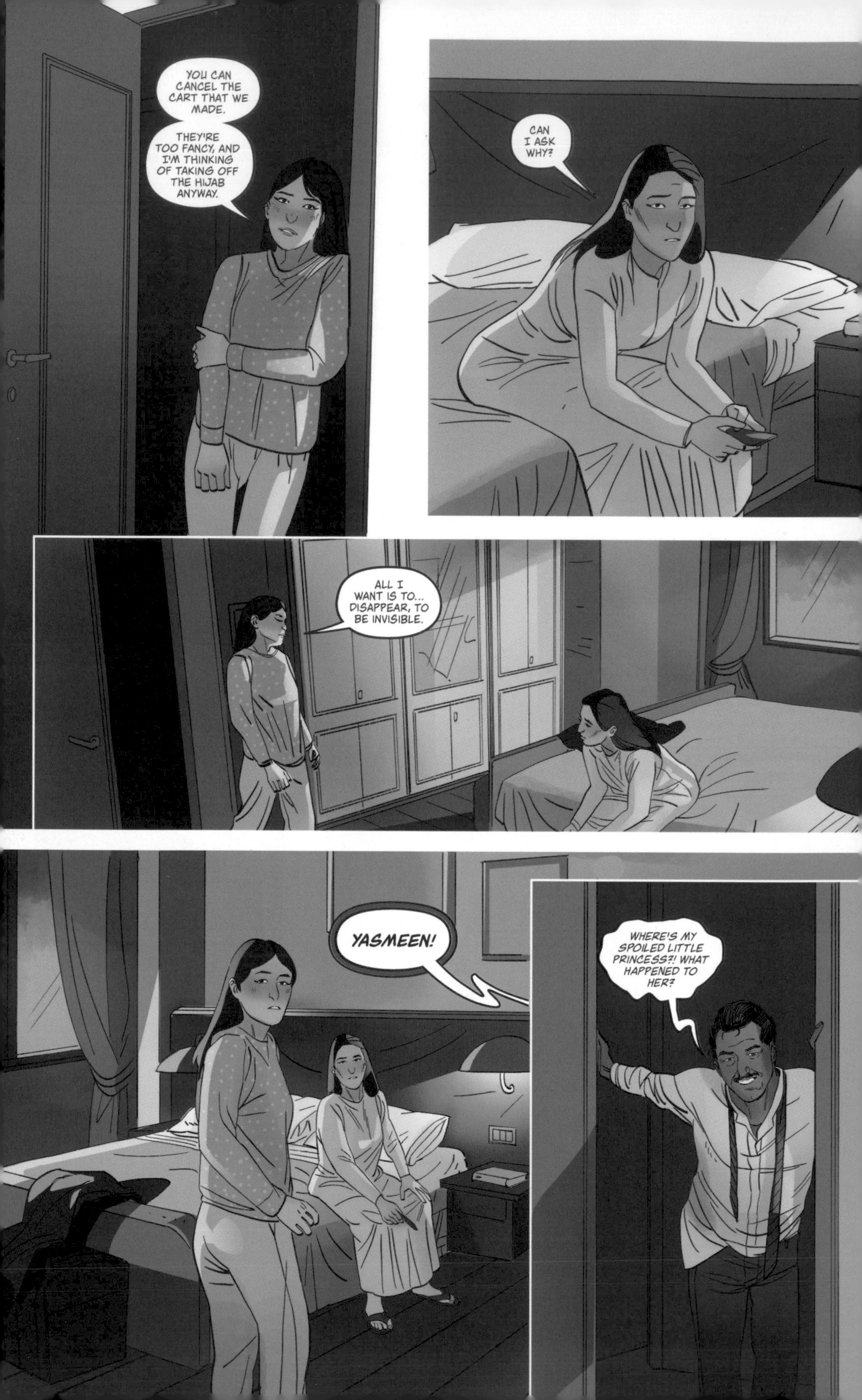
YOU CAN CANCEL THE CART THAT WE MADE.
THEY'RE TOO FANCY, AND I'M THINKING OF TAKING OFF THE HIJAB ANYWAY.
CAN I ASK WHY?
ALL I WANT IS TO... DISAPPEAR, TO BE INVISIBLE.
YASMEEN!
WHERE'S MY SPOILED LITTLE PRINCESS?! WHAT HAPPENED TO HER?

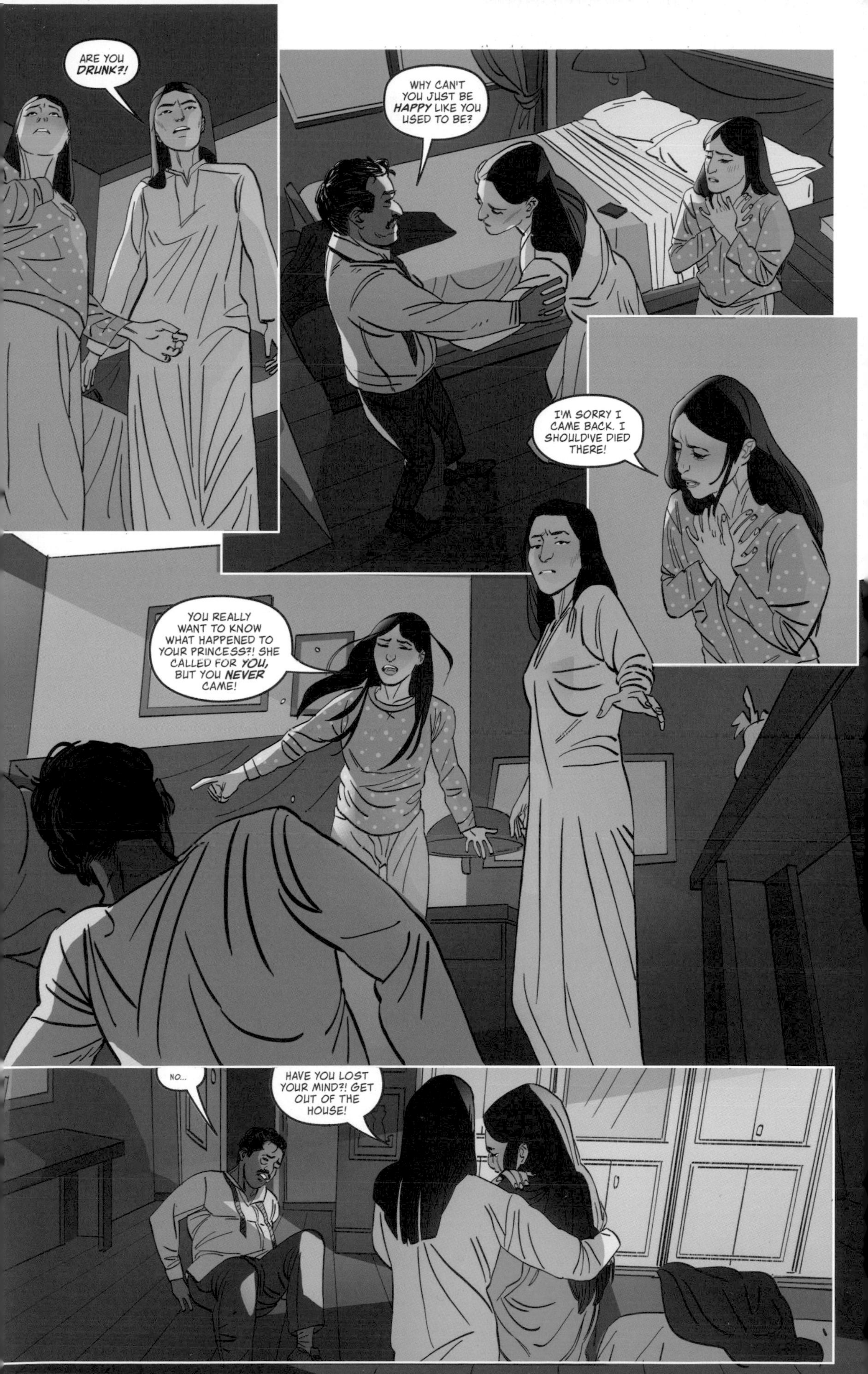
ARE YOU DRUNK?!
WHY CAN'T YOU JUST BE HAPPY LIKE YOU USED TO BE?
I'M SORRY I CAME BACK. I SHOULD'VE DIED THERE!
YOU REALLY WANT TO KNOW WHAT HAPPENED TO YOUR PRINCESS?! SHE CALLED FOR YOU, BUT YOU NEVER CAME!
NO...
HAVE YOU LOST YOUR MIND?! GET OUT OF THE HOUSE!

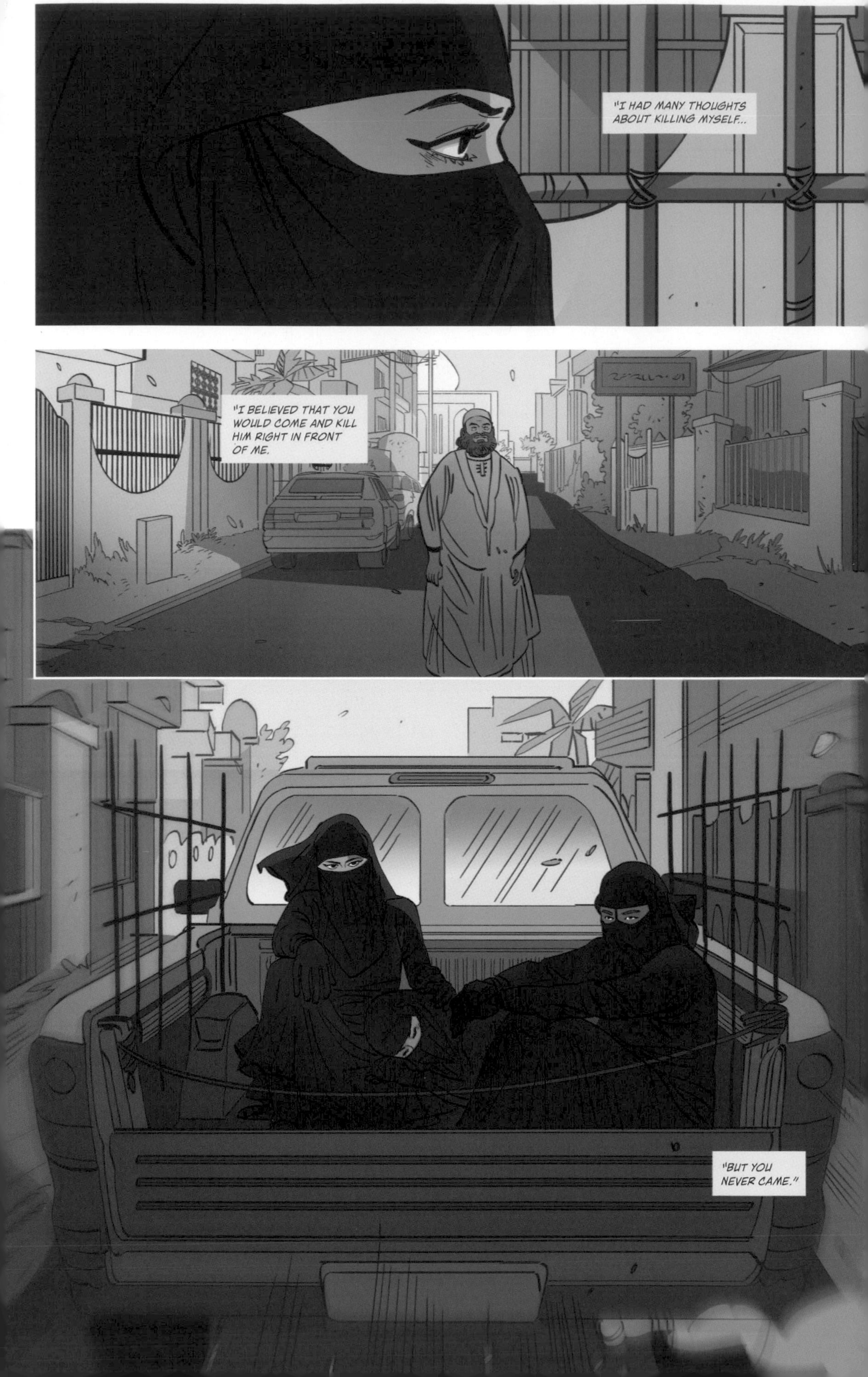
"I HAD MANY THOUGHTS ABOUT KILLING MYSELF...
"I BELIEVED THAT YOU WOULD COME AND KILL HIM RIGHT IN FRONT OF ME.
"BUT YOU NEVER CAME."

CHAPTER 4

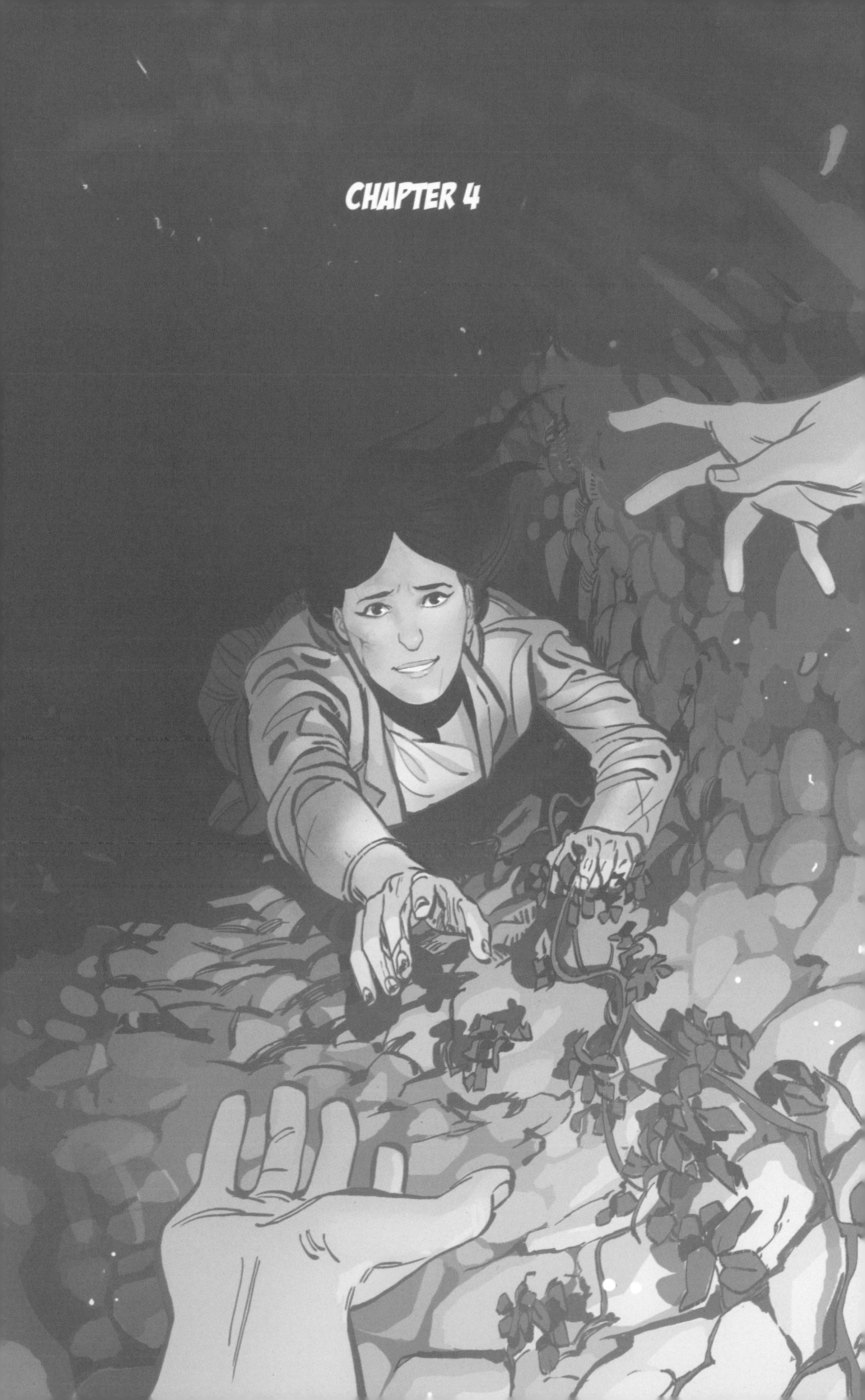

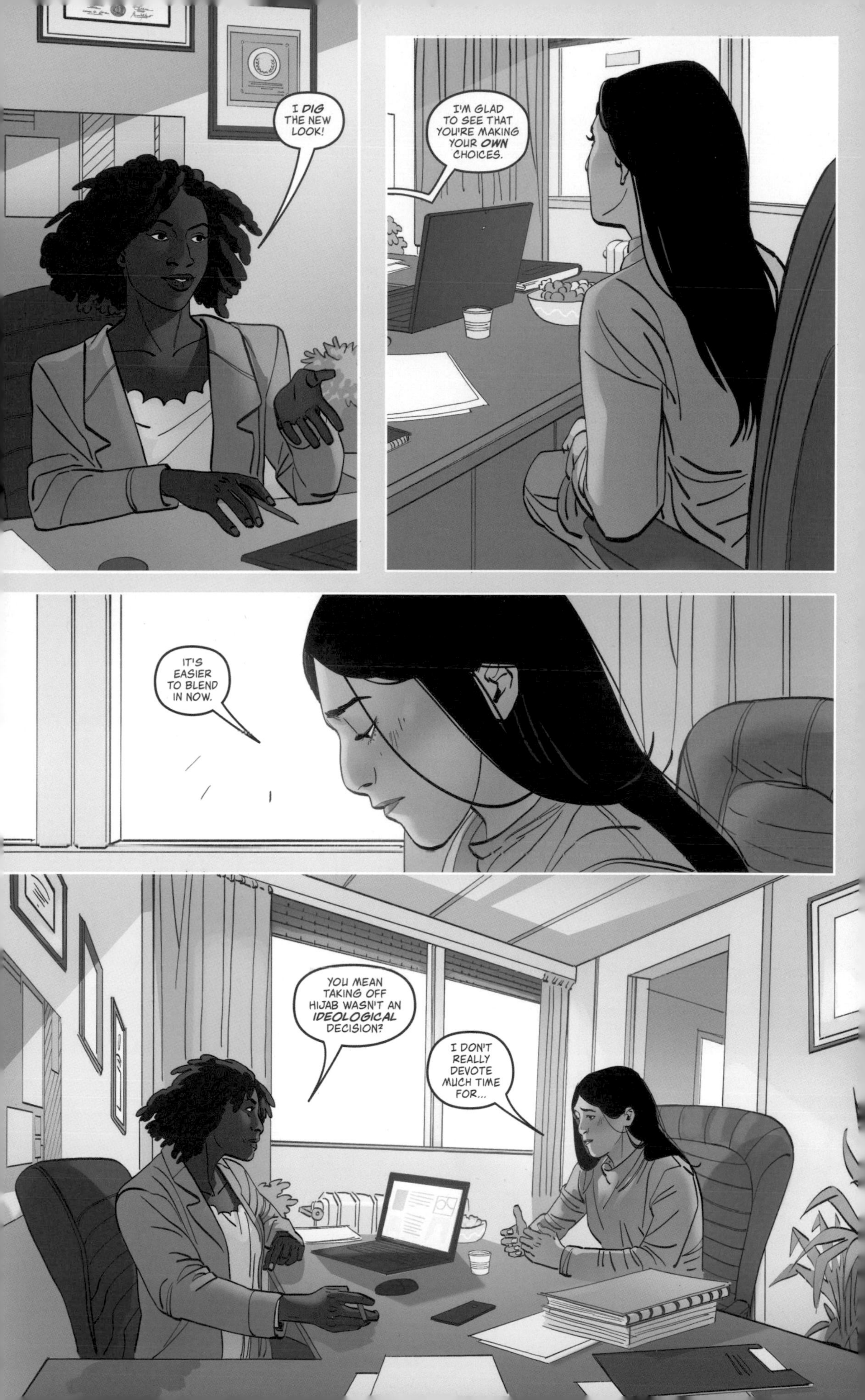
I DIG THE NEW LOOK!
I'M GLAD TO SEE THAT YOU'RE MAKING YOUR OWN CHOICES.
IT'S EASIER TO BLEND IN NOW.
YOU MEAN TAKING OFF HIJAB WASN'T AN IDEOLOGICAL DECISION?
I DON'T REALLY DEVOTE MUCH TIME FOR...

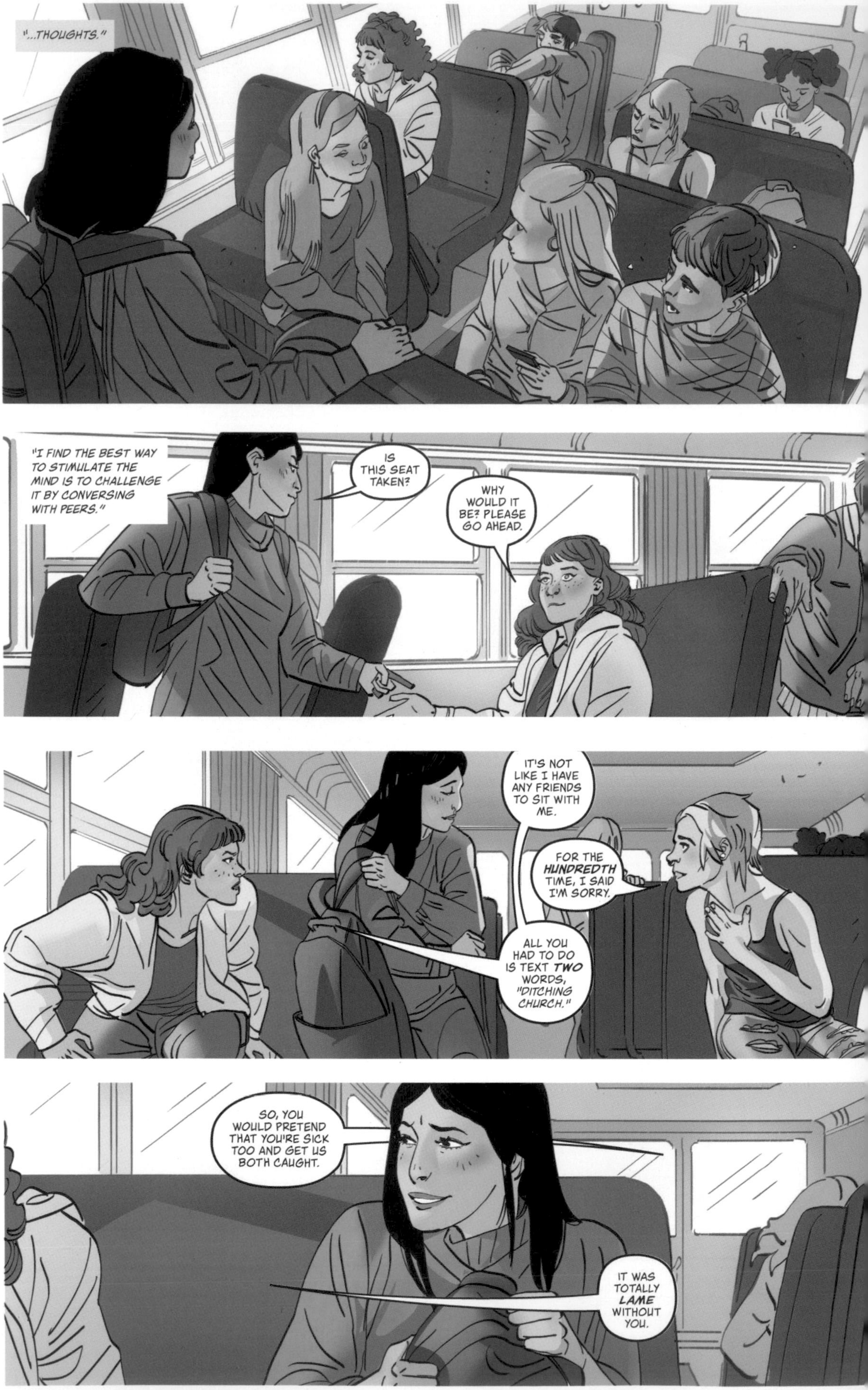
"...THOUGHTS."
"I FIND THE BEST WAY TO STIMULATE THE MIND IS TO CHALLENGE IT BY CONVERSING WITH PEERS."
IS THIS SEAT TAKEN?
WHY WOULD IT BE? PLEASE GO AHEAD.
IT'S NOT LIKE I HAVE ANY FRIENDS TO SIT WITH ME.
FOR THE HUNDREDTH TIME, I SAID I'M SORRY.
ALL YOU HAD TO DO IS TEXT TWO WORDS, "DITCHING CHURCH."
SO, YOU WOULD PRETEND THAT YOU'RE SICK TOO AND GET US BOTH CAUGHT.
IT WAS TOTALLY LAME WITHOUT YOU.

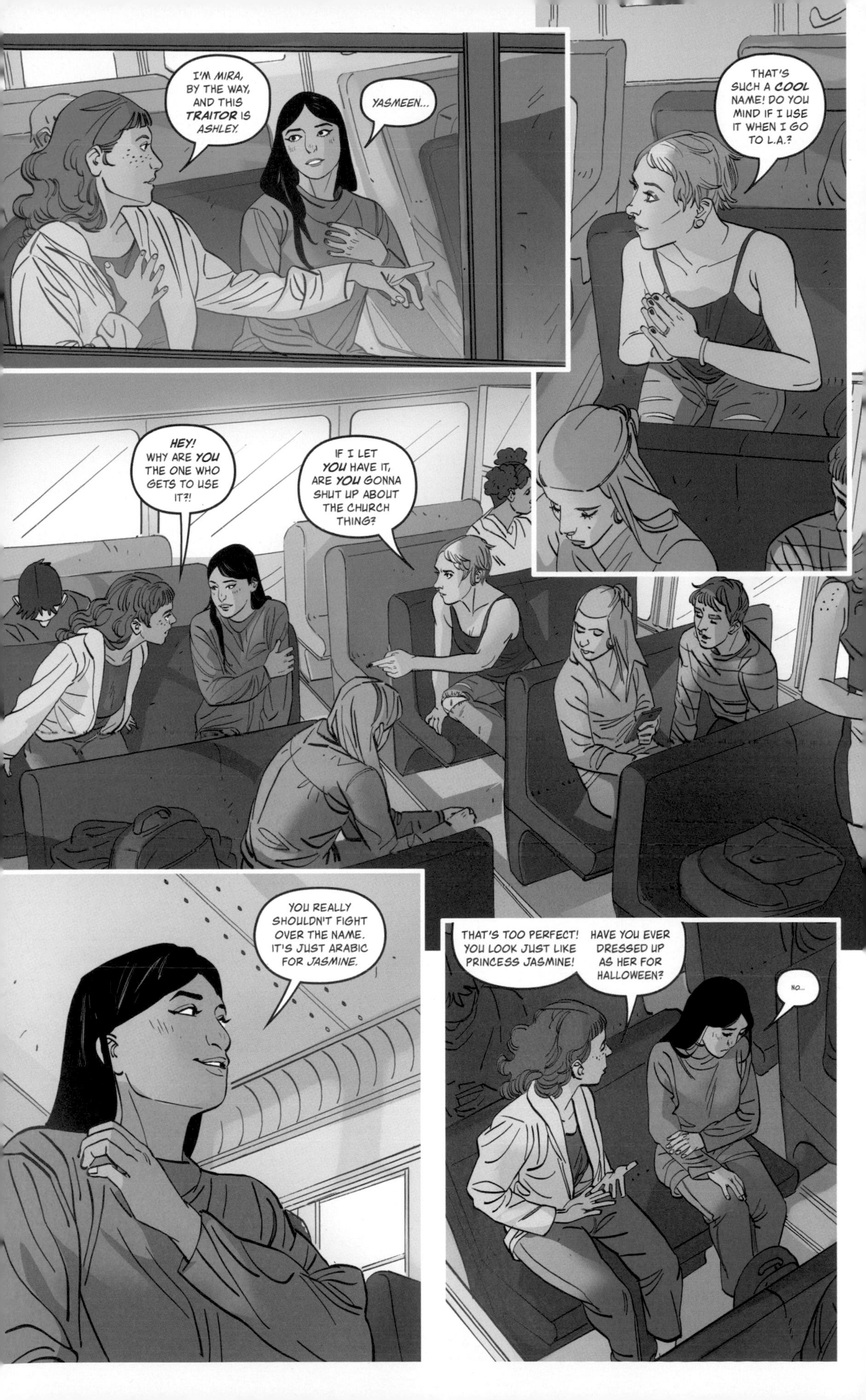
I'M MIRA, BY THE WAY, AND THIS TRAITOR IS ASHLEY.
YASMEEN...
THAT'S SUCH A COOL NAME! DO YOU MIND IF I USE IT WHEN I GO TO L.A.?
HEY! WHY ARE YOU THE ONE WHO GETS TO USE IT?!
IF I LET YOU HAVE IT, ARE YOU GONNA SHUT UP ABOUT THE CHURCH THING?
YOU REALLY SHOULDN'T FIGHT OVER THE NAME. IT'S JUST ARABIC FOR JASMINE.
THAT'S TOO PERFECT! YOU LOOK JUST LIKE PRINCESS JASMINE!
HAVE YOU EVER DRESSED UP AS HER FOR HALLOWEEN?
NO...

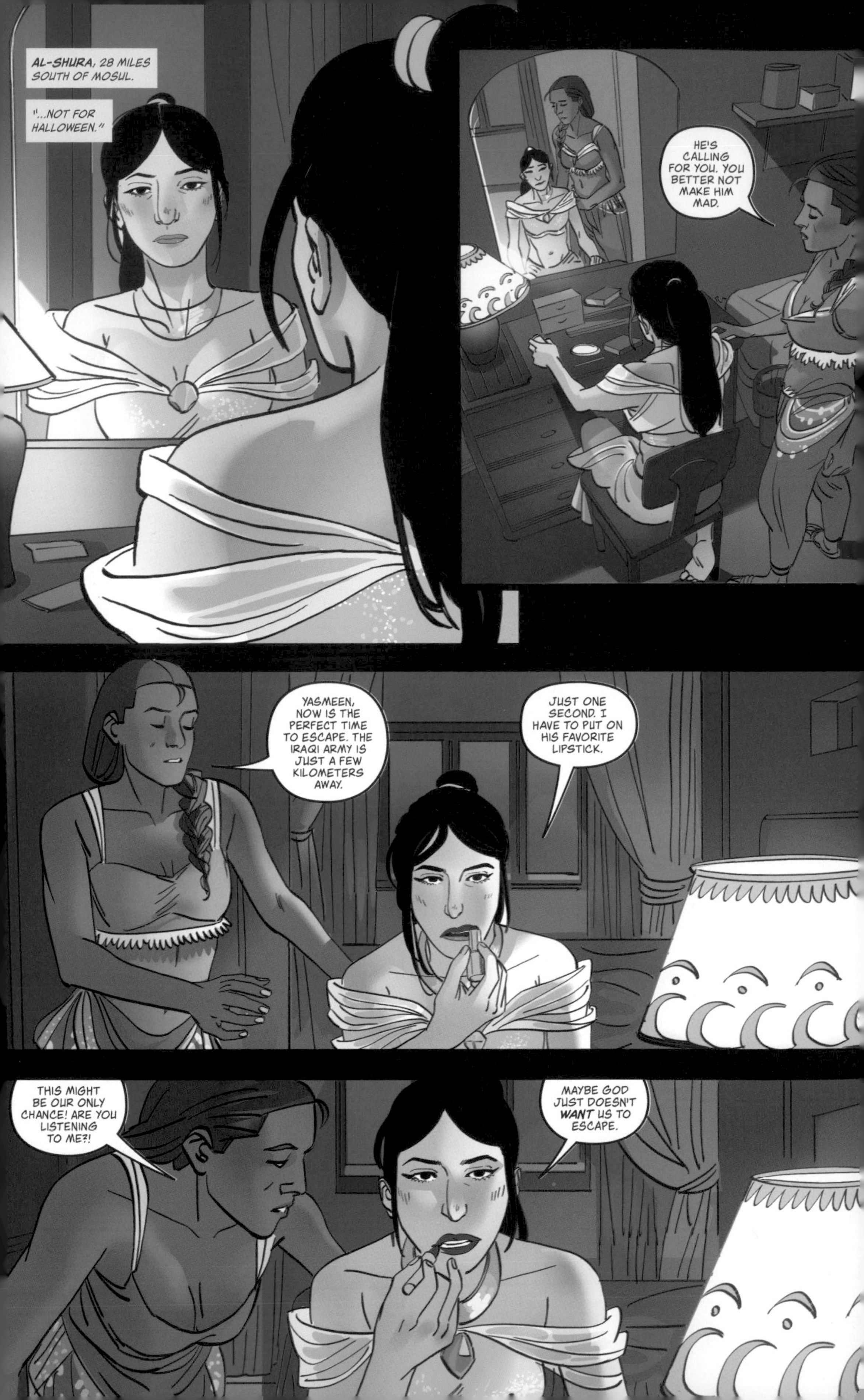

AL-SHURA, 28 MILES SOUTH OF MOSUL.
"...NOT FOR HALLOWEEN."
HE'S CALLING FOR YOU. YOU BETTER NOT MAKE HIM MAD.
YASMEEN, NOW IS THE PERFECT TIME TO ESCAPE. THE IRAQI ARMY IS JUST A FEW KILOMETERS AWAY.
JUST ONE SECOND. I HAVE TO PUT ON HIS FAVORITE LIPSTICK.
THIS MIGHT BE OUR ONLY CHANCE! ARE YOU LISTENING TO ME?!
MAYBE GOD JUST DOESN'T WANT US TO ESCAPE.

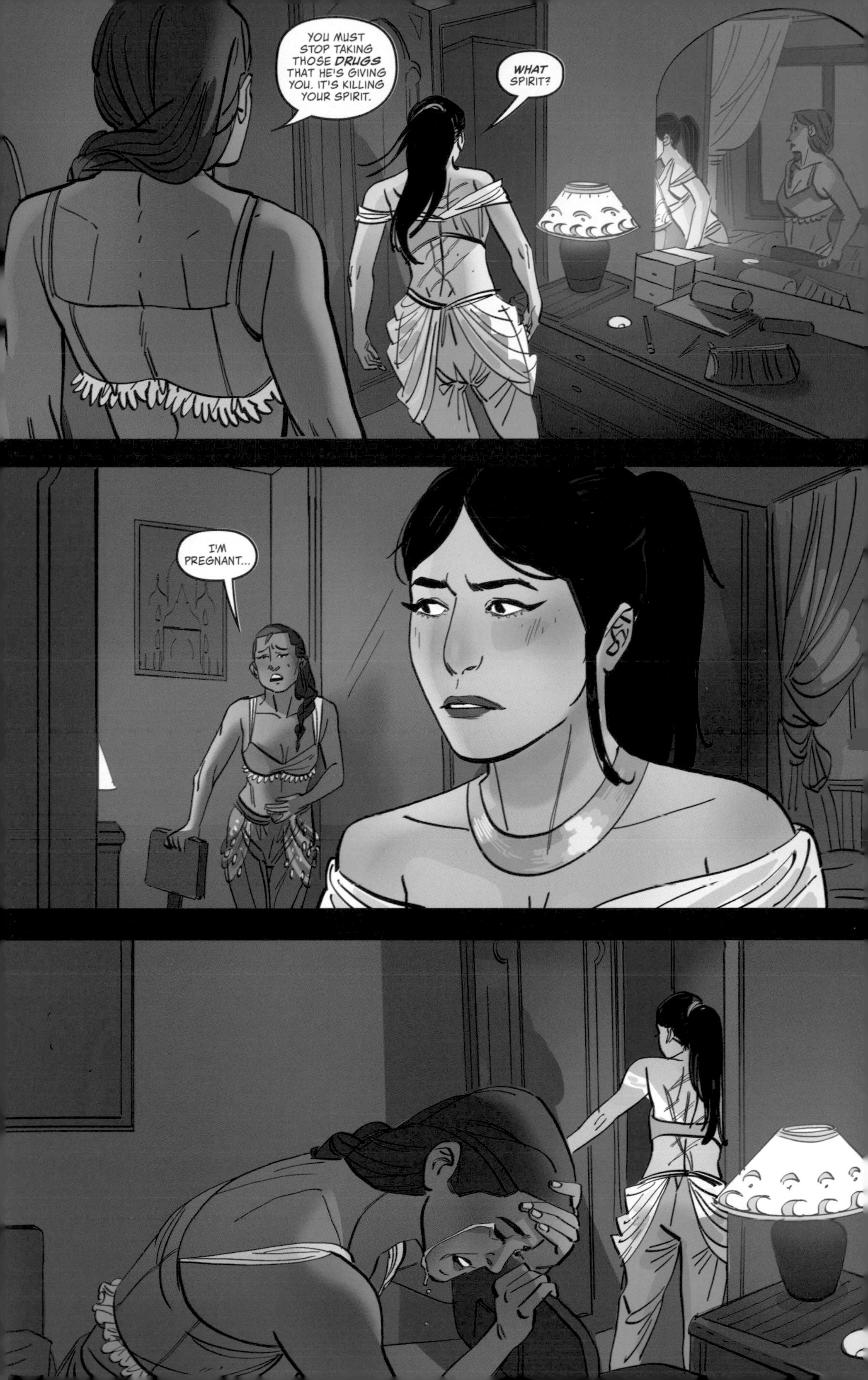
YOU MUST STOP TAKING THOSE DRUGS THAT HE'S GIVING YOU. IT'S KILLING YOUR SPIRIT.
WHAT SPIRIT?
I'M PREGNANT...

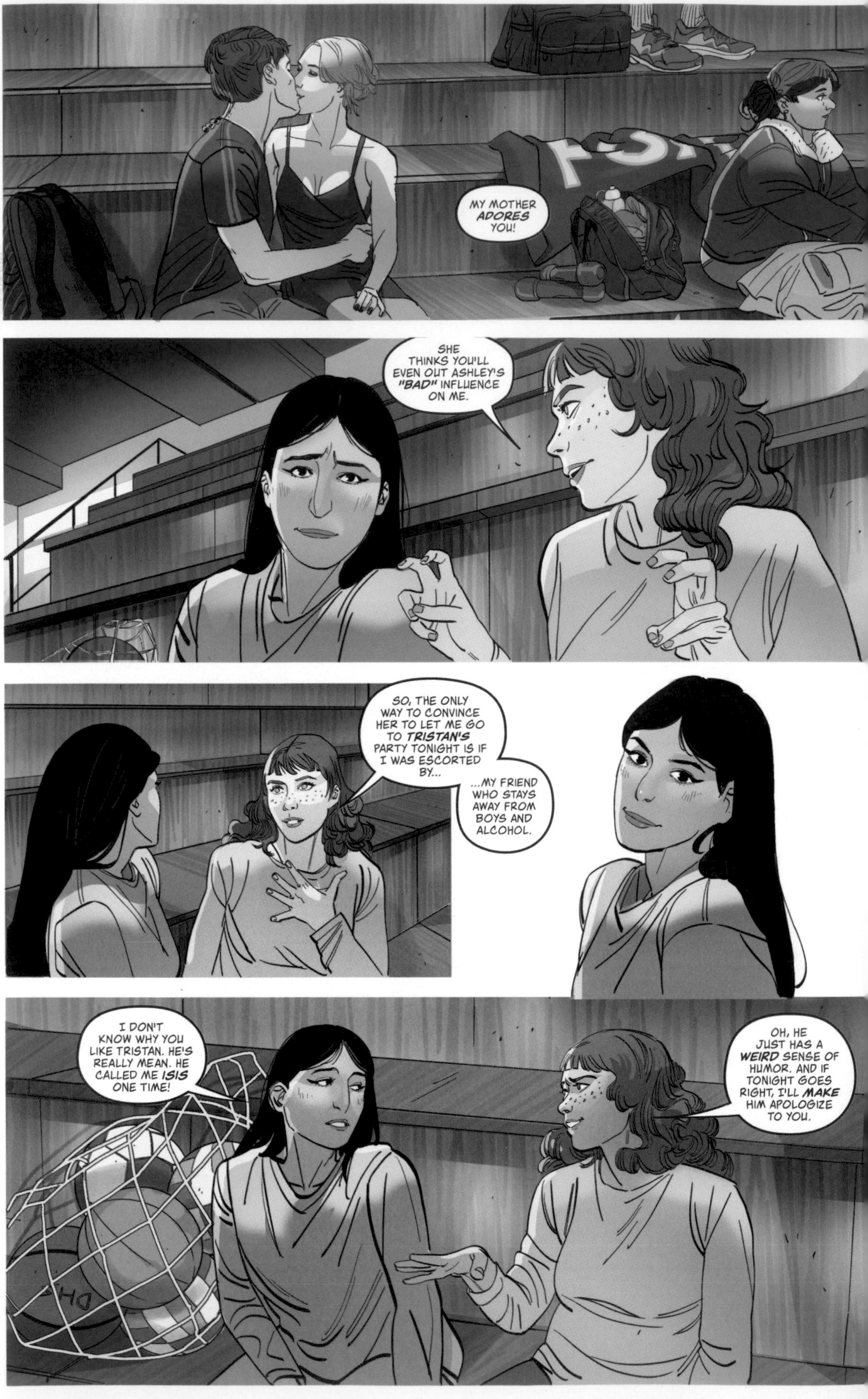
MY MOTHER ADORES YOU!
SHE THINKS YOU'LL EVEN OUT ASHLEY'S "BAD" INFLUENCE ON ME.
SO, THE ONLY WAY TO CONVINCE HER TO LET ME GO TO TRISTAN'S PARTY TONIGHT IS IF I WAS ESCORTED BY...
...MY FRIEND WHO STAYS AWAY FROM BOYS AND ALCOHOL.
I DON'T KNOW WHY YOU LIKE TRISTAN. HE'S REALLY MEAN. HE CALLED ME ISIS ONE TIME!
OH, HE JUST HAS A WEIRD SENSE OF HUMOR. AND IF TONIGHT GOES RIGHT, I'LL MAKE HIM APOLOGIZE TO YOU.

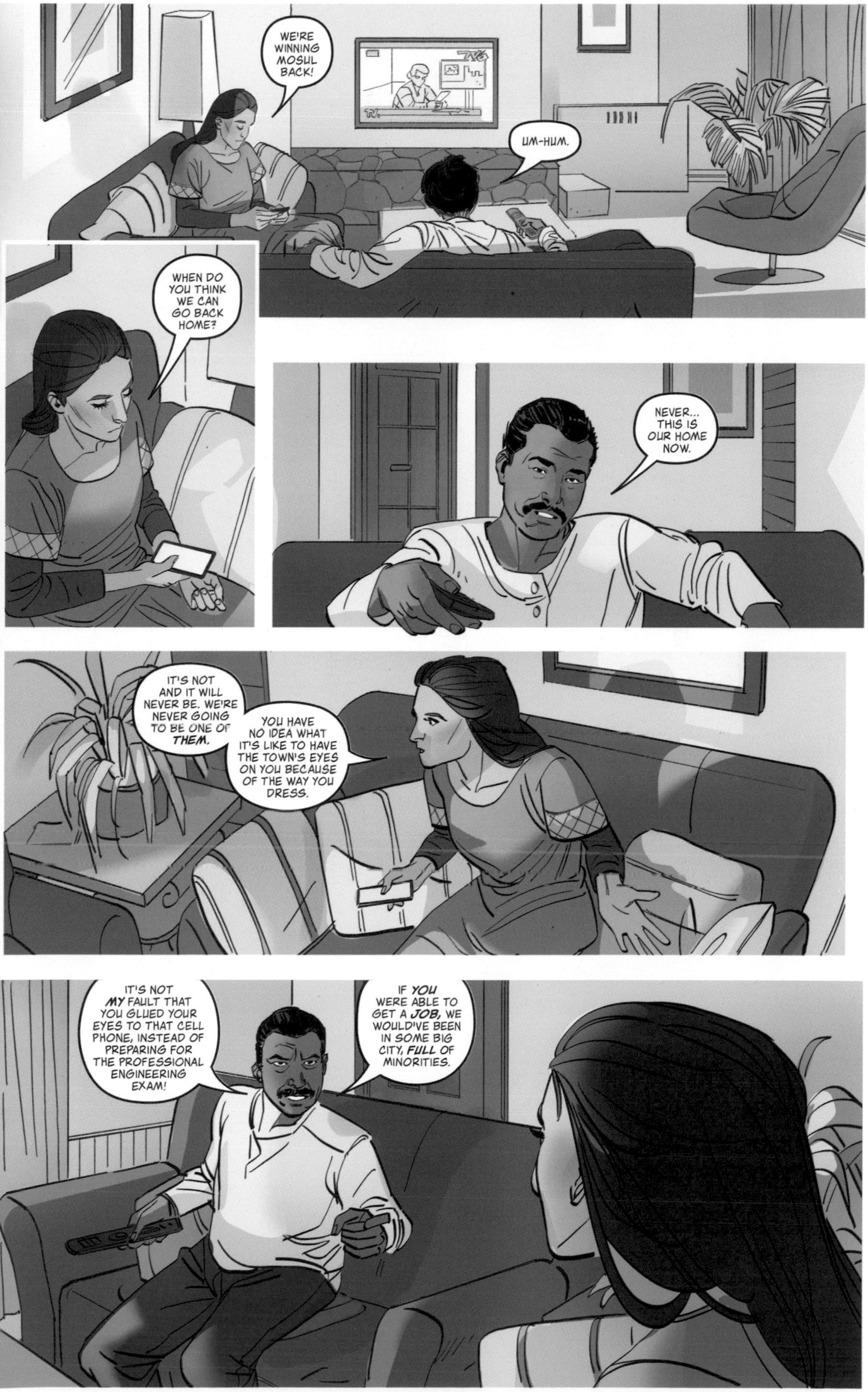
WE'RE WINNING MOSUL BACK!
UM-HUM.
WHEN DO YOU THINK WE CAN GO BACK HOME?
NEVER... THIS IS OUR HOME NOW.
IT'S NOT AND IT WILL NEVER BE. WE'RE NEVER GOING TO BE ONE OF THEM.
YOU HAVE NO IDEA WHAT IT'S LIKE TO HAVE THE TOWN'S EYES ON YOU BECAUSE OF THE WAY YOU DRESS.
IT'S NOT MY FAULT THAT YOU GLUED YOUR EYES TO THAT CELL PHONE, INSTEAD OF PREPARING FOR THE PROFESSIONAL ENGINEERING EXAM!
IF YOU WERE ABLE TO GET A JOB, WE WOULD'VE BEEN IN SOME BIG CITY, FULL OF MINORITIES.

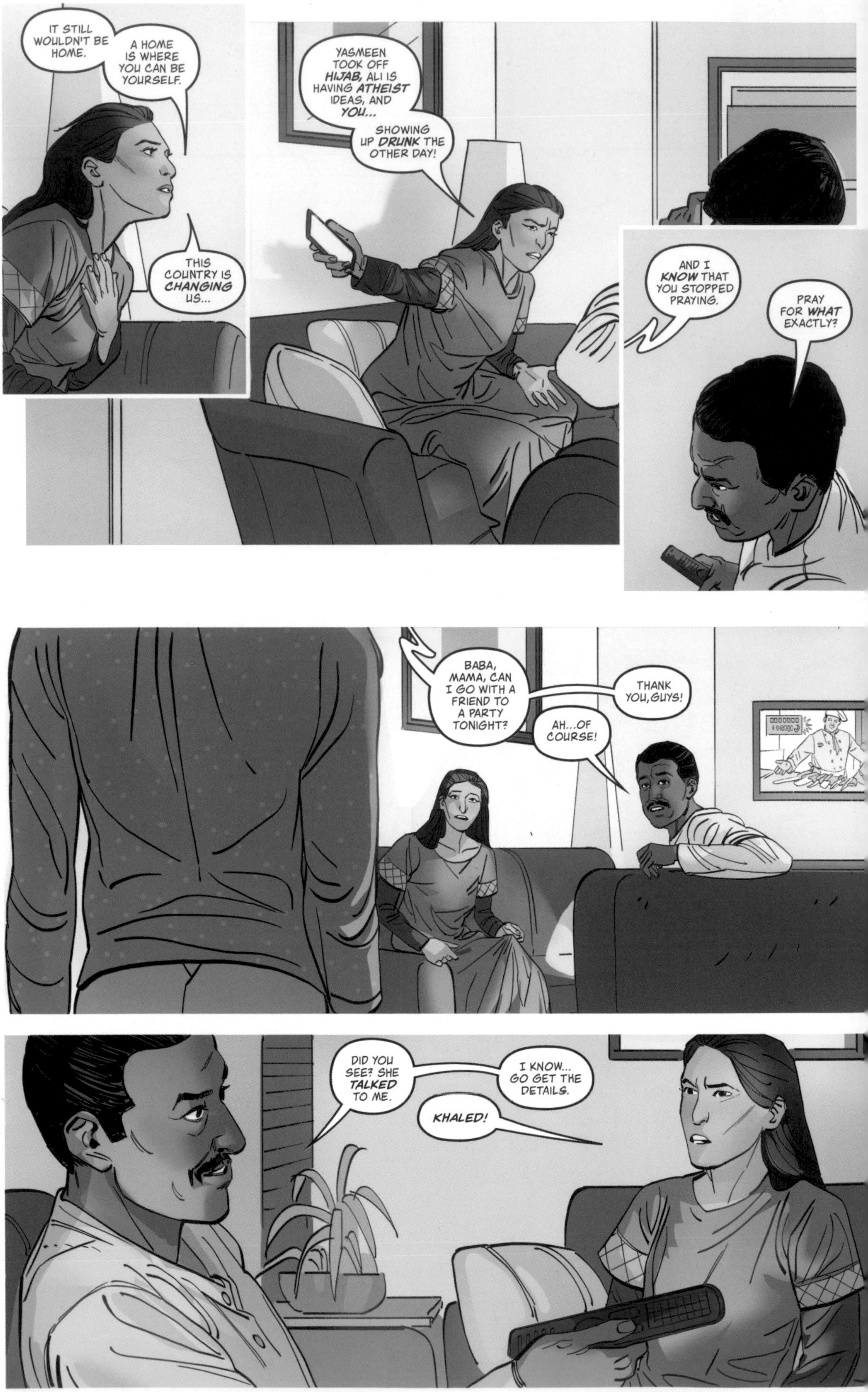
IT STILL WOULDN'T BE HOME.
A HOME IS WHERE YOU CAN BE YOURSELF.
THIS COUNTRY IS CHANGING US...
YASMEEN TOOK OFF HIJAB, ALI IS HAVING ATHEIST IDEAS, AND YOU...
SHOWING UP DRUNK THE OTHER DAY!
AND I KNOW THAT YOU STOPPED PRAYING.
PRAY FOR WHAT EXACTLY?
BABA, MAMA, CAN I GO WITH A FRIEND TO A PARTY TONIGHT?
AH...OF COURSE!
THANK YOU,GUYS!
DID YOU SEE? SHE TALKED TO ME.
I KNOW... GO GET THE DETAILS.
KHALED!

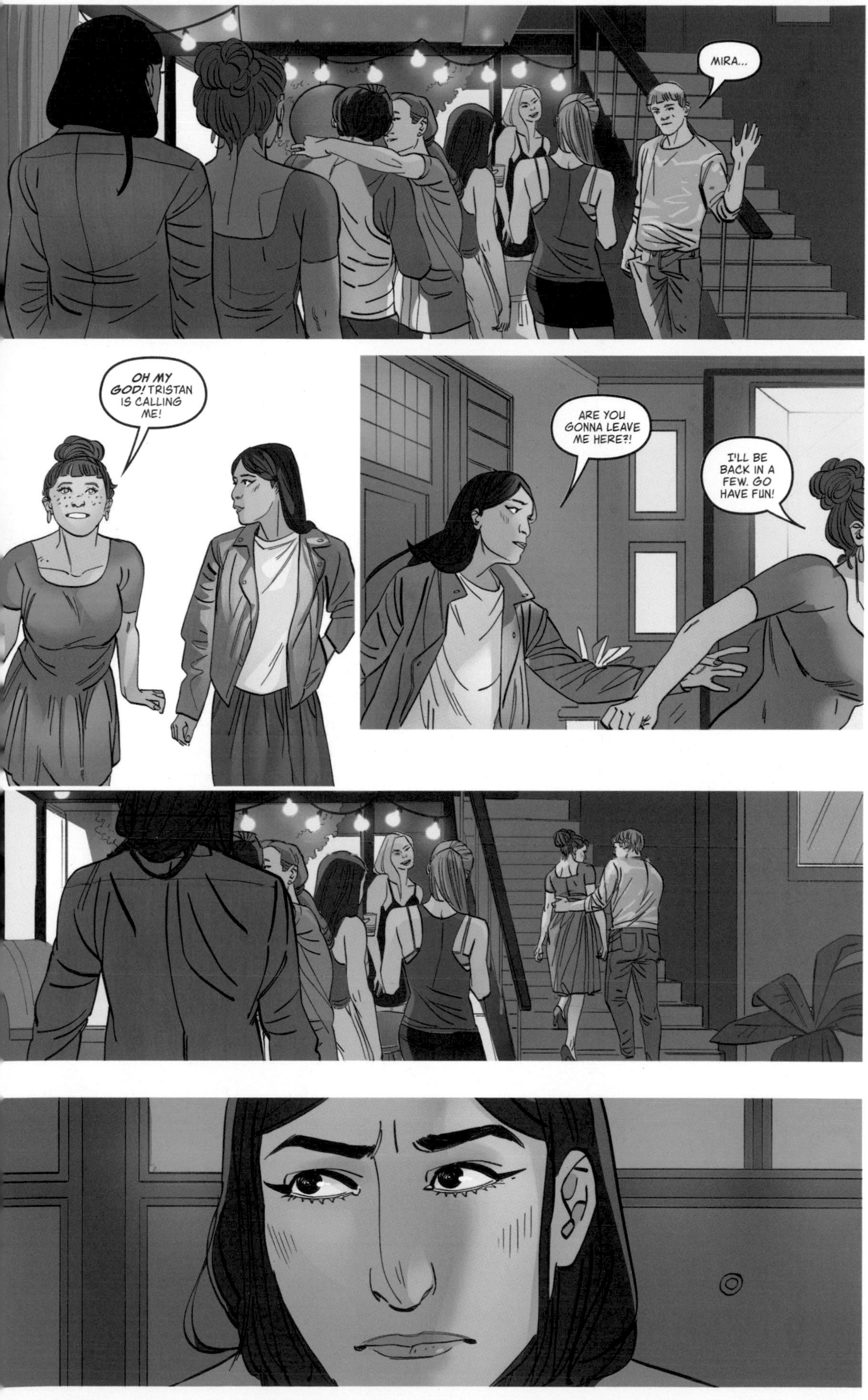
MIRA...
OH MY GOD! TRISTAN IS CALLING ME!
ARE YOU GONNA LEAVE ME HERE?!
I'LL BE BACK IN A FEW. GO HAVE FUN!

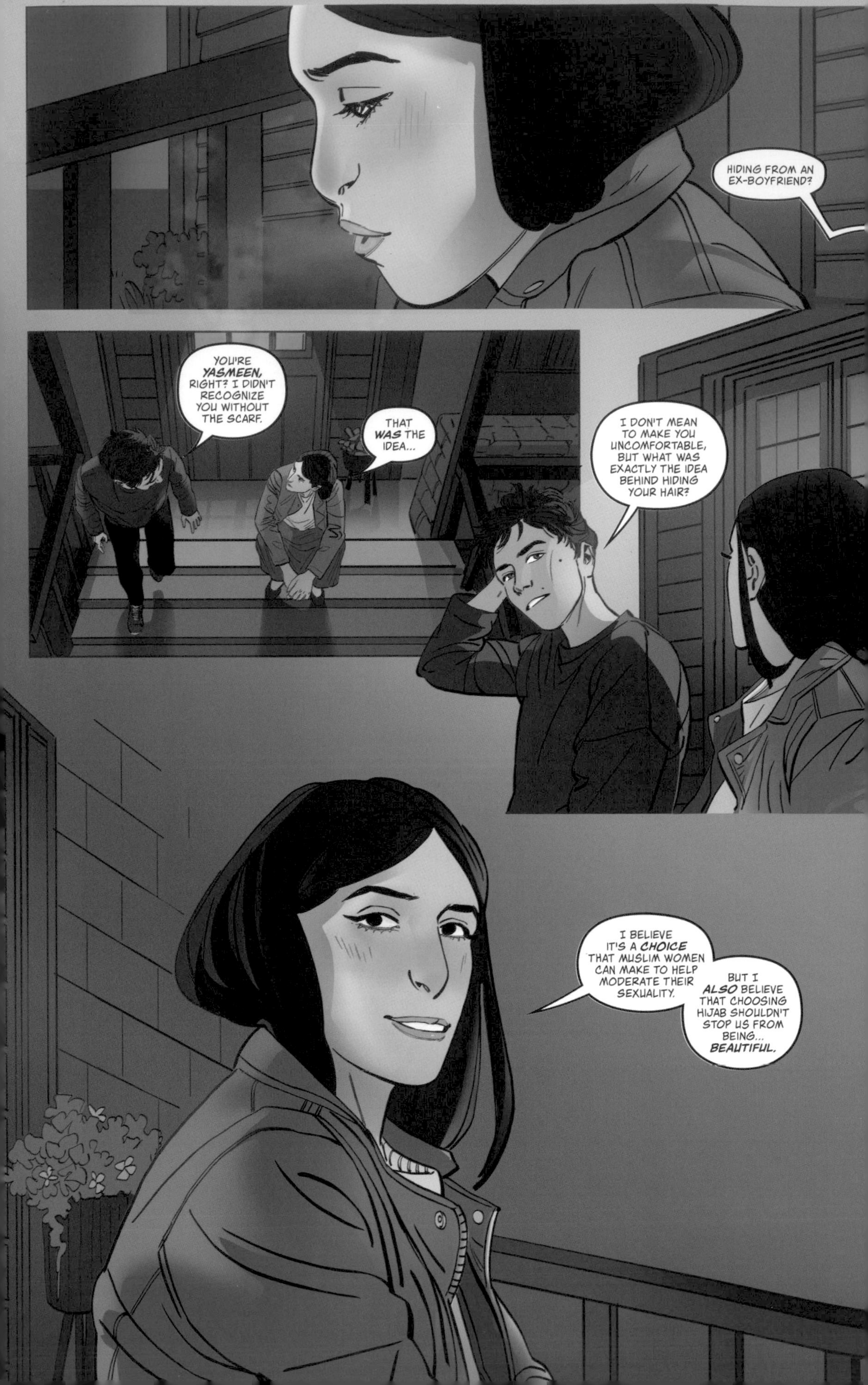
HIDING FROM AN EX-BOYFRIEND?
YOU'RE YASMEEN, RIGHT? I DIDN'T RECOGNIZE YOU WITHOUT THE SCARF.
THAT WAS THE IDEA...
I DON'T MEAN TO MAKE YOU UNCOMFORTABLE, BUT WHAT WAS EXACTLY THE IDEA BEHIND HIDING YOUR HAIR?
I BELIEVE IT'S A CHOICE THAT MUSLIM WOMEN CAN MAKE TO HELP MODERATE THEIR SEXUALITY.
BUT I ALSO BELIEVE THAT CHOOSING HIJAB SHOULDN'T STOP US FROM BEING... BEAUTIFUL.

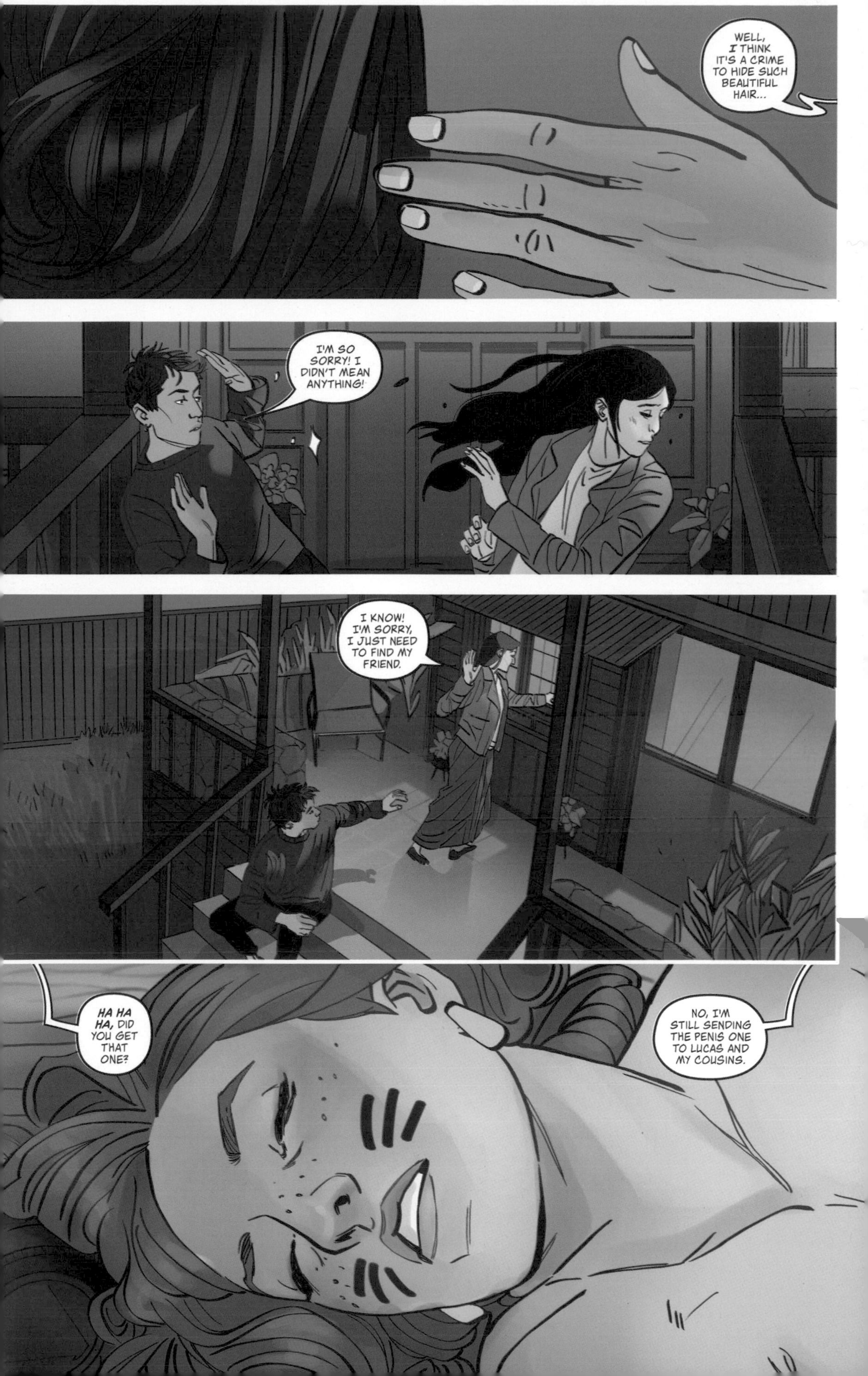
WELL, I THINK IT'S A CRIME TO HIDE SUCH BEAUTIFUL HAIR...
I'M SO SORRY! I DIDN'T MEAN ANYTHING!
I KNOW! I'M SORRY, I JUST NEED TO FIND MY FRIEND.
HA HA HA, DID YOU GET THAT ONE?
NO, I'M STILL SENDING THE PENIS ONE TO LUCAS AND MY COUSINS.

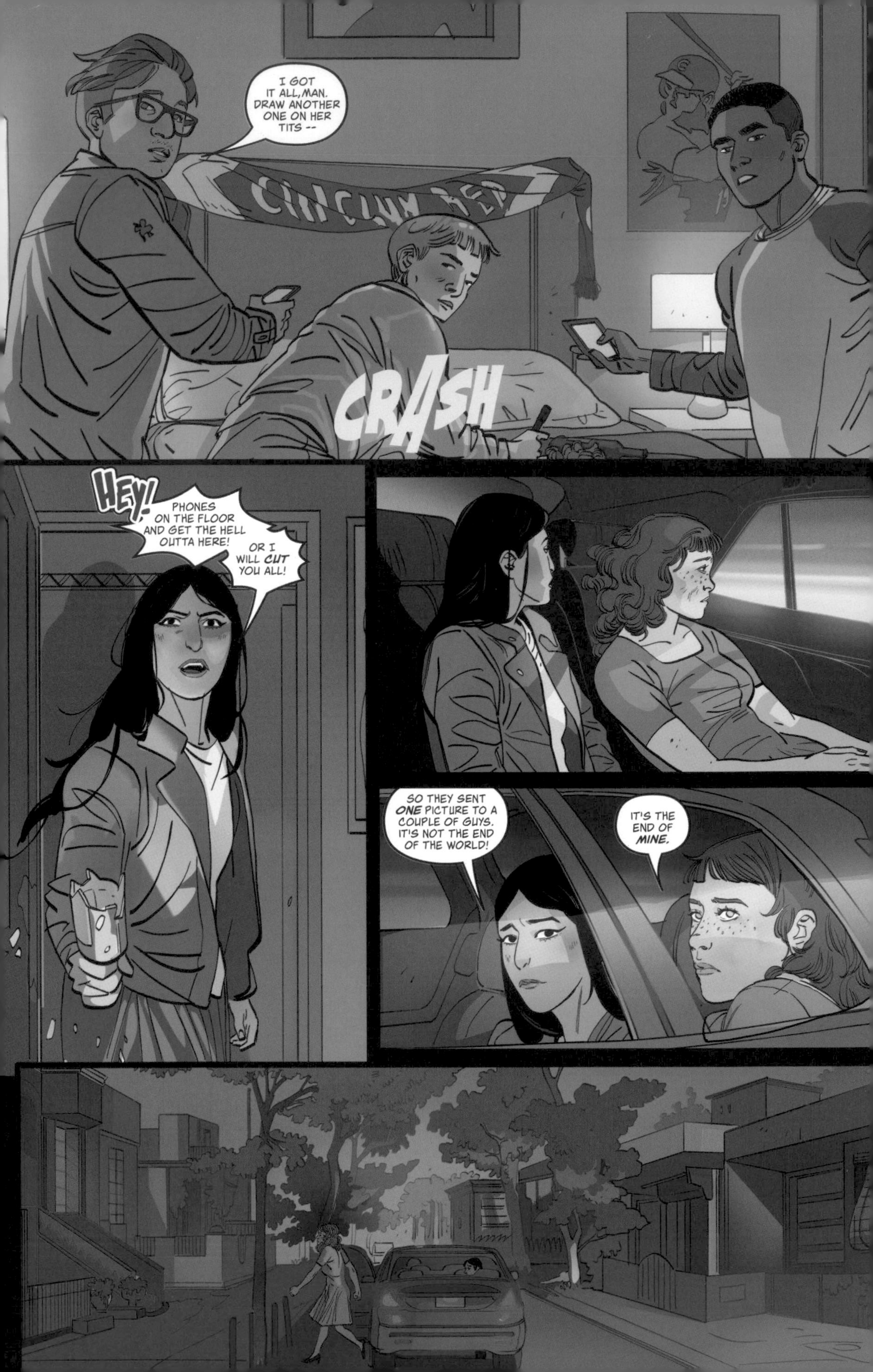
I GOT IT ALL, MAN. DRAW ANOTHER ONE ON HER TITS --
CRASH
HEY!
PHONES ON THE FLOOR AND GET THE HELL OUTTA HERE!
OR I WILL CUT YOU ALL!
SO THEY SENT ONE PICTURE TO A COUPLE OF GUYS. IT'S NOT THE END OF THE WORLD!
IT'S THE END OF MINE.

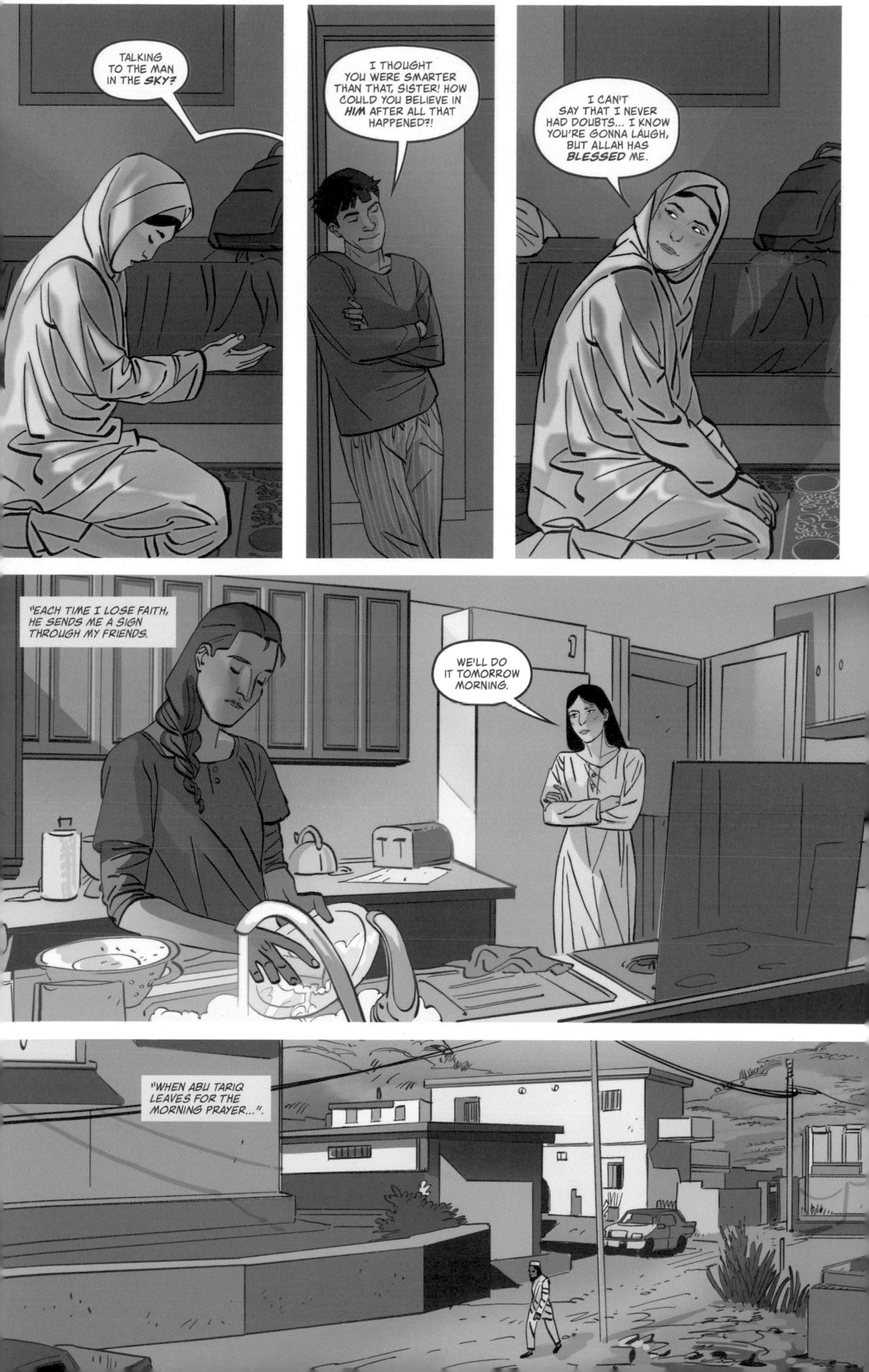
TALKING TO THE MAN IN THE SKY?
I THOUGHT YOU WERE SMARTER THAN THAT, SISTER! HOW COULD YOU BELIEVE IN HIM AFTER ALL THAT HAPPENED?!
I CAN'T SAY THAT I NEVER HAD DOUBTS... I KNOW YOU'RE GONNA LAUGH, BUT ALLAH HAS BLESSED ME.
"EACH TIME I LOSE FAITH, HE SENDS ME A SIGN THROUGH MY FRIENDS.
WE'LL DO IT TOMORROW MORNING.
"WHEN ABU TARIQ LEAVES FOR THE MORNING PRAYER...".

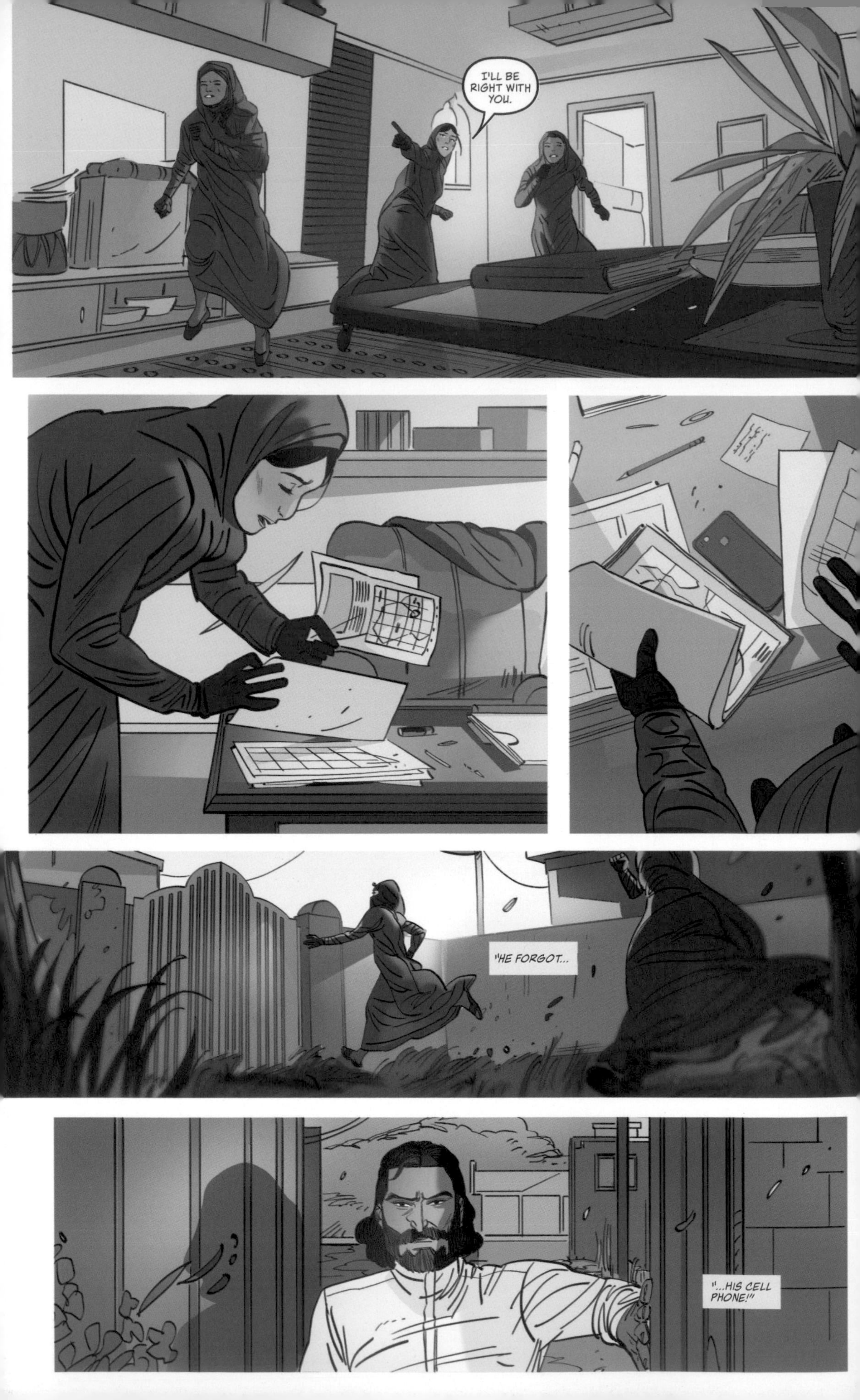
I'LL BE RIGHT WITH YOU.
"HE FORGOT...
"...HIS CELL PHONE!"

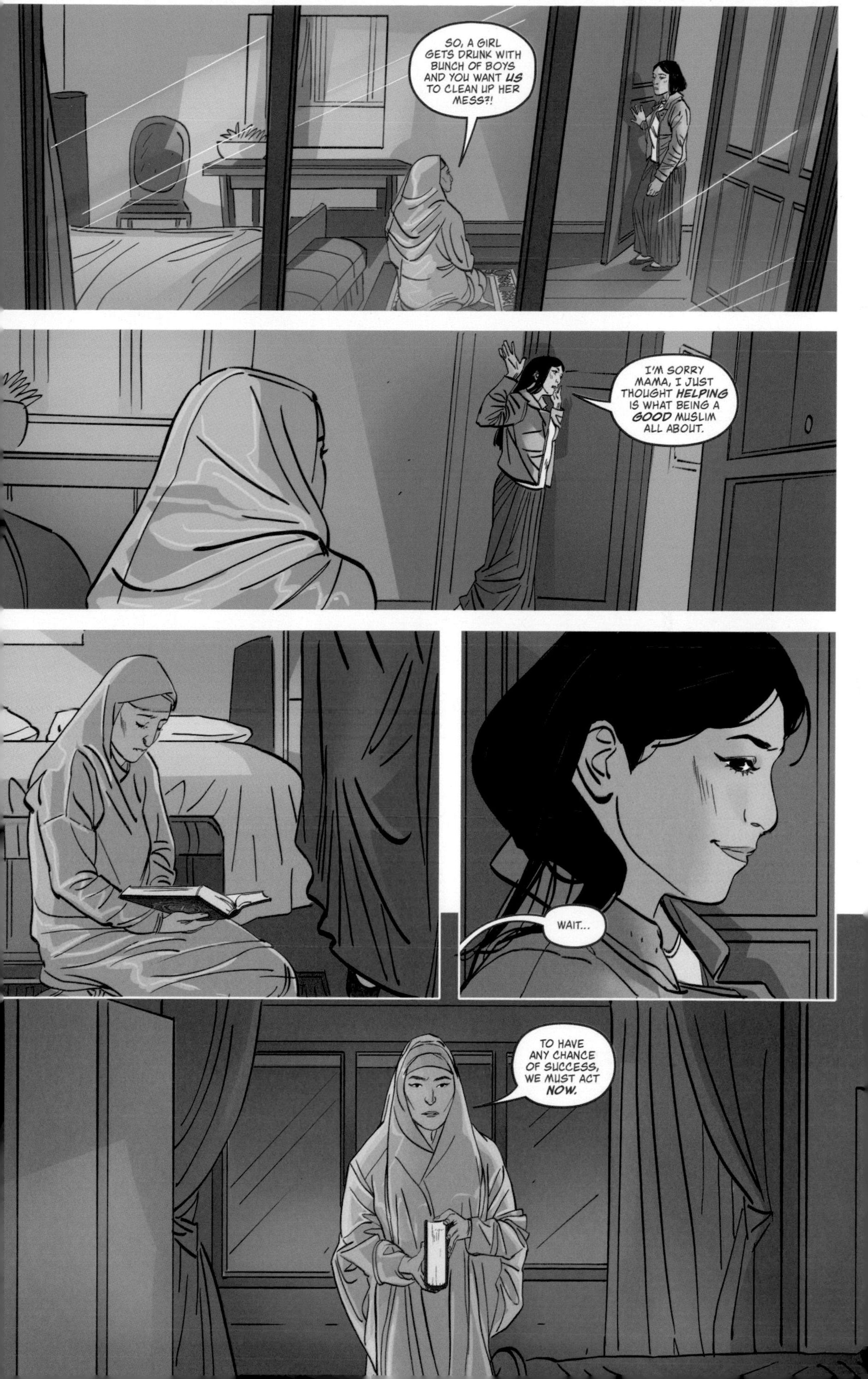
SO, A GIRL GETS DRUNK WITH BUNCH OF BOYS AND YOU WANT US TO CLEAN UP HER MESS?!
I'M SORRY MAMA, I JUST THOUGHT HELPING IS WHAT BEING A GOOD MUSLIM ALL ABOUT.
WAIT...
TO HAVE ANY CHANCE OF SUCCESS, WE MUST ACT NOW.

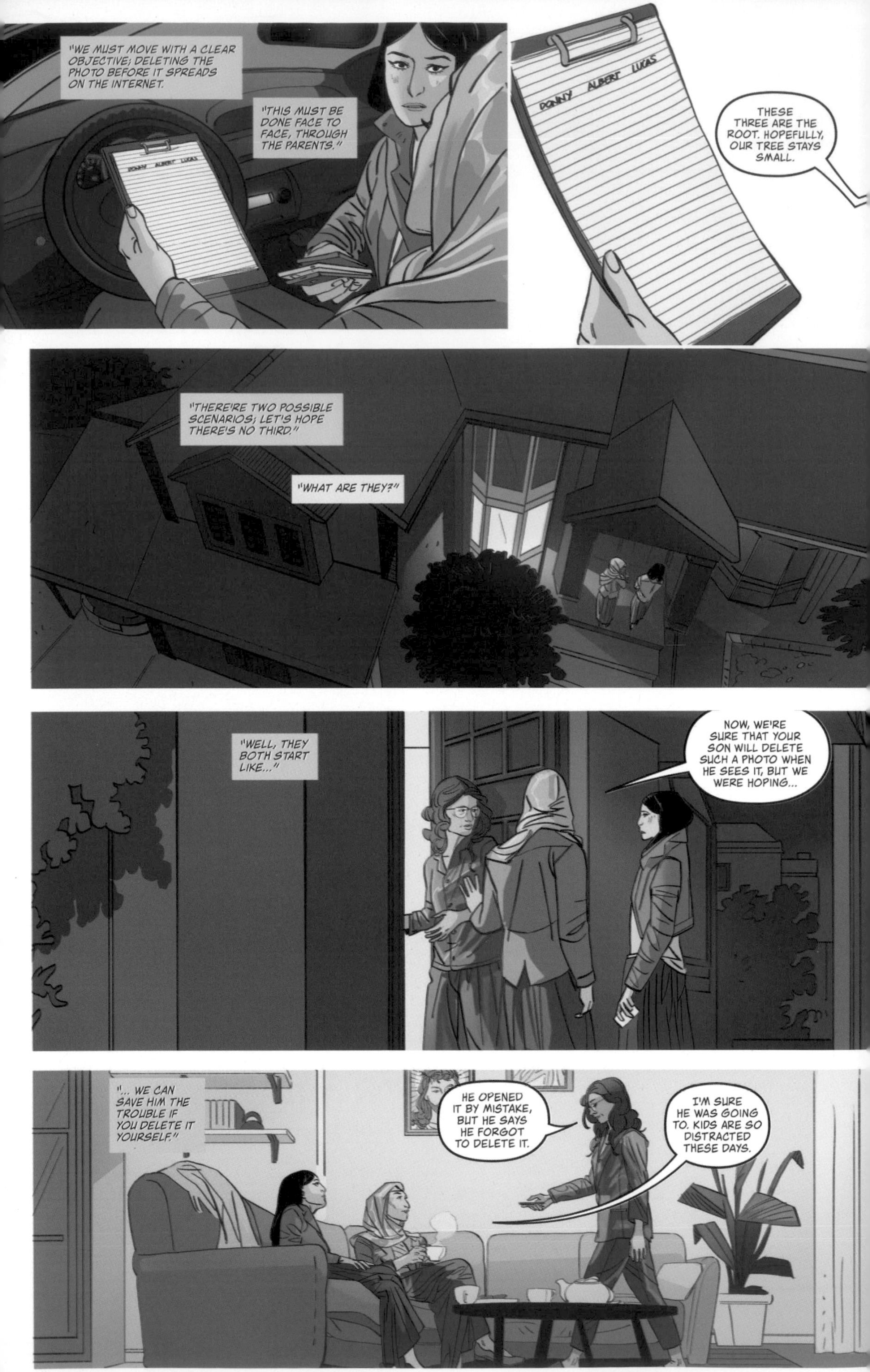
"WE MUST MOVE WITH A CLEAR OBJECTIVE; DELETING THE PHOTO BEFORE IT SPREADS ON THE INTERNET.
"THIS MUST BE DONE FACE TO FACE, THROUGH THE PARENTS."
DONNY ALBERT LUCAS
DONNY ALBERT LUCAS
THESE THREE ARE THE ROOT. HOPEFULLY, OUR TREE STAYS SMALL.
"THERE'RE TWO POSSIBLE SCENARIOS; LET'S HOPE THERE'S NO THIRD."
"WHAT ARE THEY?"
"WELL, THEY BOTH START LIKE..."
NOW, WE'RE SURE THAT YOUR SON WILL DELETE SUCH A PHOTO WHEN HE SEES IT, BUT WE WERE HOPING...
"... WE CAN SAVE HIM THE TROUBLE IF YOU DELETE IT YOURSELF."
HE OPENED IT BY MISTAKE, BUT HE SAYS HE FORGOT TO DELETE IT.
I'M SURE HE WAS GOING TO. KIDS ARE SO DISTRACTED THESE DAYS.

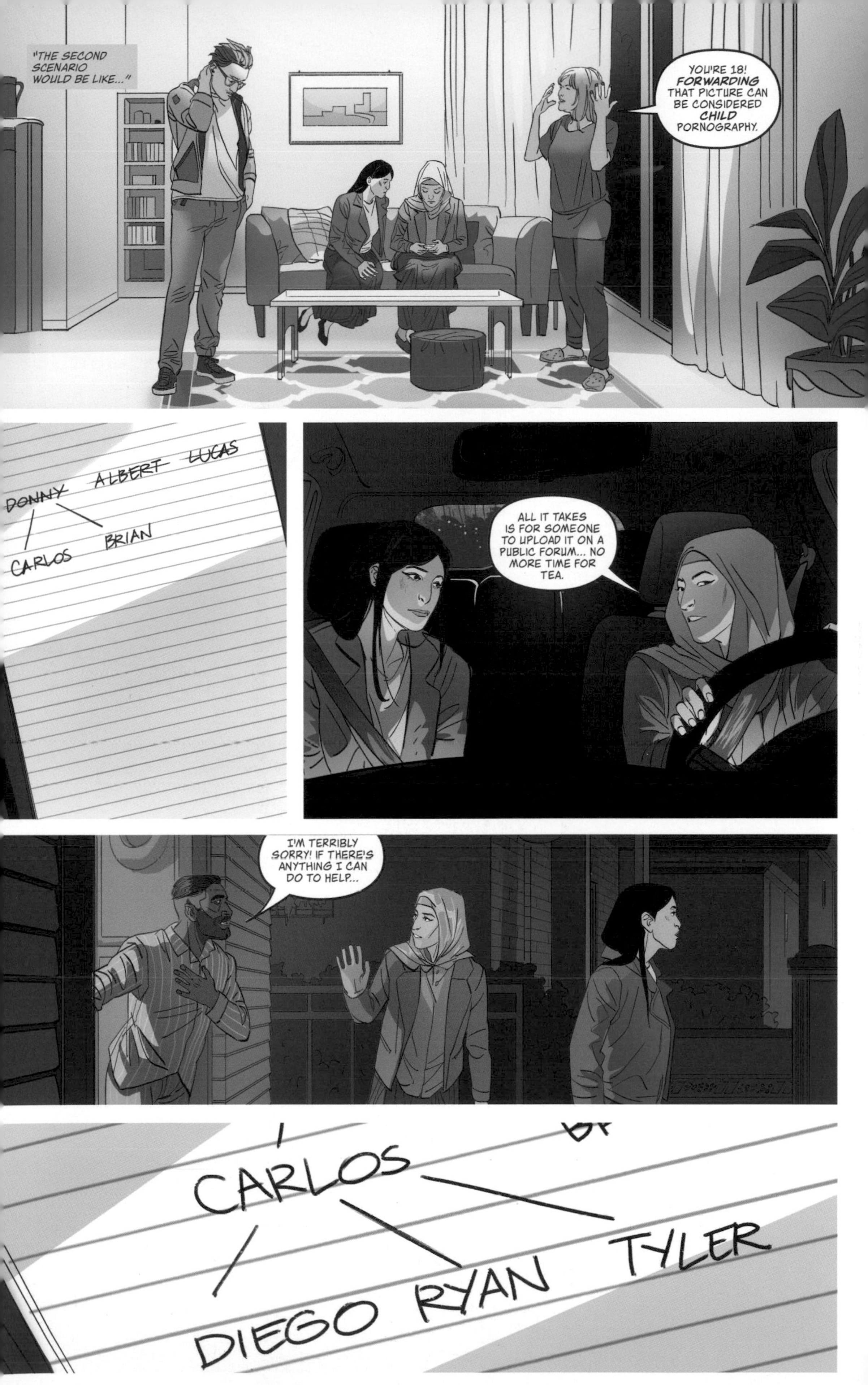

"THE SECOND SCENARIO WOULD BE LIKE..."
YOU'RE 18! FORWARDING THAT PICTURE CAN BE CONSIDERED CHILD PORNOGRAPHY.
DONNY ALBERT LUCAS
CARLOS BRIAN
ALL IT TAKES IS FOR SOMEONE TO UPLOAD IT ON A PUBLIC FORUM... NO MORE TIME FOR TEA.
I'M TERRIBLY SORRY! IF THERE'S ANYTHING I CAN DO TO HELP...
CARLOS
DIEGO RYAN TYLER

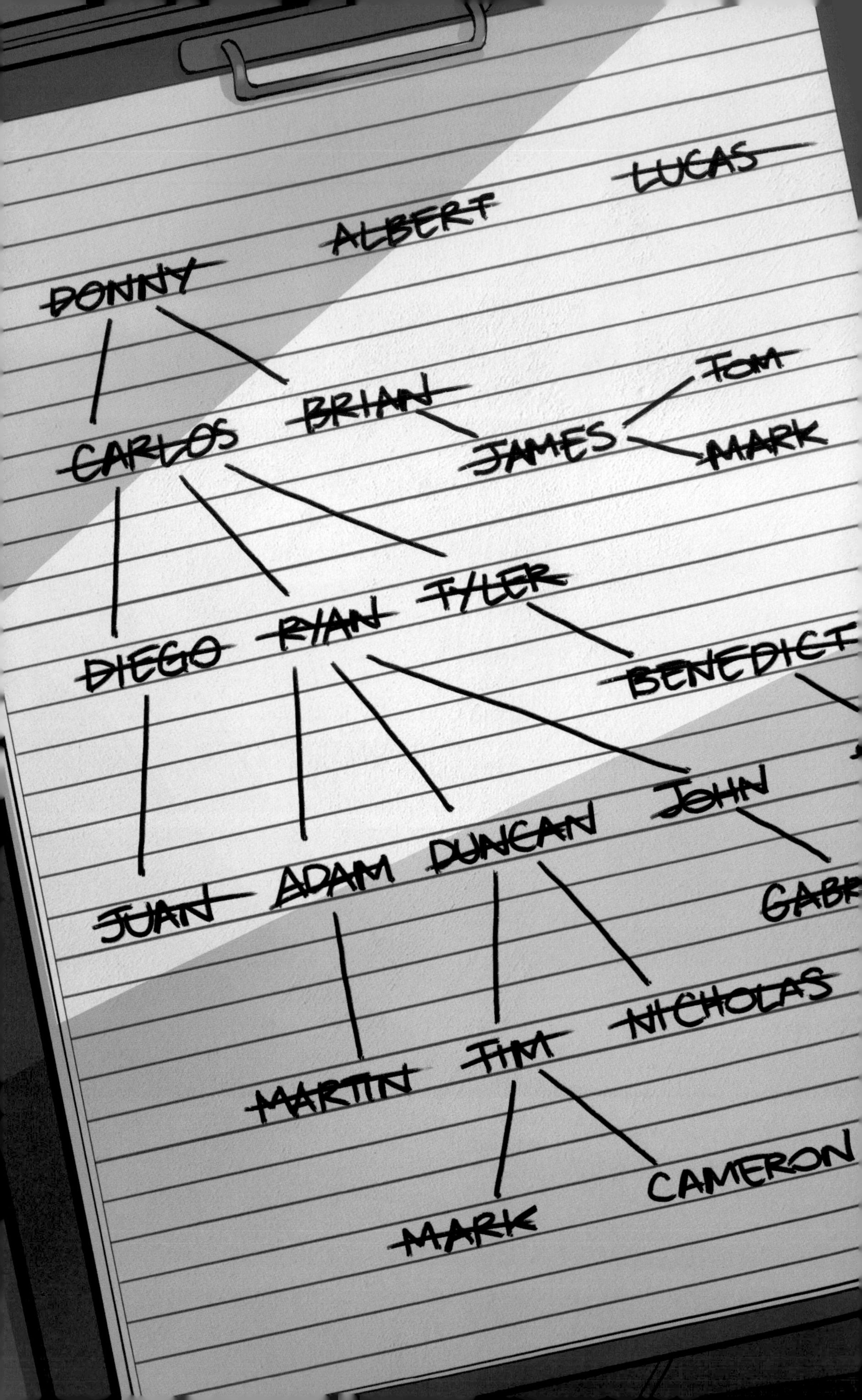
LUCAS
ALBERT
DONNY
CARLOS
BRIAN
TOM
JAMES
MARK
TYLER
DIEGO
RYAN
BENEDICT
JOHN
DUNCAN
ADAM
JUAN
NICHOLAS
TIM
MARTIN
CAMERON
MARK

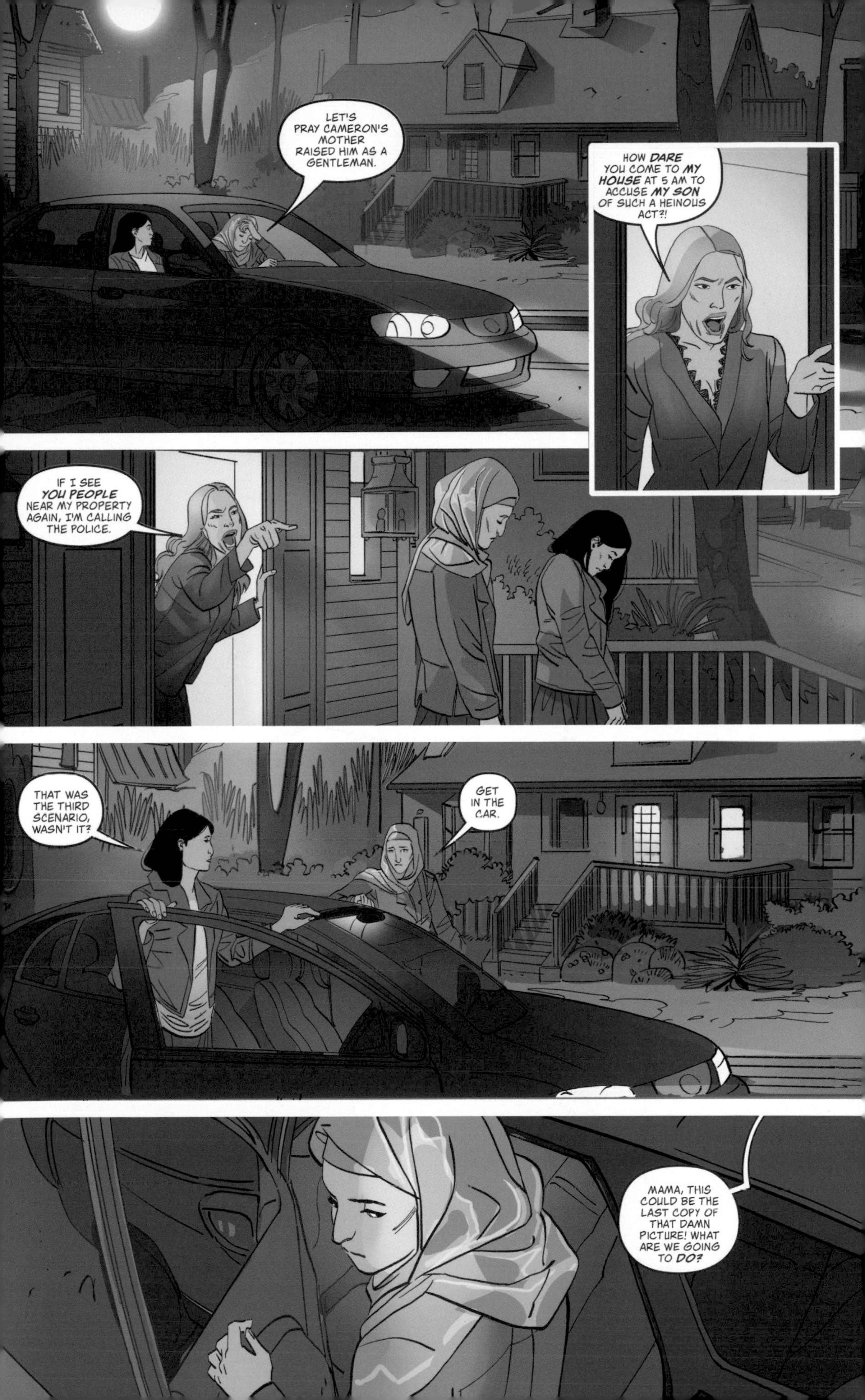
LET'S PRAY CAMERON'S MOTHER RAISED HIM AS A GENTLEMAN.
HOW DARE YOU COME TO MY HOUSE AT 5 AM TO ACCUSE MY SON OF SUCH A HEINOUS ACT?!
IF I SEE YOU PEOPLE NEAR MY PROPERTY AGAIN, I'M CALLING THE POLICE.
THAT WAS THE THIRD SCENARIO, WASN'T IT?
GET IN THE CAR.
MAMA, THIS COULD BE THE LAST COPY OF THAT DAMN PICTURE! WHAT ARE WE GOING TO DO?

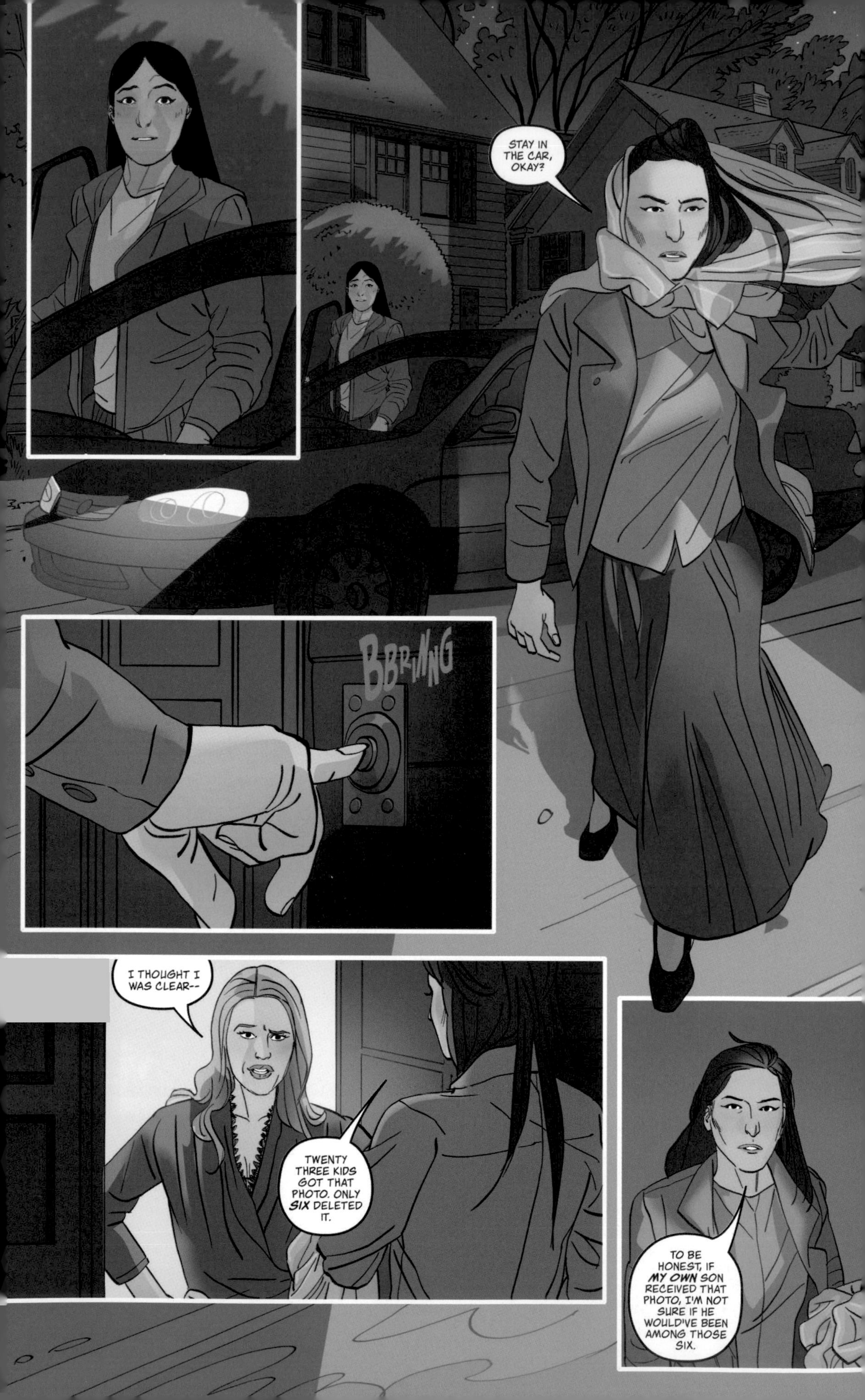
STAY IN THE CAR, OKAY?
BBRIING
I THOUGHT I WAS CLEAR--
TWENTY THREE KIDS GOT THAT PHOTO. ONLY SIX DELETED IT.
TO BE HONEST, IF MY OWN SON RECEIVED THAT PHOTO, I'M NOT SURE IF HE WOULD'VE BEEN AMONG THOSE SIX.

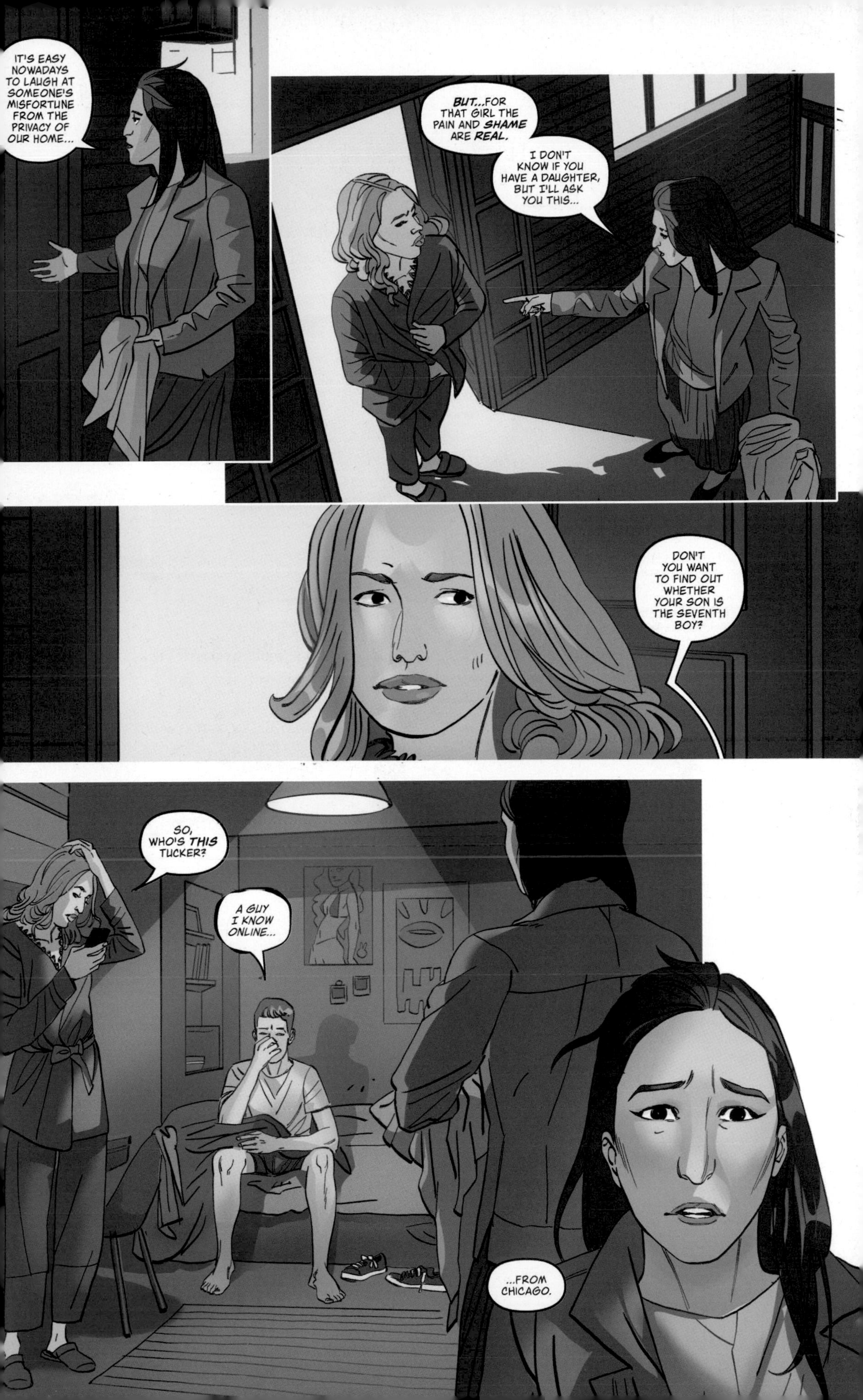
IT'S EASY NOWADAYS TO LAUGH AT SOMEONE'S MISFORTUNE FROM THE PRIVACY OF OUR HOME...
BUT...FOR THAT GIRL THE PAIN AND SHAME ARE REAL.
I DON'T KNOW IF YOU HAVE A DAUGHTER, BUT I'LL ASK YOU THIS...
DON'T YOU WANT TO FIND OUT WHETHER YOUR SON IS THE SEVENTH BOY?
SO, WHO'S THIS TUCKER?
A GUY I KNOW ONLINE...
...FROM CHICAGO.

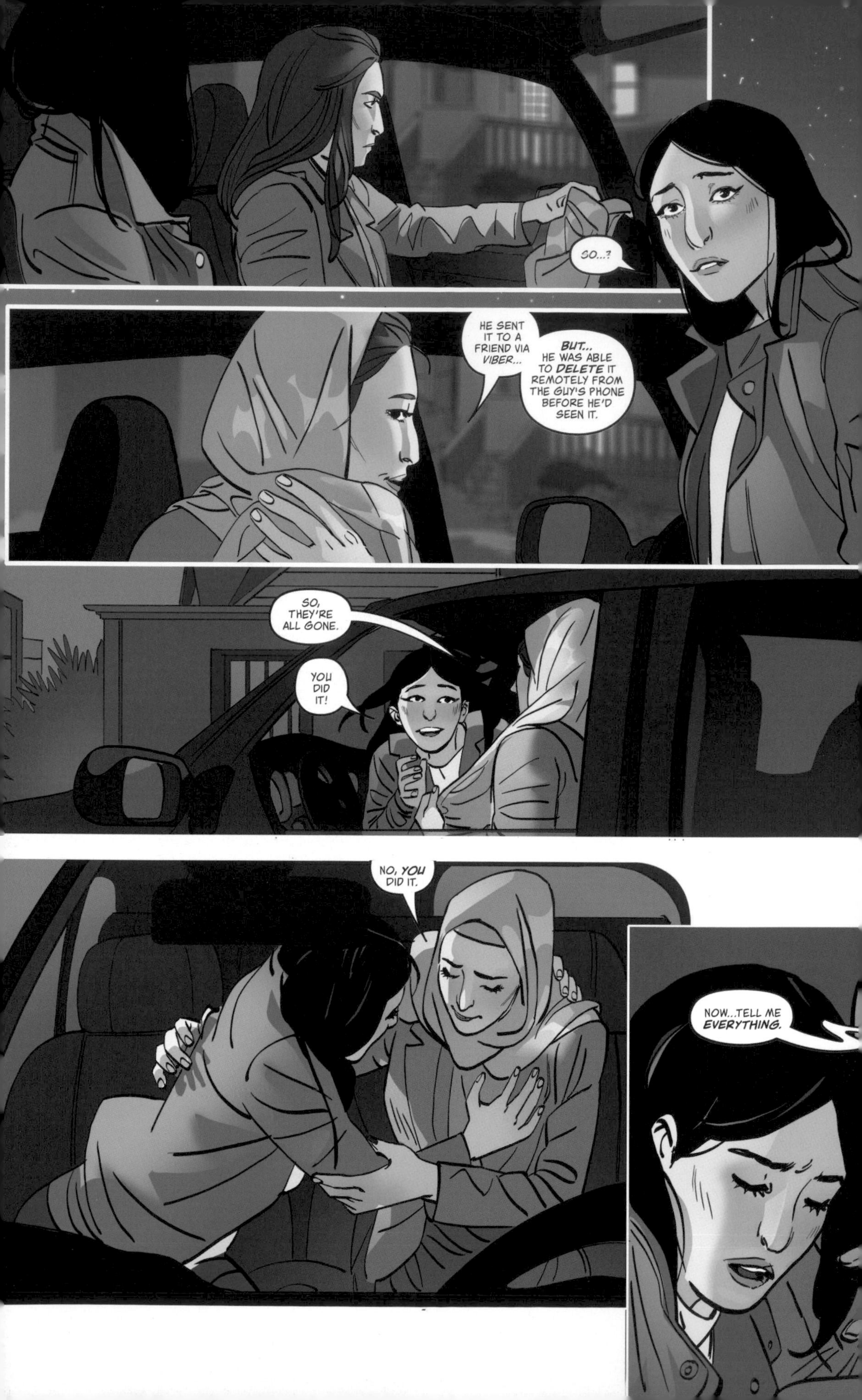
SO...?
HE SENT IT TO A FRIEND VIA VIBER...
BUT... HE WAS ABLE TO DELETE IT REMOTELY FROM THE GUY'S PHONE BEFORE HE'D SEEN IT.
SO, THEY'RE ALL GONE.
YOU DID IT!
NO, YOU DID IT.
NOW...TELL ME EVERYTHING.

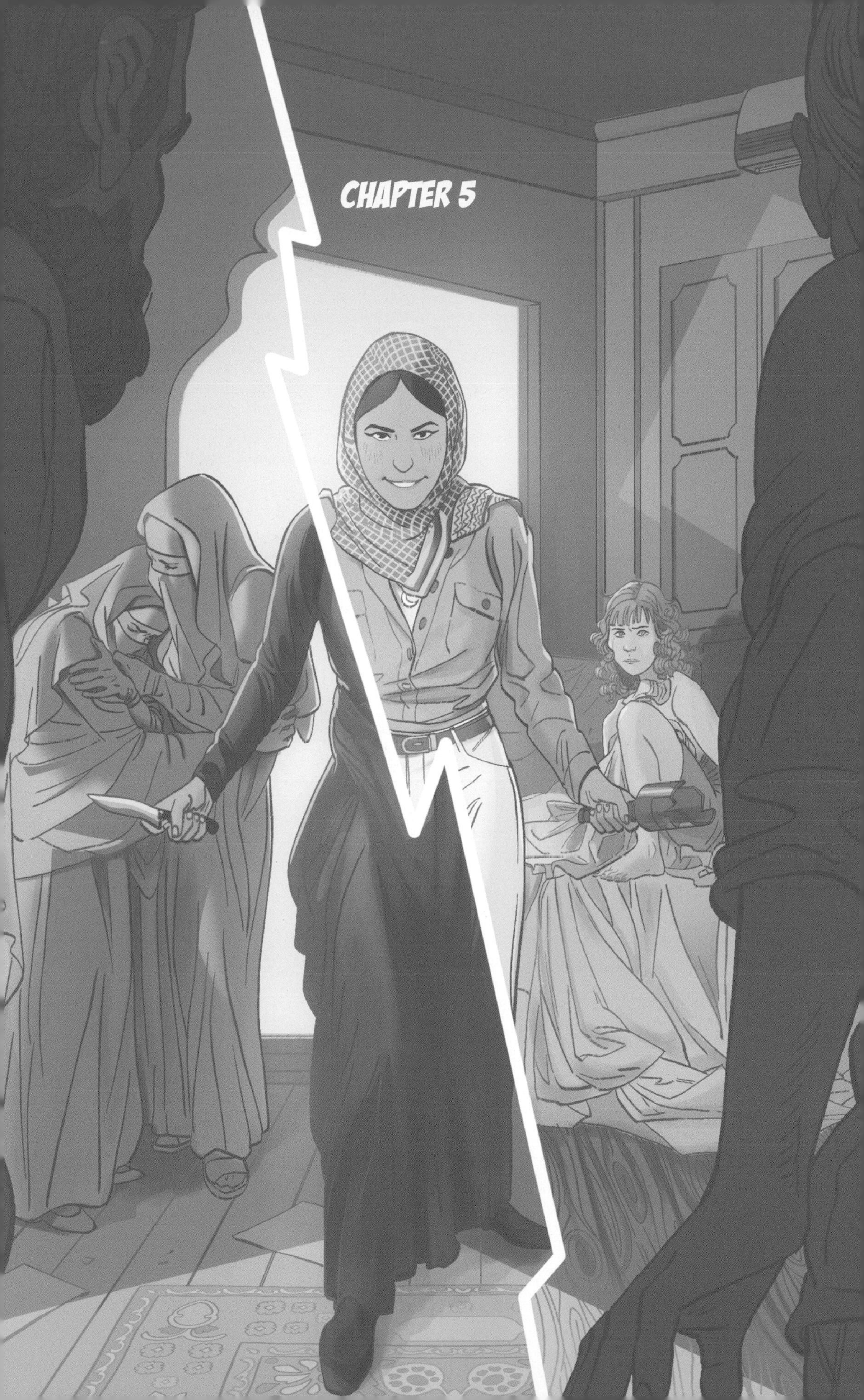
CHAPTER 5

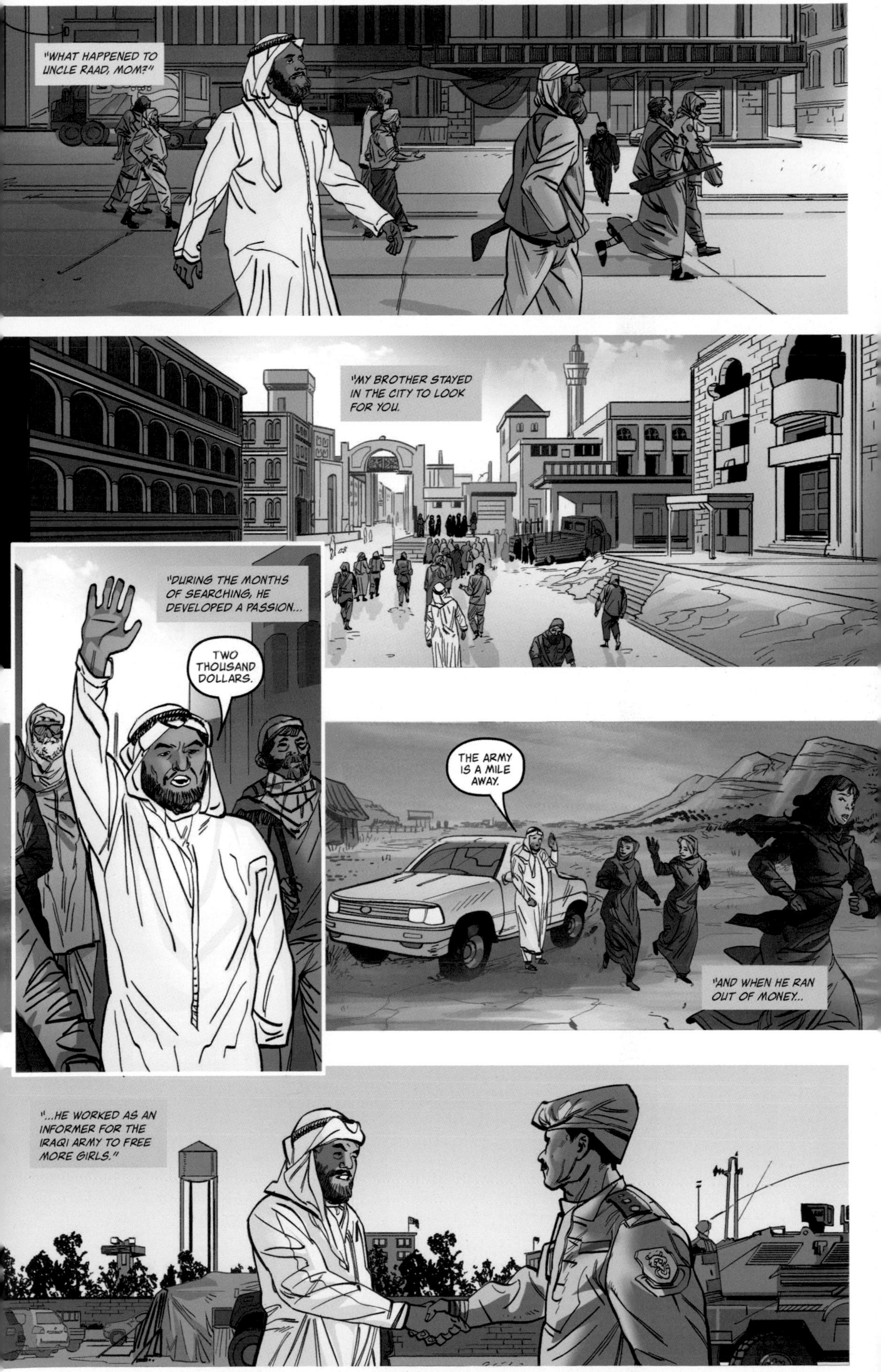
"WHAT HAPPENED TO UNCLE RAAD, MOM?"
"MY BROTHER STAYED IN THE CITY TO LOOK FOR YOU.
"DURING THE MONTHS OF SEARCHING, HE DEVELOPED A PASSION...
TWO THOUSAND DOLLARS.
THE ARMY IS A MILE AWAY.
"AND WHEN HE RAN OUT OF MONEY...
"...HE WORKED AS AN INFORMER FOR THE IRAQI ARMY TO FREE MORE GIRLS."

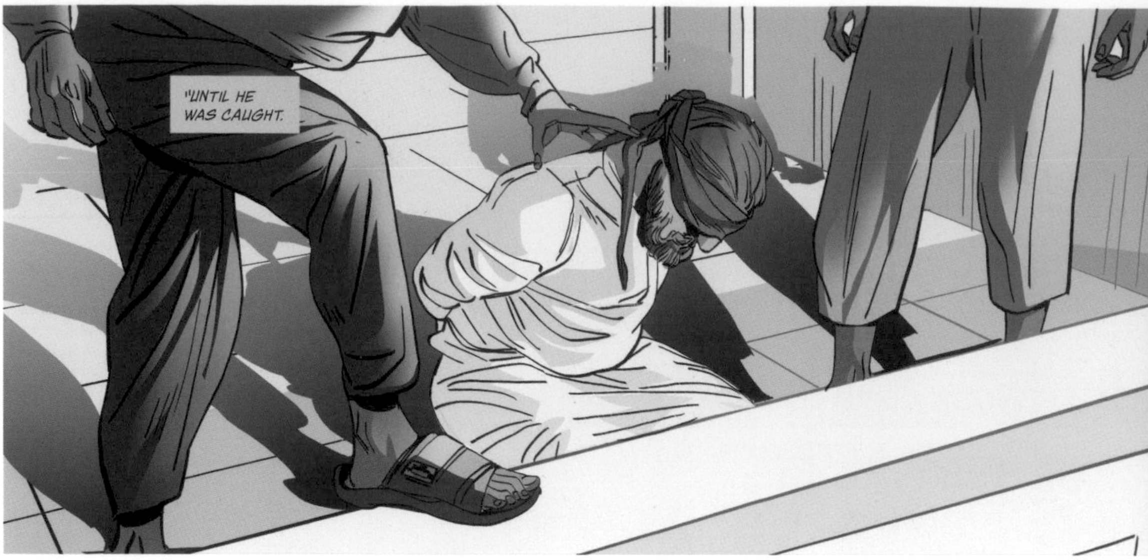
"UNTIL HE WAS CAUGHT.

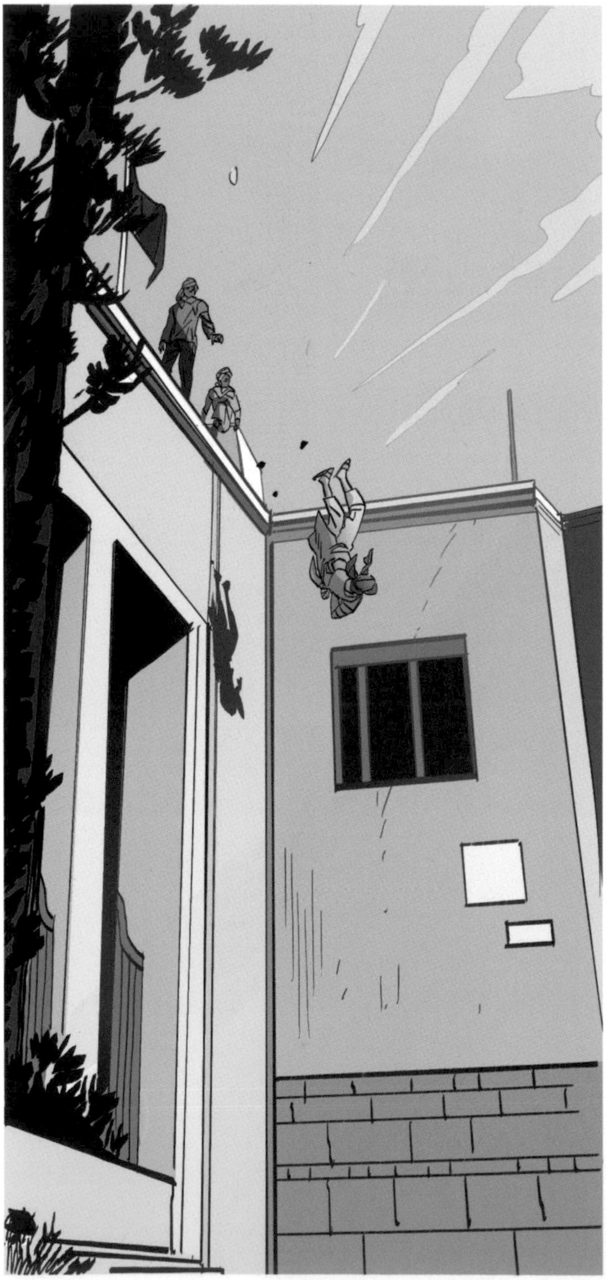

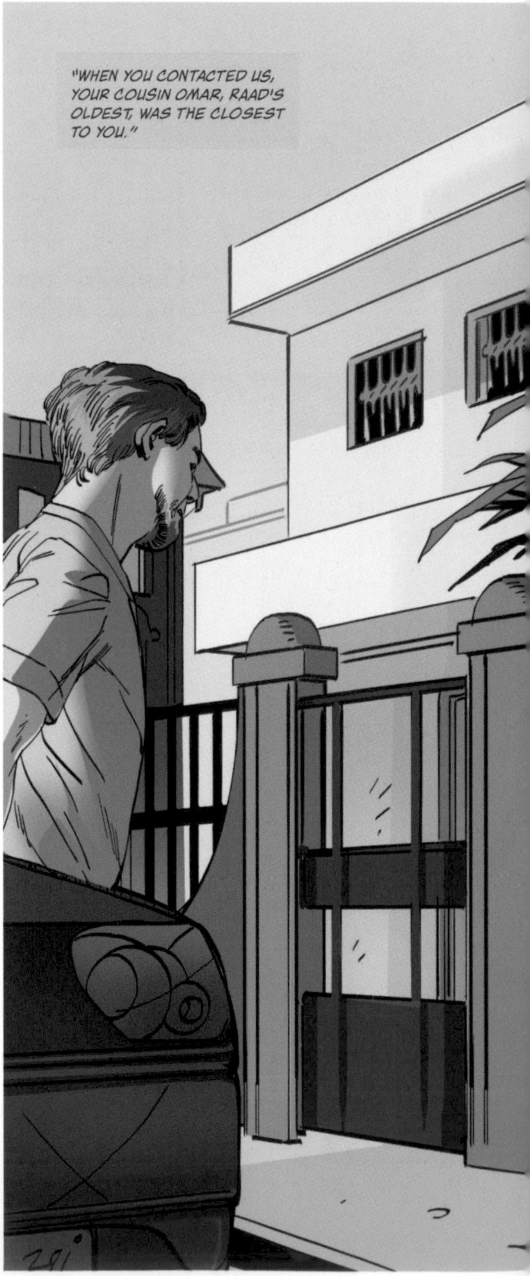
"WHEN YOU CONTACTED US, YOUR COUSIN OMAR, RAAD'S OLDEST, WAS THE CLOSEST TO YOU."

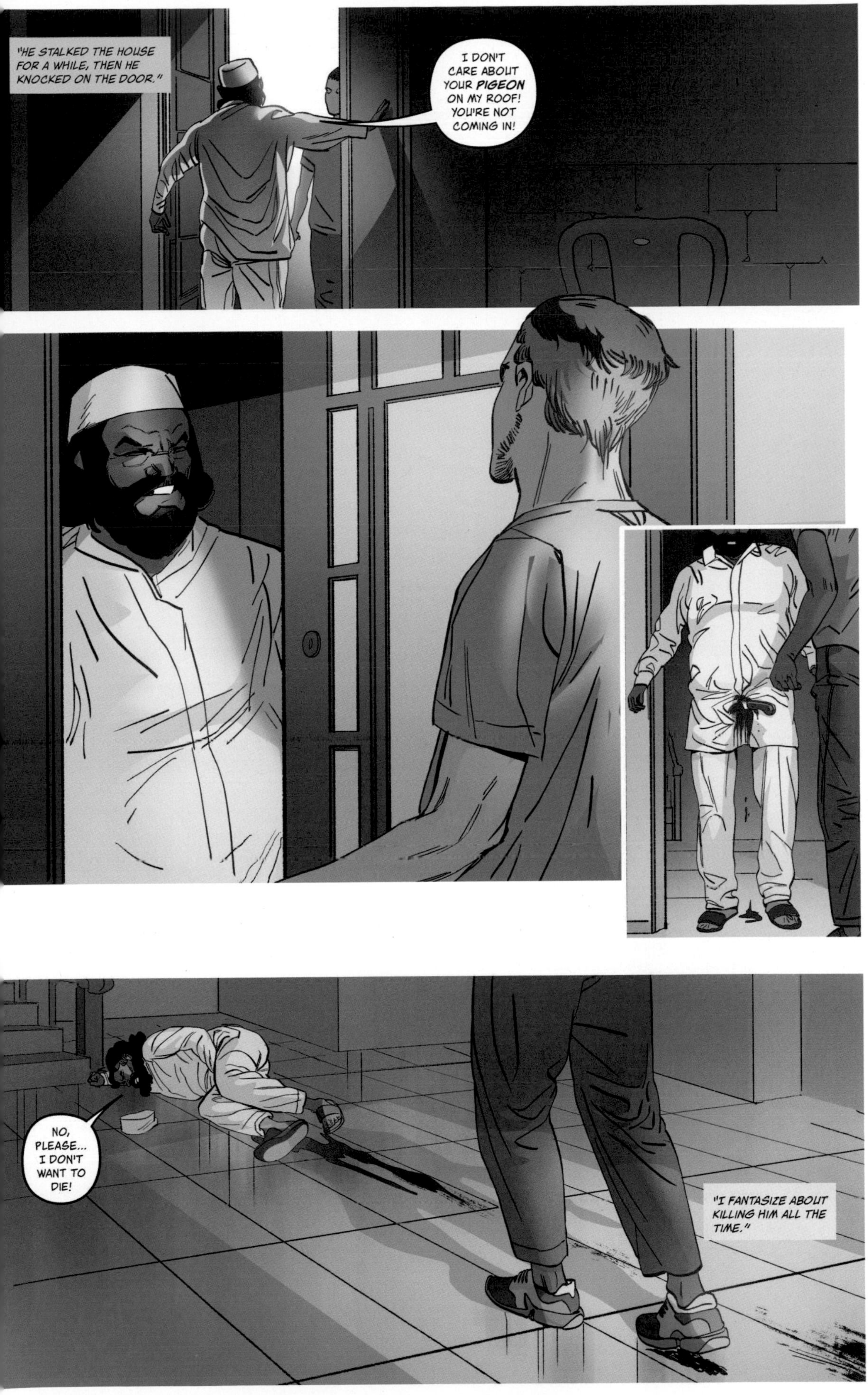
"HE STALKED THE HOUSE FOR A WHILE, THEN HE KNOCKED ON THE DOOR."
I DON'T CARE ABOUT YOUR PIGEON ON MY ROOF! YOU'RE NOT COMING IN!
NO, PLEASE... I DON'T WANT TO DIE!
"I FANTASIZE ABOUT KILLING HIM ALL THE TIME."

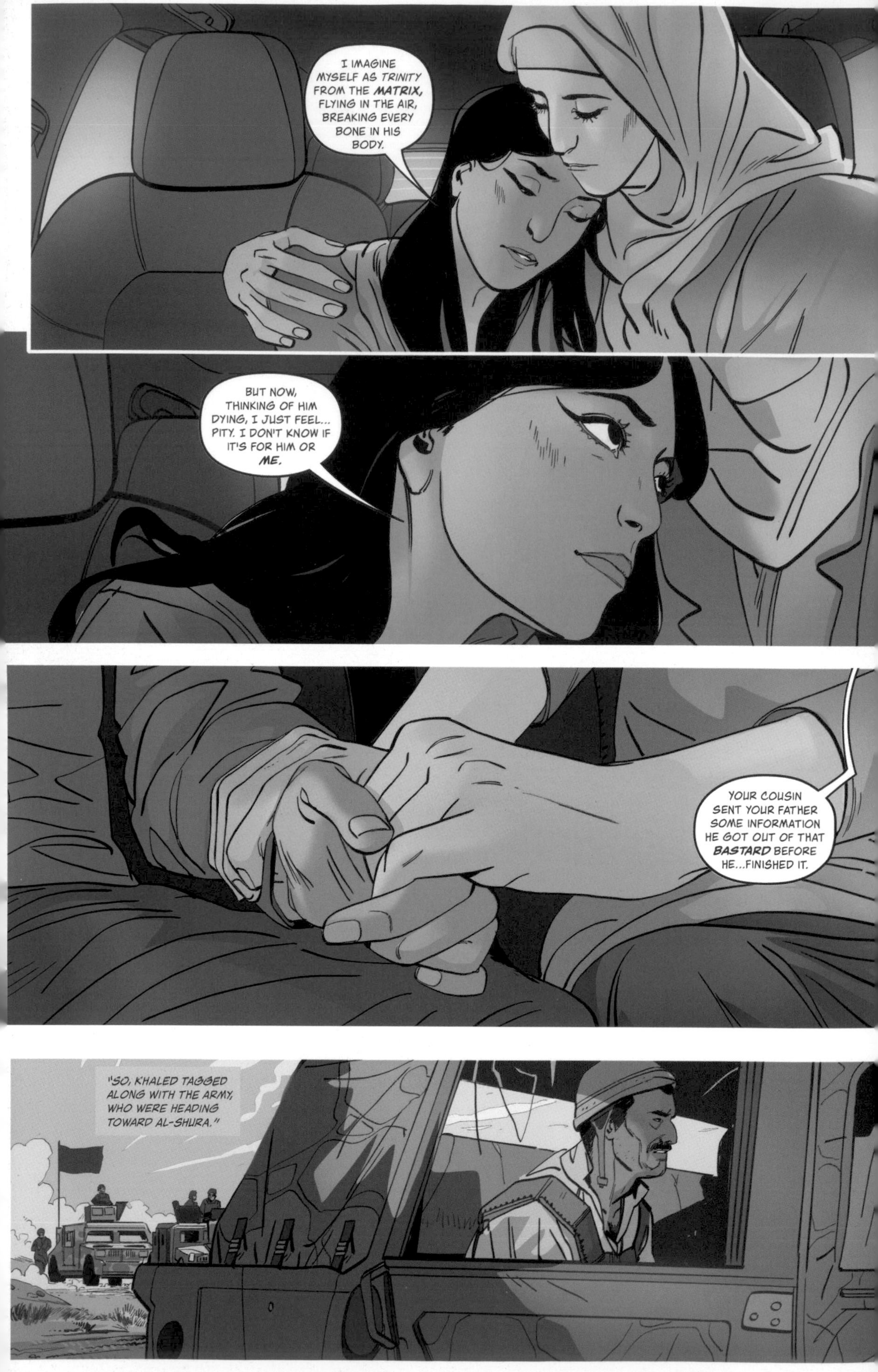
I IMAGINE MYSELF AS TRINITY FROM THE MATRIX, FLYING IN THE AIR, BREAKING EVERY BONE IN HIS BODY.
BUT NOW, THINKING OF HIM DYING, I JUST FEEL... PITY. I DON'T KNOW IF IT'S FOR HIM OR ME.
YOUR COUSIN SENT YOUR FATHER SOME INFORMATION HE GOT OUT OF THAT BASTARD BEFORE HE...FINISHED IT.
"SO, KHALED TAGGED ALONG WITH THE ARMY, WHO WERE HEADING TOWARD AL-SHURA."

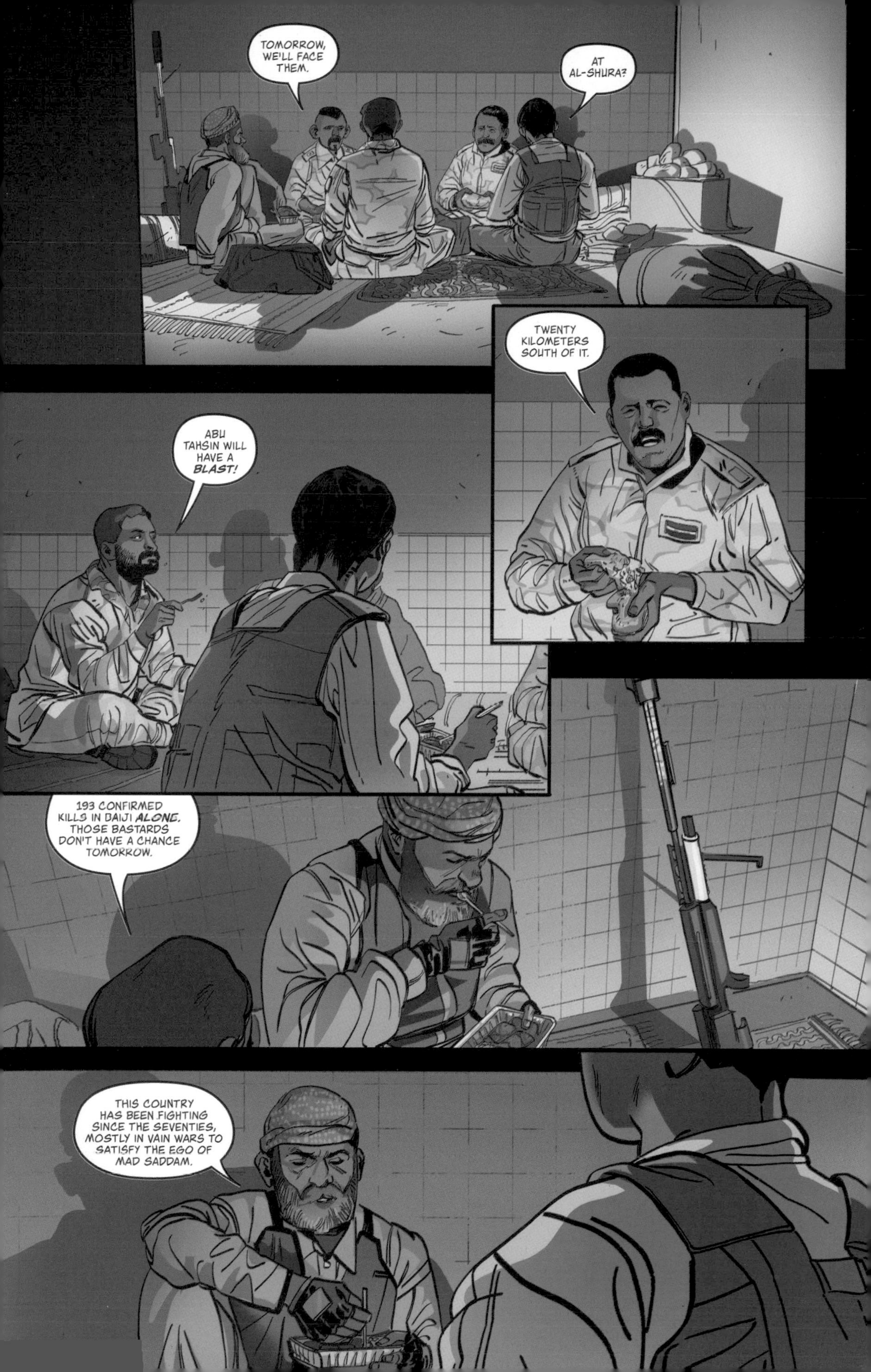
TOMORROW, WE'LL FACE THEM.
AT AL-SHURA?
TWENTY KILOMETERS SOUTH OF IT.
ABU TAHSIN WILL HAVE A *BLAST!*
193 CONFIRMED KILLS IN BAIJI *ALONE.* THOSE BASTARDS DON'T HAVE A CHANCE TOMORROW.
THIS COUNTRY HAS BEEN FIGHTING SINCE THE SEVENTIES, MOSTLY IN VAIN WARS TO SATISFY THE EGO OF MAD SADDAM.

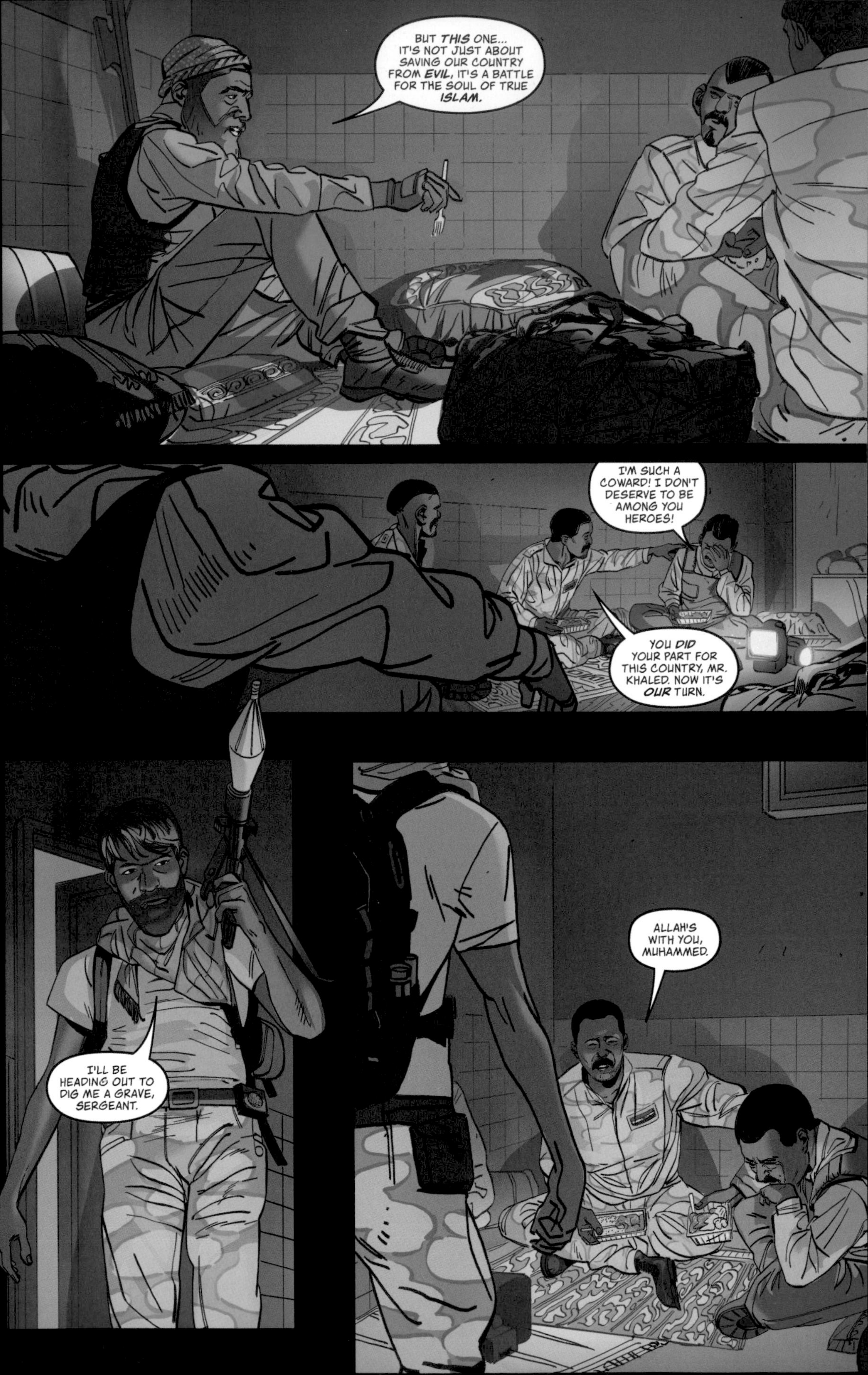
BUT THIS ONE... IT'S NOT JUST ABOUT SAVING OUR COUNTRY FROM EVIL, IT'S A BATTLE FOR THE SOUL OF TRUE ISLAM.
I'M SUCH A COWARD! I DON'T DESERVE TO BE AMONG YOU HEROES!
YOU DID YOUR PART FOR THIS COUNTRY, MR. KHALED. NOW IT'S OUR TURN.
I'LL BE HEADING OUT TO DIG ME A GRAVE, SERGEANT.
ALLAH'S WITH YOU, MUHAMMED.

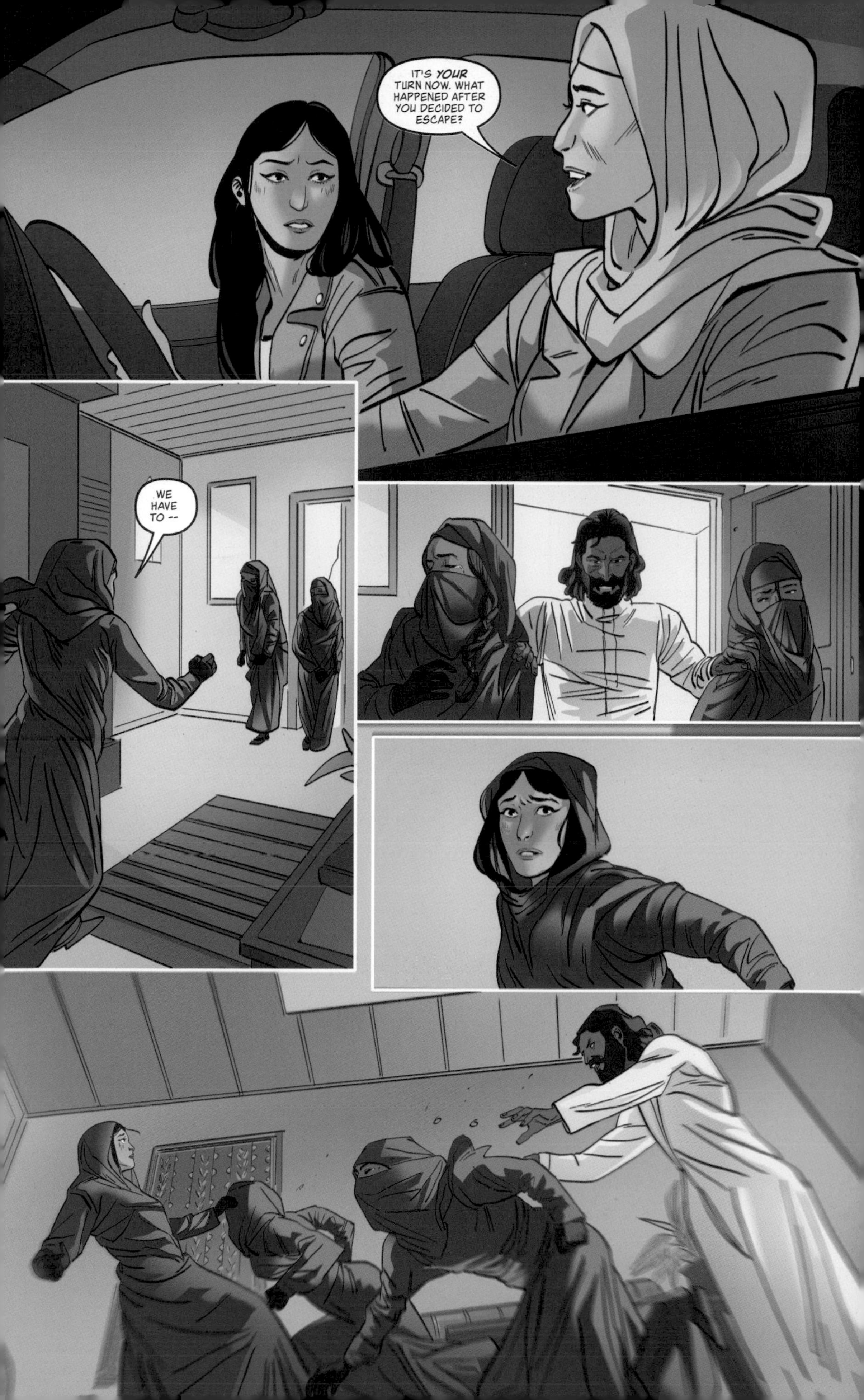
IT'S *YOUR* TURN NOW. WHAT HAPPENED AFTER YOU DECIDED TO ESCAPE?
WE HAVE TO --

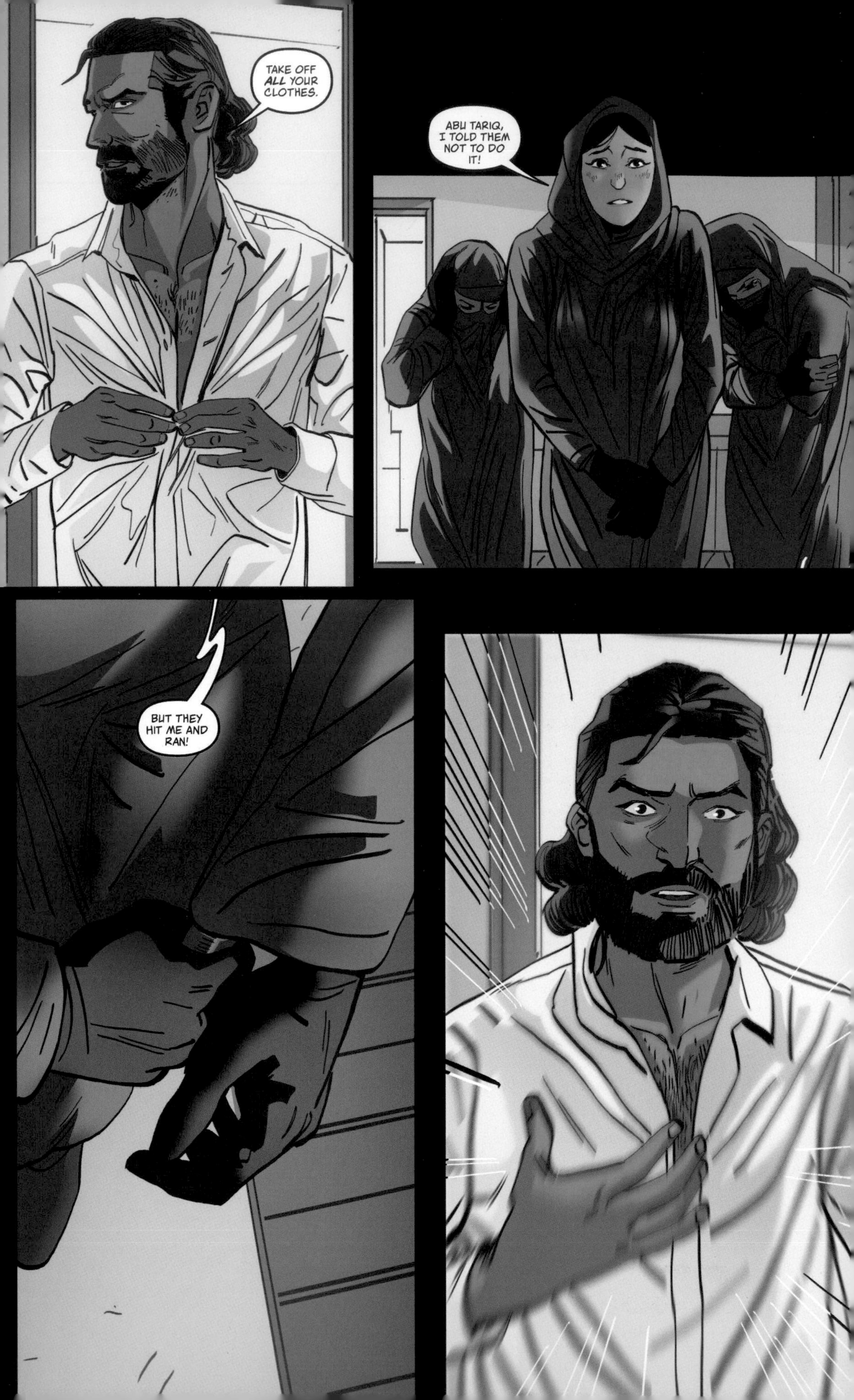
TAKE OFF ALL YOUR CLOTHES.
ABU TARIQ, I TOLD THEM NOT TO DO IT!
BUT THEY HIT ME AND RAN!

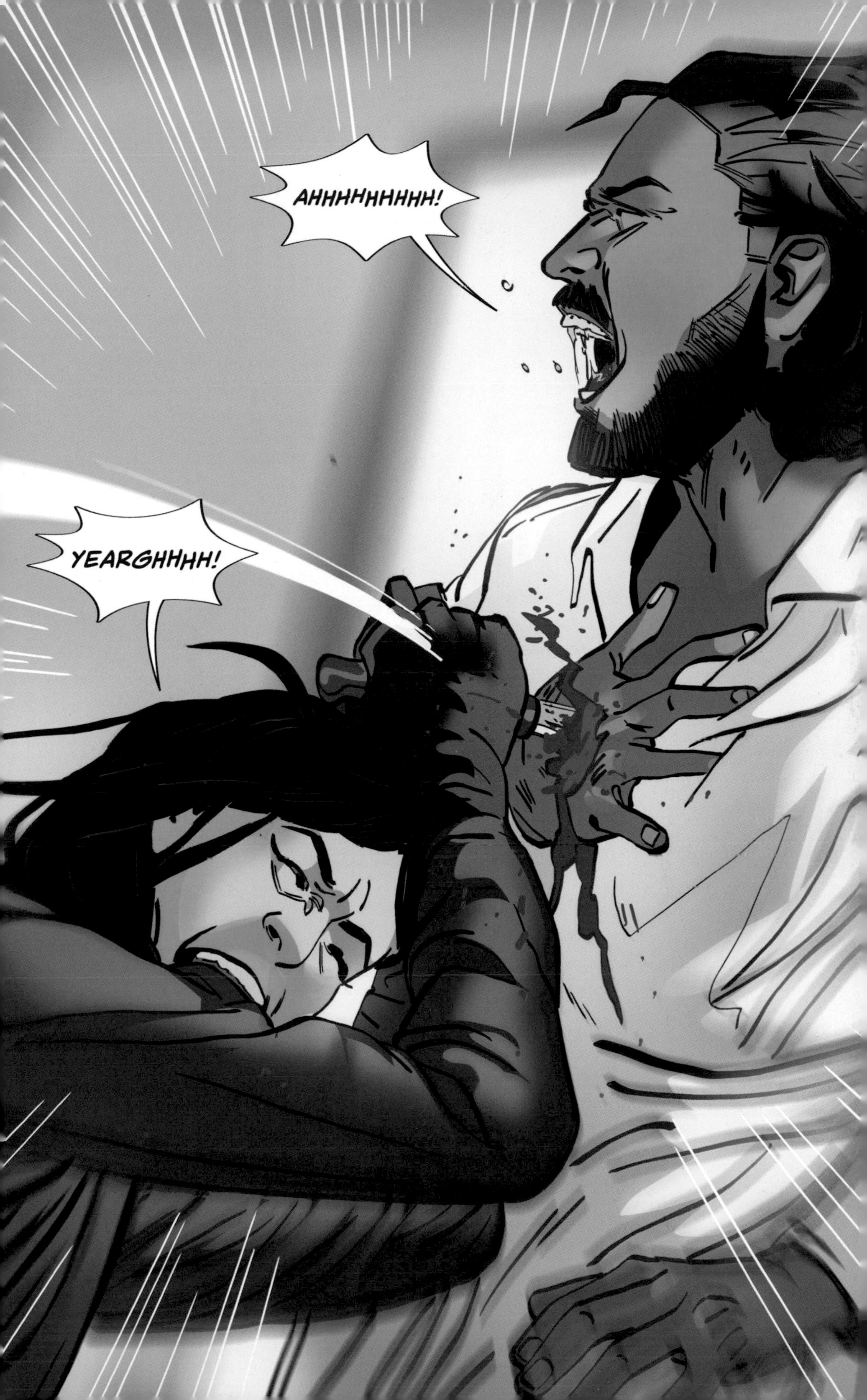
AHHHHHHHHH!
YEARGHHHH!

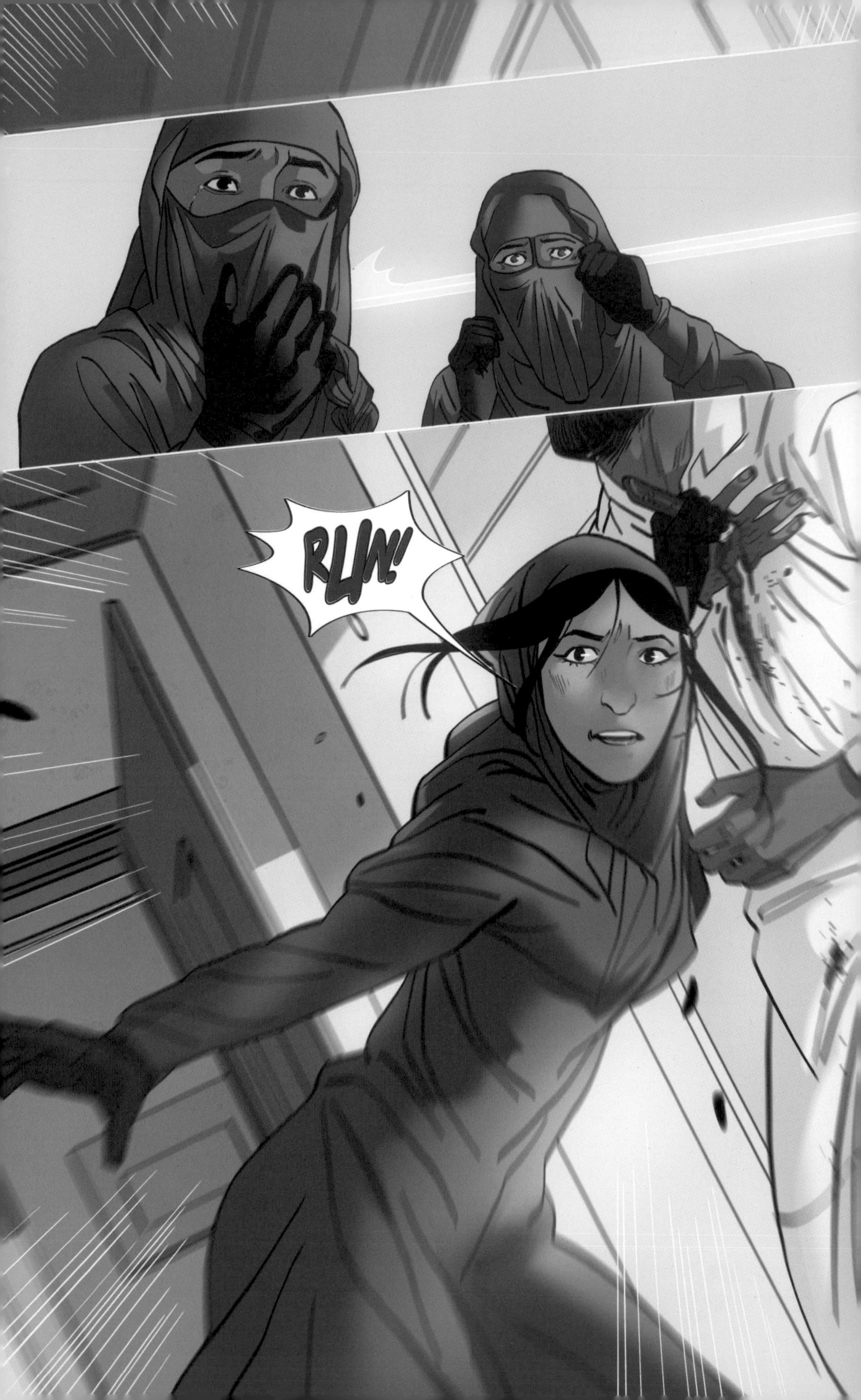
RUN!

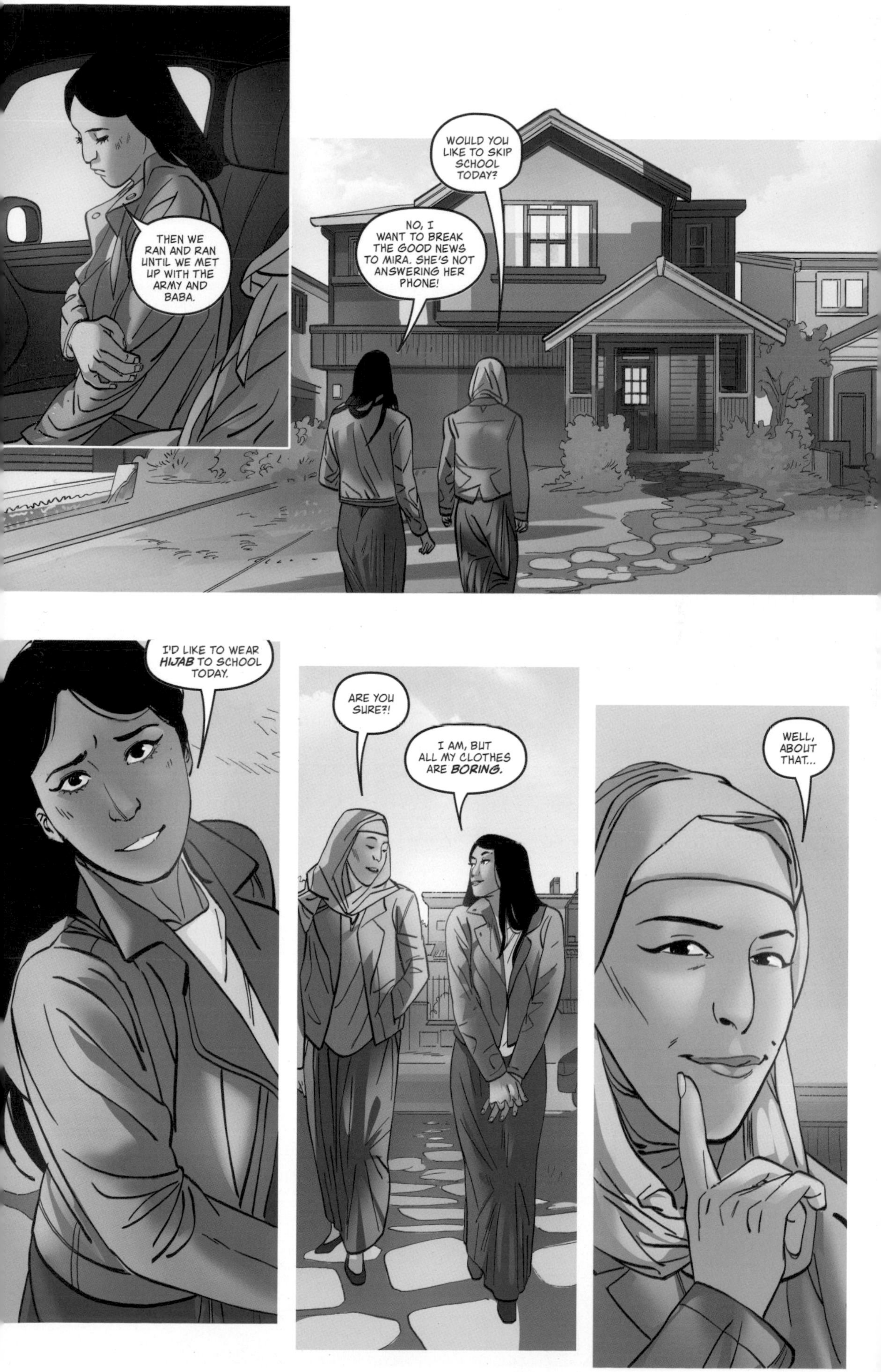
THEN WE RAN AND RAN UNTIL WE MET UP WITH THE ARMY AND BABA.
WOULD YOU LIKE TO SKIP SCHOOL TODAY?
NO, I WANT TO BREAK THE GOOD NEWS TO MIRA. SHE'S NOT ANSWERING HER PHONE!
I'D LIKE TO WEAR HIJAB TO SCHOOL TODAY.
ARE YOU SURE?!
I AM, BUT ALL MY CLOTHES ARE BORING.
WELL, ABOUT THAT...

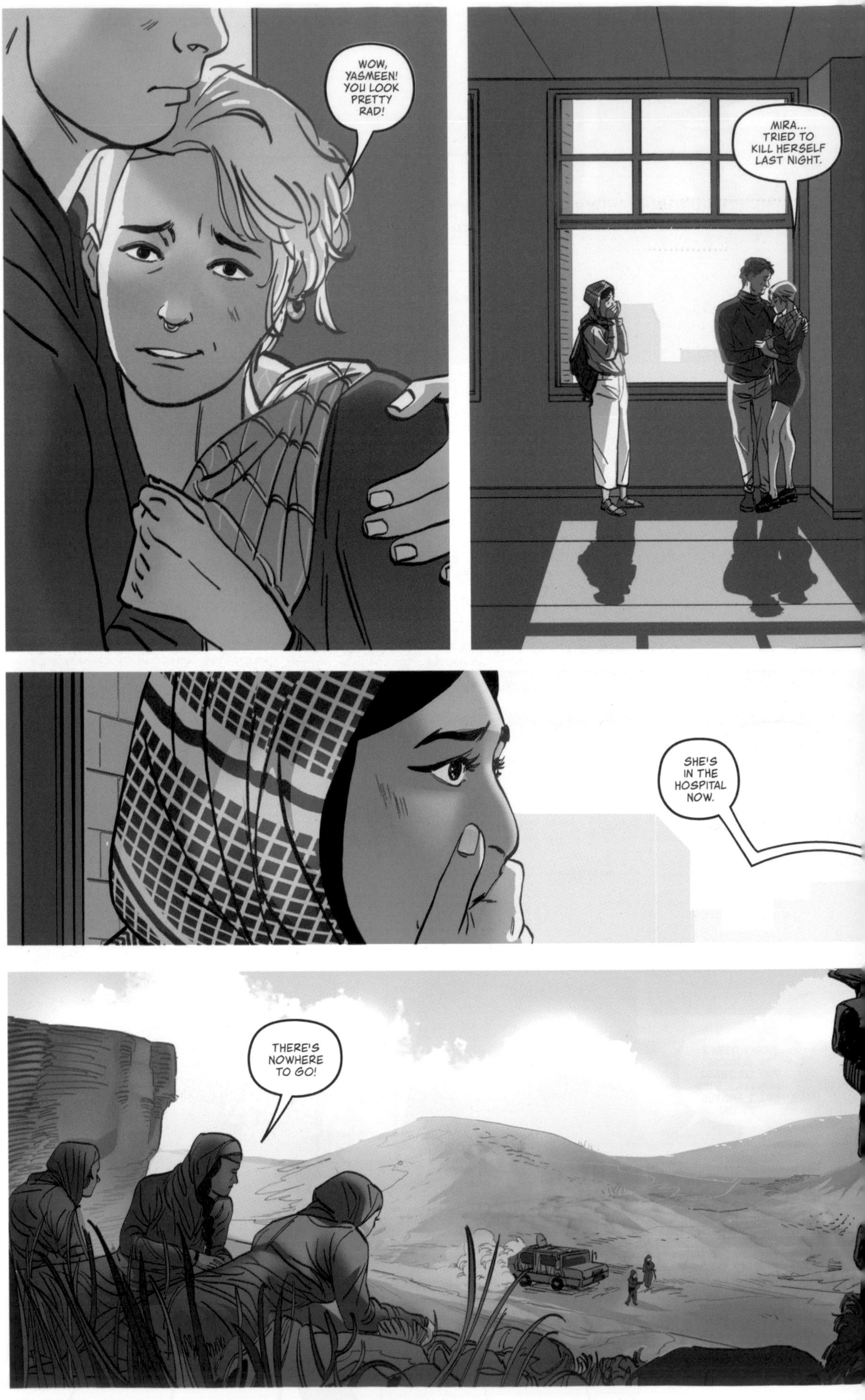
WOW, YASMEEN! YOU LOOK PRETTY RAD!
MIRA... TRIED TO KILL HERSELF LAST NIGHT.
SHE'S IN THE HOSPITAL NOW.
THERE'S NOWHERE TO GO!

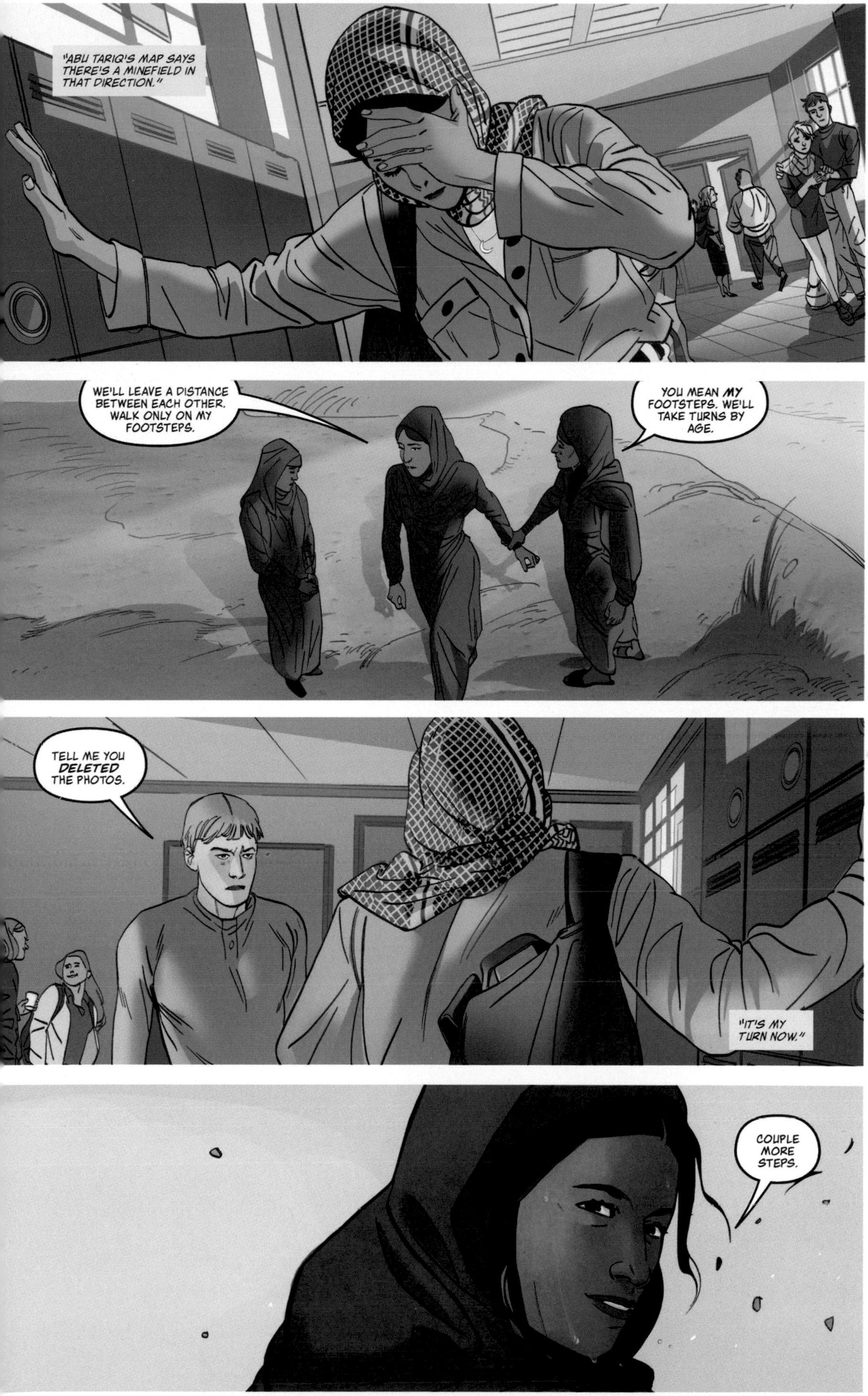
"ABU TARIQ'S MAP SAYS THERE'S A MINEFIELD IN THAT DIRECTION."
WE'LL LEAVE A DISTANCE BETWEEN EACH OTHER. WALK ONLY ON MY FOOTSTEPS.
YOU MEAN MY FOOTSTEPS. WE'LL TAKE TURNS BY AGE.
TELL ME YOU DELETED THE PHOTOS.
"IT'S MY TURN NOW."
COUPLE MORE STEPS.

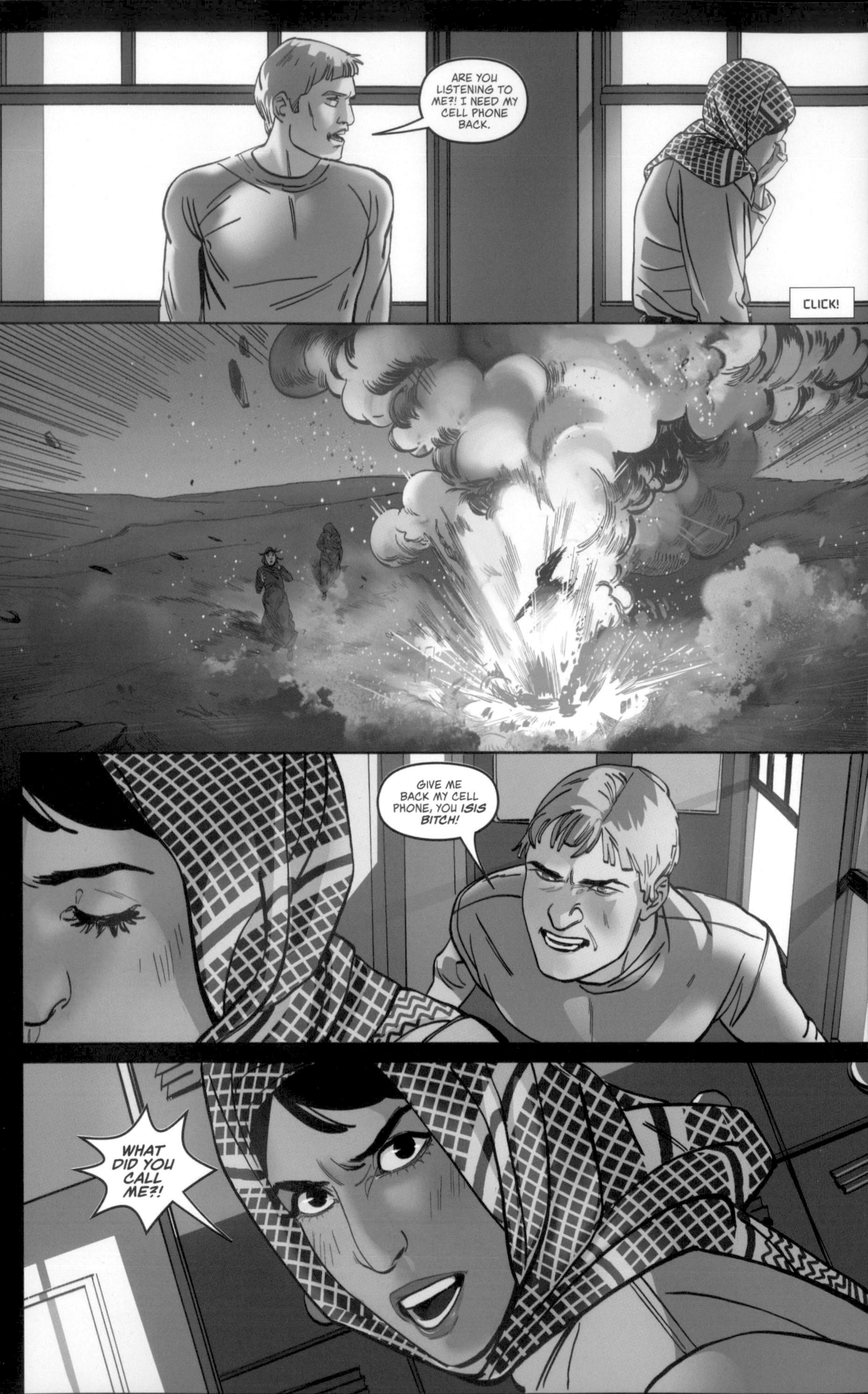
ARE YOU LISTENING TO ME?! I NEED MY CELL PHONE BACK.
CLICK!
GIVE ME BACK MY CELL PHONE, YOU ISIS BITCH!
WHAT DID YOU CALL ME?!

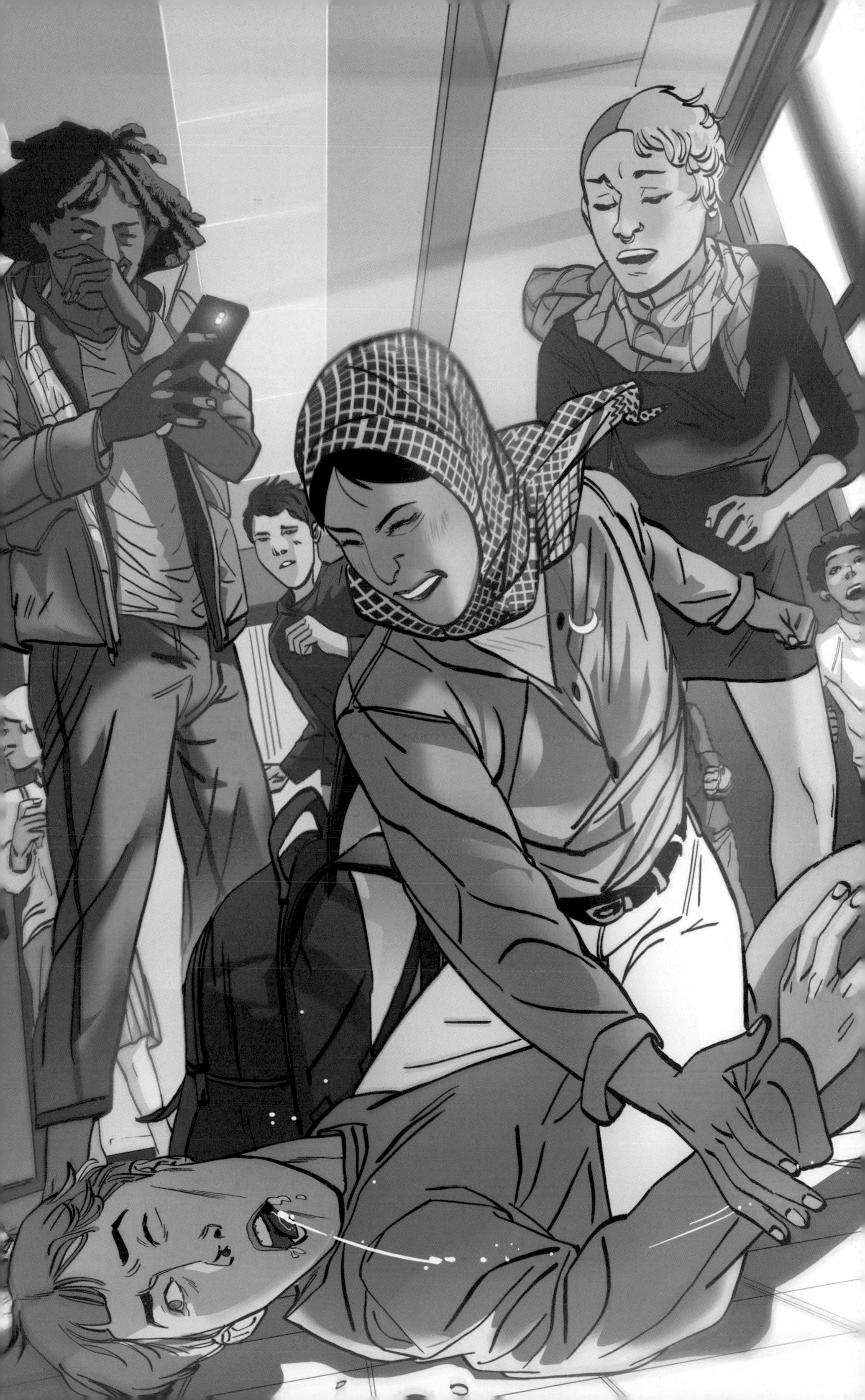

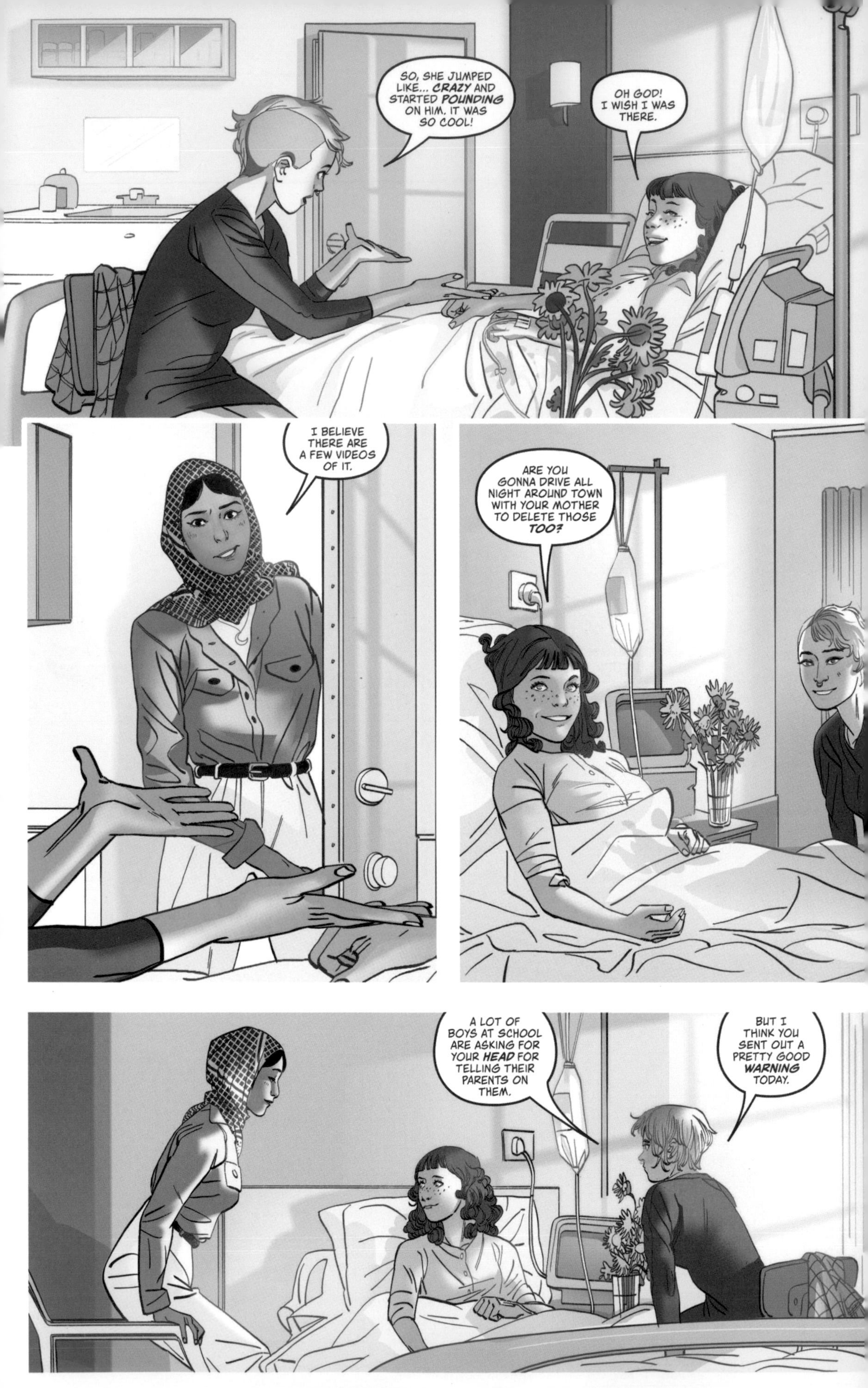
SO, SHE JUMPED LIKE... CRAZY AND STARTED POUNDING ON HIM. IT WAS SO COOL!
OH GOD! I WISH I WAS THERE.
I BELIEVE THERE ARE A FEW VIDEOS OF IT.
ARE YOU GONNA DRIVE ALL NIGHT AROUND TOWN WITH YOUR MOTHER TO DELETE THOSE TOO?
A LOT OF BOYS AT SCHOOL ARE ASKING FOR YOUR HEAD FOR TELLING THEIR PARENTS ON THEM.
BUT I THINK YOU SENT OUT A PRETTY GOOD WARNING TODAY.

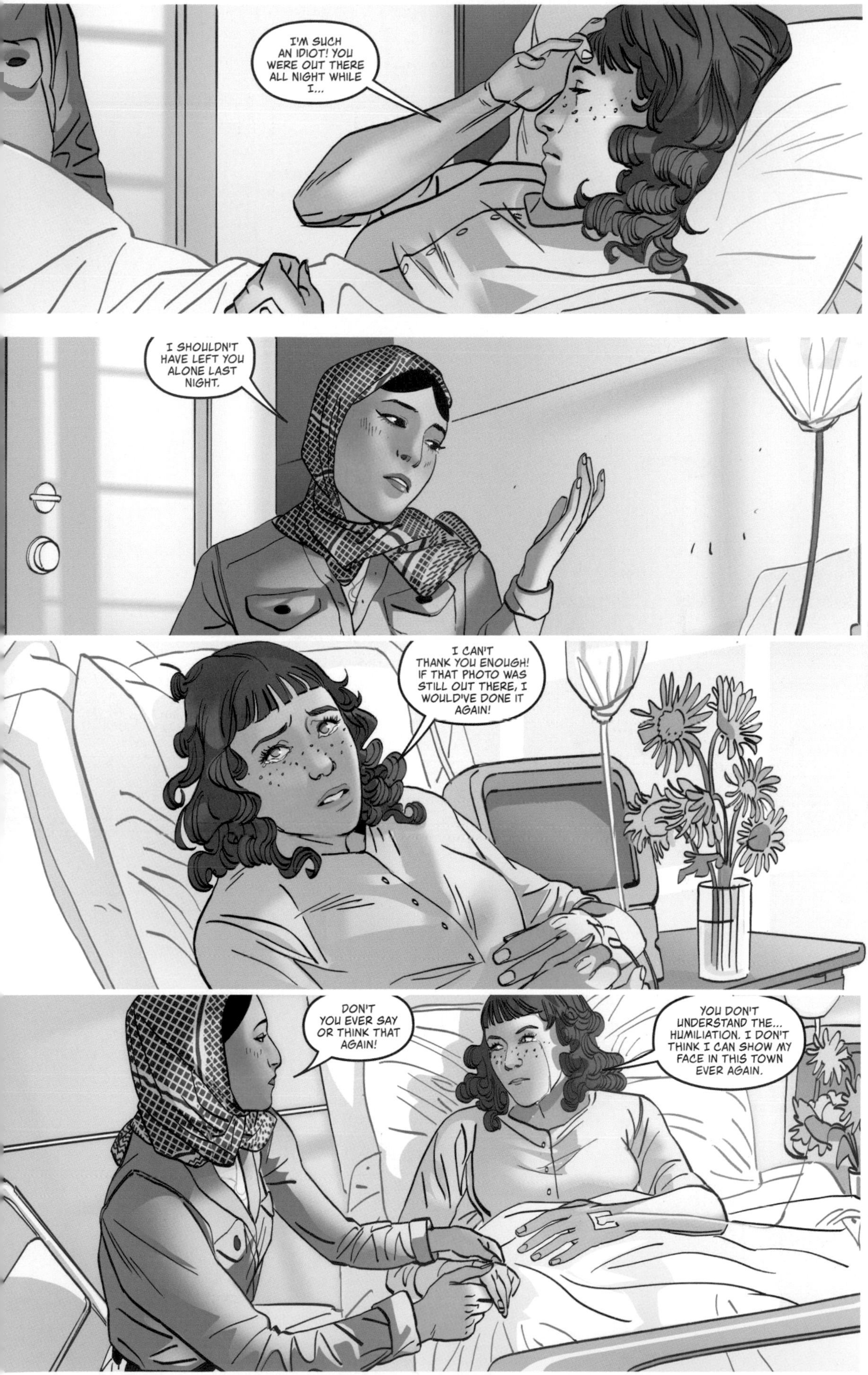
I'M SUCH AN IDIOT! YOU WERE OUT THERE ALL NIGHT WHILE I...
I SHOULDN'T HAVE LEFT YOU ALONE LAST NIGHT.
I CAN'T THANK YOU ENOUGH! IF THAT PHOTO WAS STILL OUT THERE, I WOULD'VE DONE IT AGAIN!
DON'T YOU EVER SAY OR THINK THAT AGAIN!
YOU DON'T UNDERSTAND THE... HUMILIATION. I DON'T THINK I CAN SHOW MY FACE IN THIS TOWN EVER AGAIN.

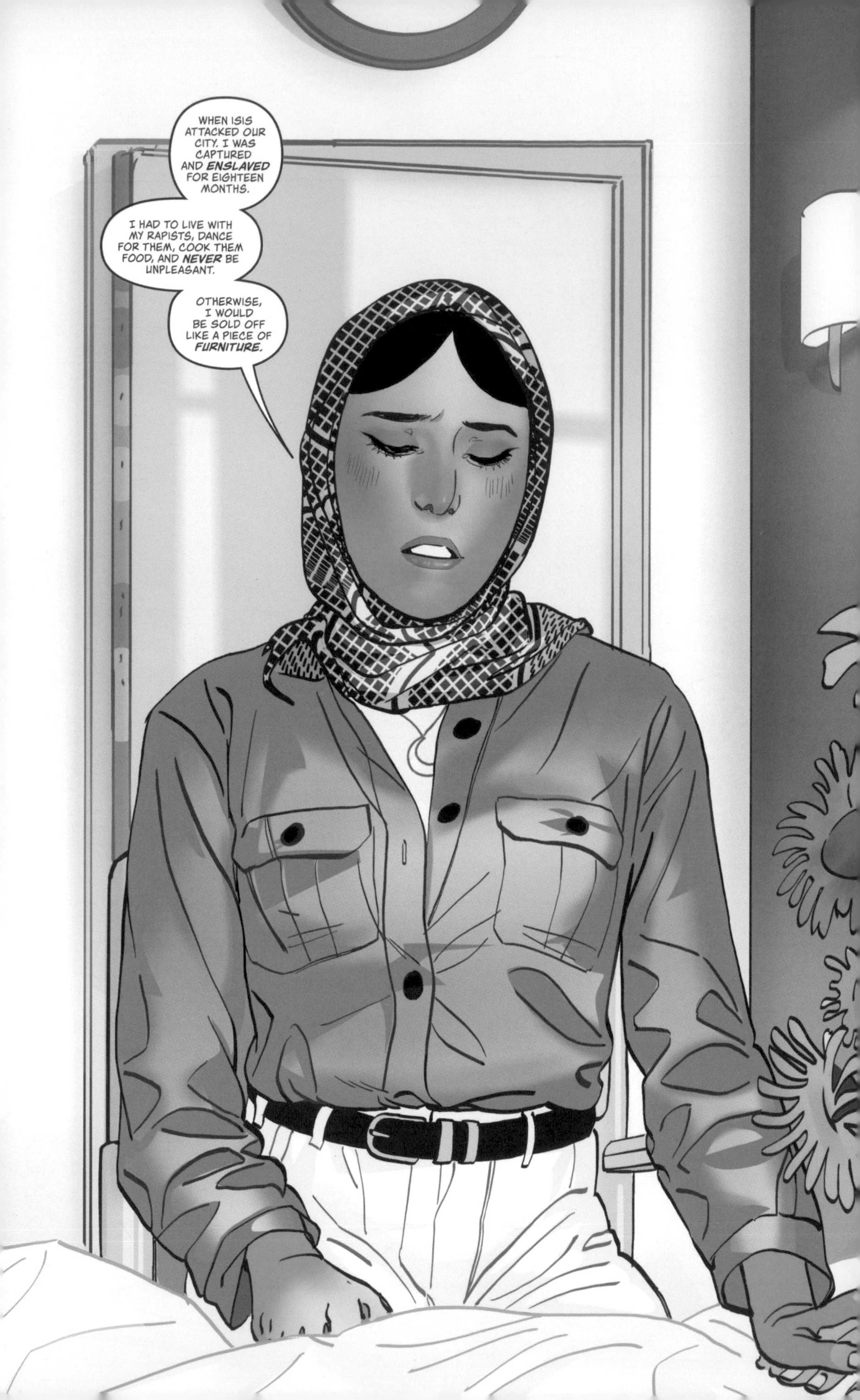
WHEN ISIS ATTACKED OUR CITY, I WAS CAPTURED AND ENSLAVED FOR EIGHTEEN MONTHS.
I HAD TO LIVE WITH MY RAPISTS, DANCE FOR THEM, COOK THEM FOOD, AND NEVER BE UNPLEASANT.
OTHERWISE, I WOULD BE SOLD OFF LIKE A PIECE OF FURNITURE.

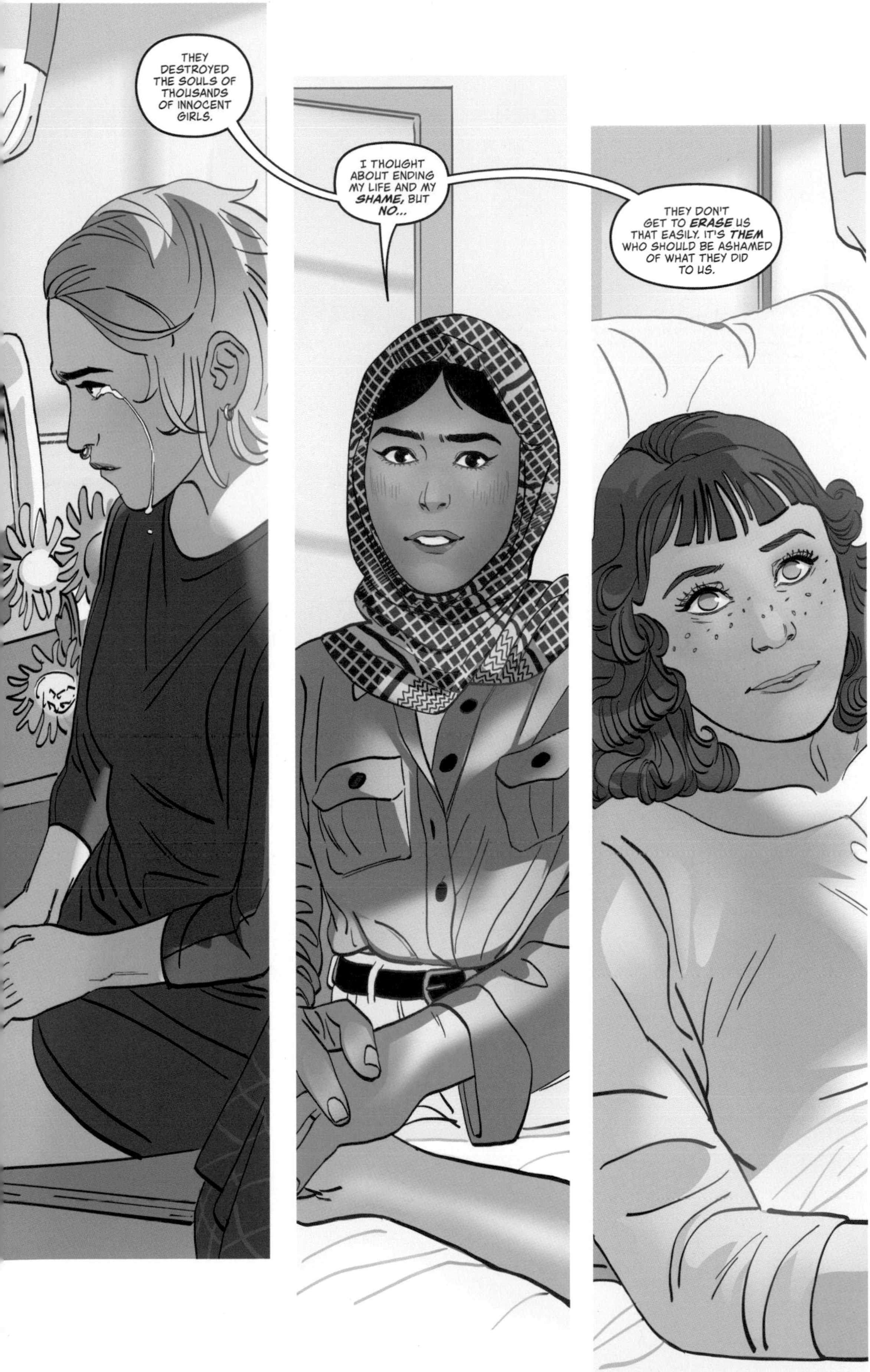
THEY DESTROYED THE SOULS OF THOUSANDS OF INNOCENT GIRLS.
I THOUGHT ABOUT ENDING MY LIFE AND MY SHAME, BUT NO...
THEY DON'T GET TO ERASE US THAT EASILY. IT'S THEM WHO SHOULD BE ASHAMED OF WHAT THEY DID TO US.

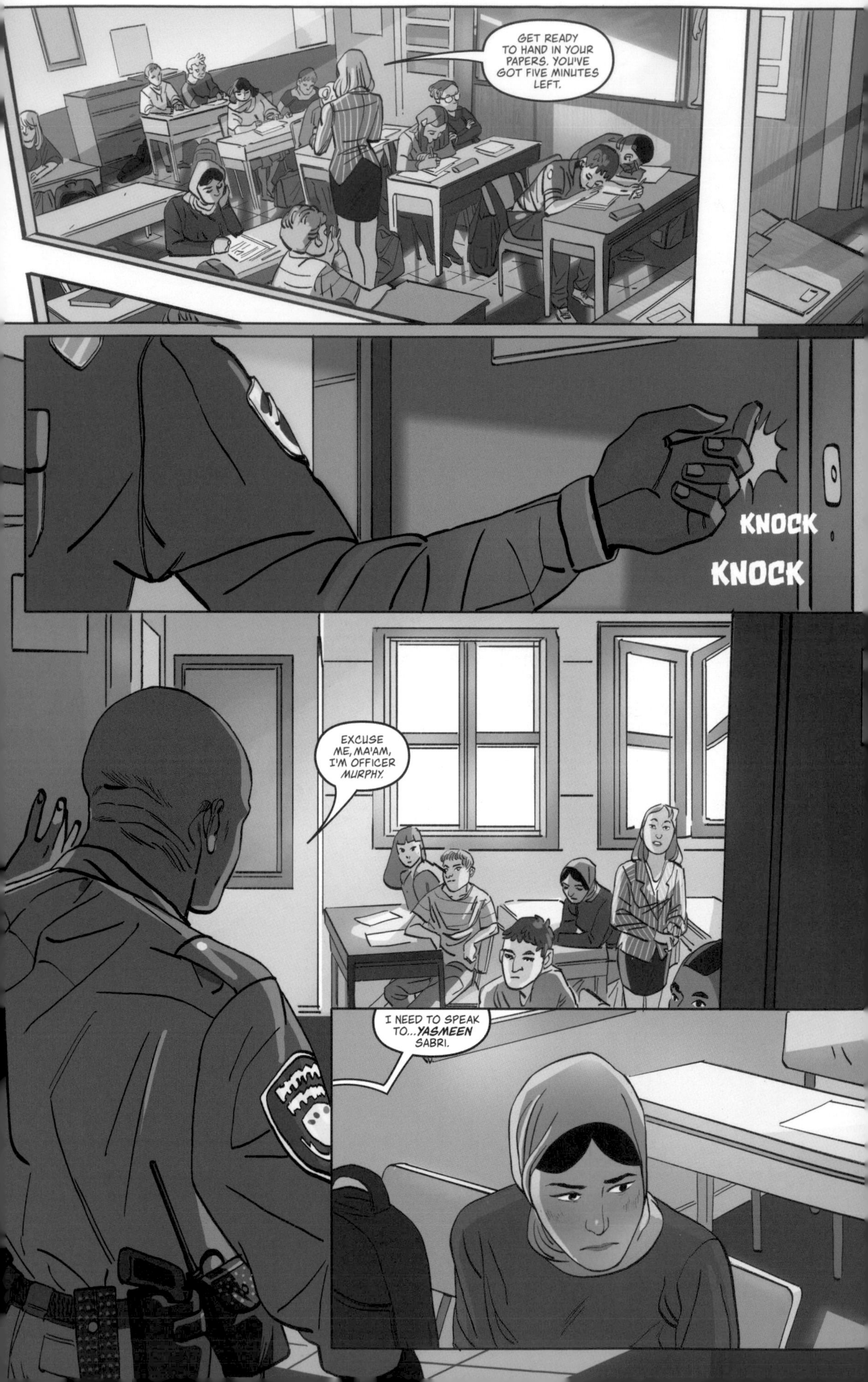
GET READY TO HAND IN YOUR PAPERS. YOU'VE GOT FIVE MINUTES LEFT.
KNOCK
KNOCK
EXCUSE ME, MA'AM, I'M OFFICER *MURPHY.*
I NEED TO SPEAK TO...***YASMEEN*** SABRI.

THE MEN WITH KHALED ARE BASED ON REAL IRAQI
FIGHTERS WHO LOST THEIR LIVES IN THE FIGHT
AGAINST ISIS, EXCEPT FOR MUHAMMAD AL-BADRI
WHO LOST HIS ARM AND LEG IN COMBAT. THIS
ISSUE IS DEDICATED TO THESE MEN AND ALL THE
BRAVE WARRIORS WHO SACRIFICED THEIR LIVES TO
FREE THEIR COUNTRY AND THE WORLD FROM EVIL.

ABU TAHSIN AL-SALHI

FIRST-LIEUTENANT
ABU BAKR AL-SAMMARAE

LIEUTENANT COLONEL
ALI SAADI

PRIVATE
MOSTAFA AL-SABEHAWY

MUHAMMAD AL-BADRI

CHAPTER 6

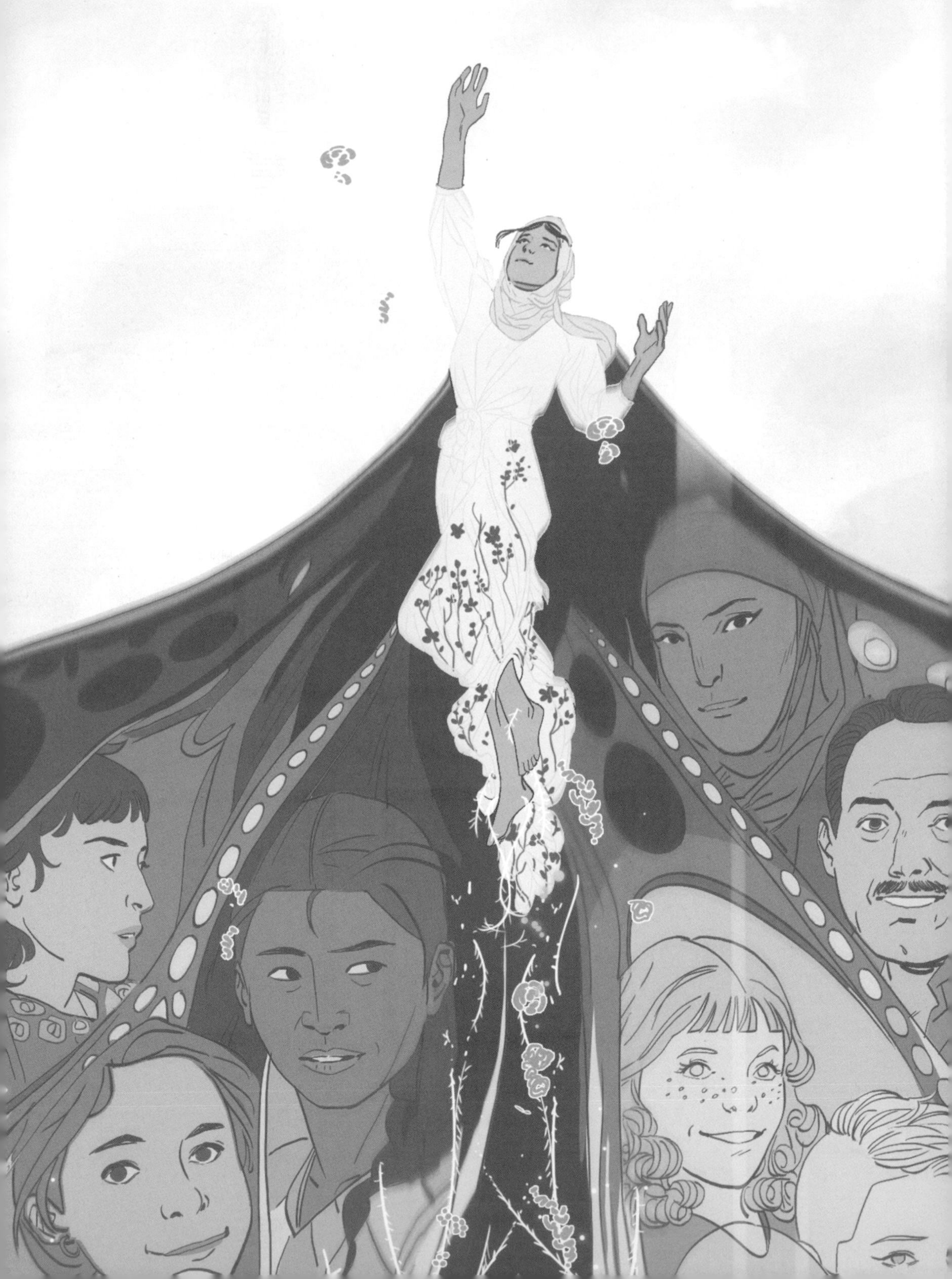

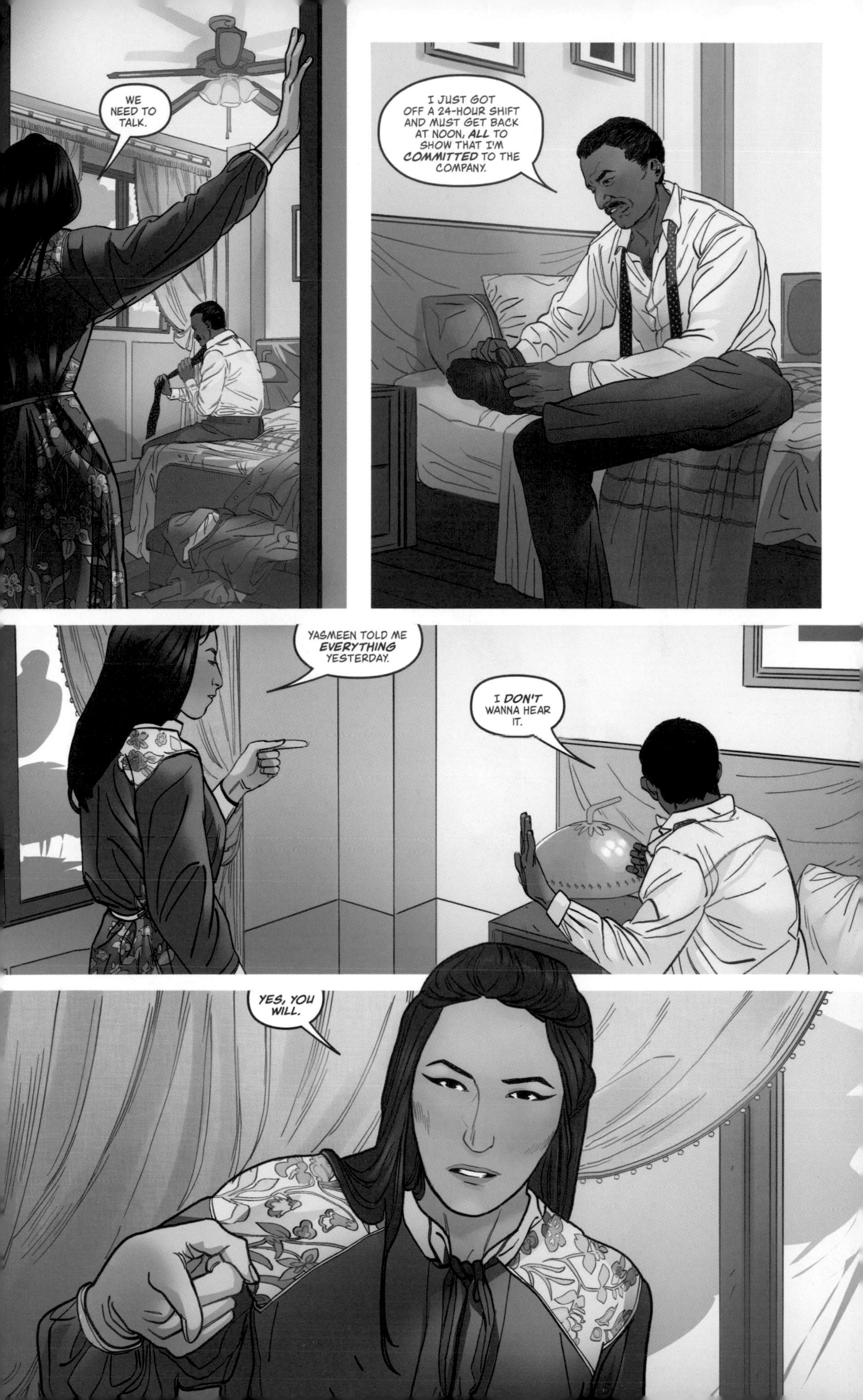
WE NEED TO TALK.
I JUST GOT OFF A 24-HOUR SHIFT AND MUST GET BACK AT NOON, **ALL** TO SHOW THAT I'M **COMMITTED** TO THE COMPANY.
YASMEEN TOLD ME **EVERYTHING** YESTERDAY.
I **DON'T** WANNA HEAR IT.
YES, YOU WILL.

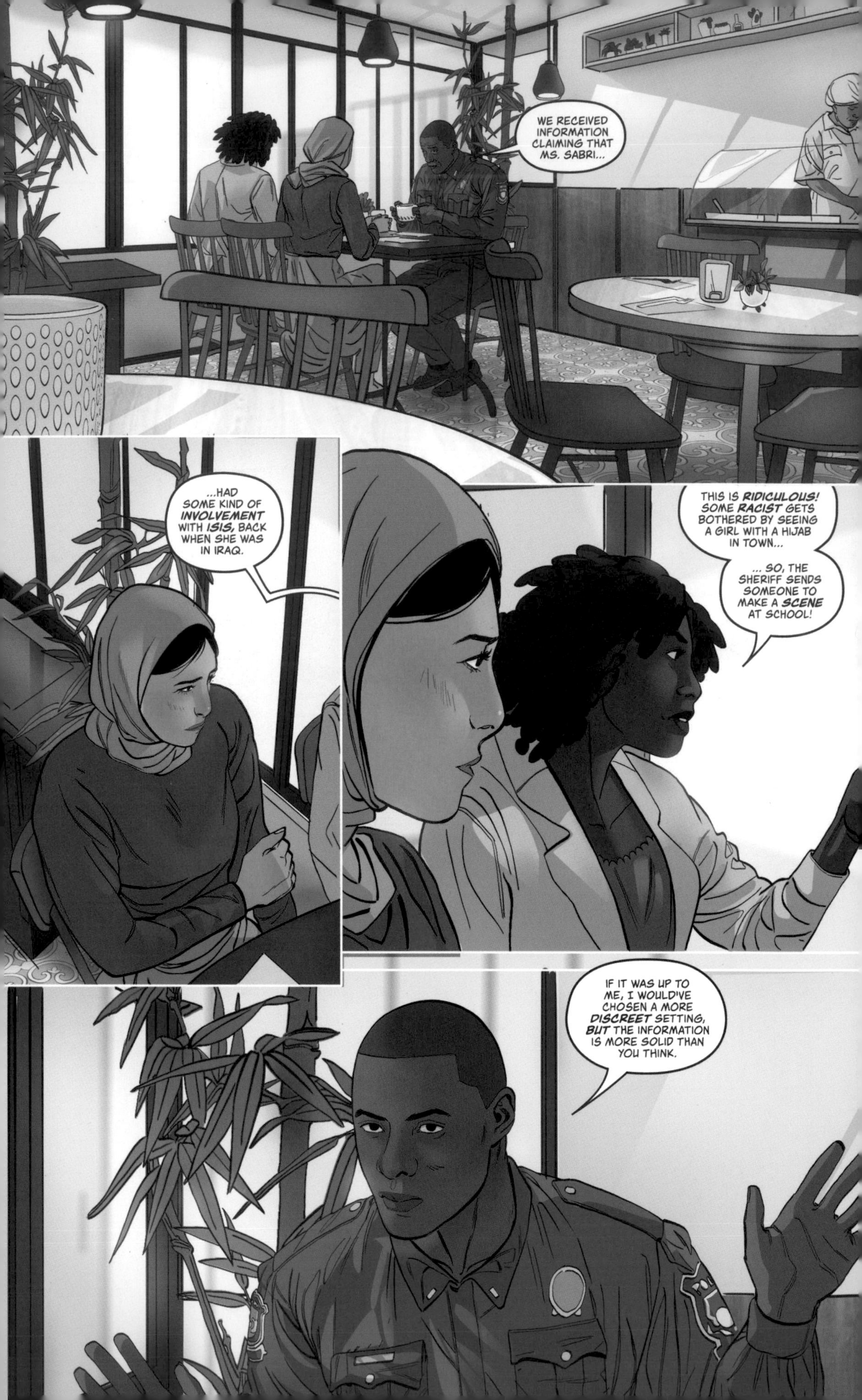
WE RECEIVED INFORMATION CLAIMING THAT MS. SABRI...
...HAD SOME KIND OF INVOLVEMENT WITH ISIS, BACK WHEN SHE WAS IN IRAQ.
THIS IS RIDICULOUS! SOME RACIST GETS BOTHERED BY SEEING A GIRL WITH A HIJAB IN TOWN...
... SO, THE SHERIFF SENDS SOMEONE TO MAKE A SCENE AT SCHOOL!
IF IT WAS UP TO ME, I WOULD'VE CHOSEN A MORE DISCREET SETTING, BUT THE INFORMATION IS MORE SOLID THAN YOU THINK.

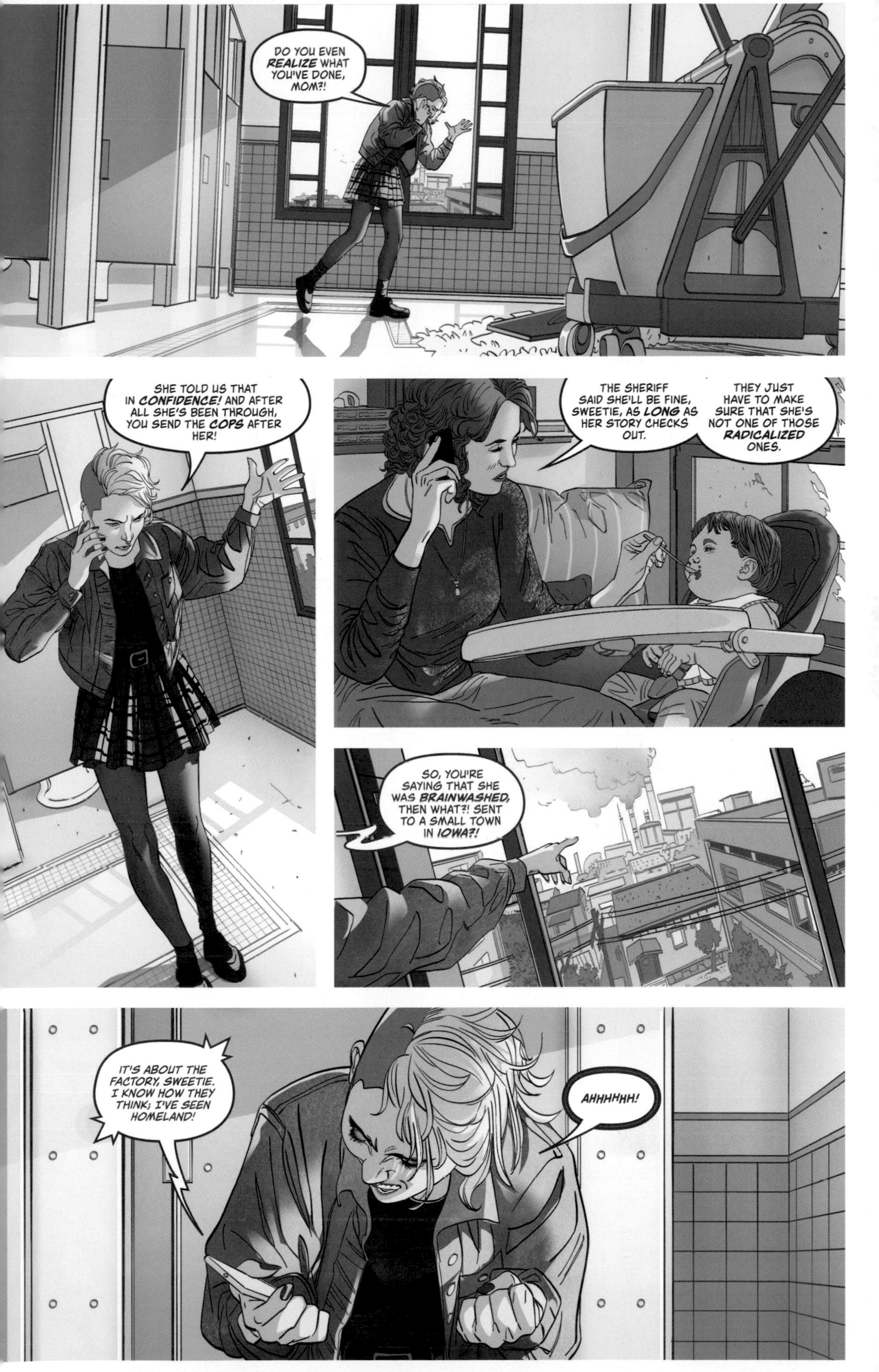
DO YOU EVEN REALIZE WHAT YOU'VE DONE, MOM?!
SHE TOLD US THAT IN CONFIDENCE! AND AFTER ALL SHE'S BEEN THROUGH, YOU SEND THE COPS AFTER HER!
THE SHERIFF SAID SHE'LL BE FINE, SWEETIE, AS LONG AS HER STORY CHECKS OUT.
THEY JUST HAVE TO MAKE SURE THAT SHE'S NOT ONE OF THOSE RADICALIZED ONES.
SO, YOU'RE SAYING THAT SHE WAS BRAINWASHED, THEN WHAT?! SENT TO A SMALL TOWN IN IOWA?!
IT'S ABOUT THE FACTORY, SWEETIE. I KNOW HOW THEY THINK; I'VE SEEN HOMELAND!
AHHHHHH!

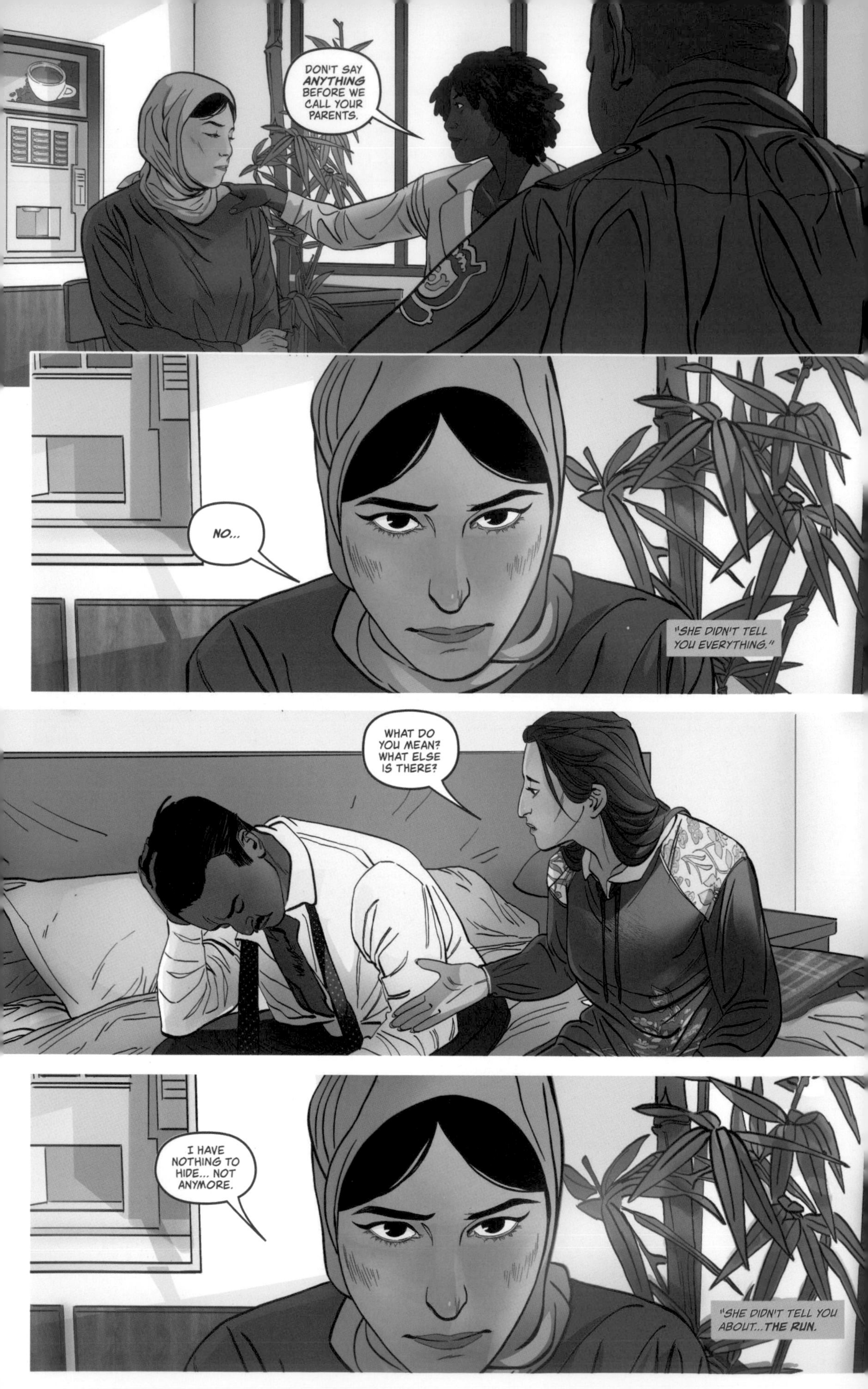
DON'T SAY ANYTHING BEFORE WE CALL YOUR PARENTS.
NO...
"SHE DIDN'T TELL YOU EVERYTHING."
WHAT DO YOU MEAN? WHAT ELSE IS THERE?
I HAVE NOTHING TO HIDE... NOT ANYMORE.
"SHE DIDN'T TELL YOU ABOUT...THE RUN.

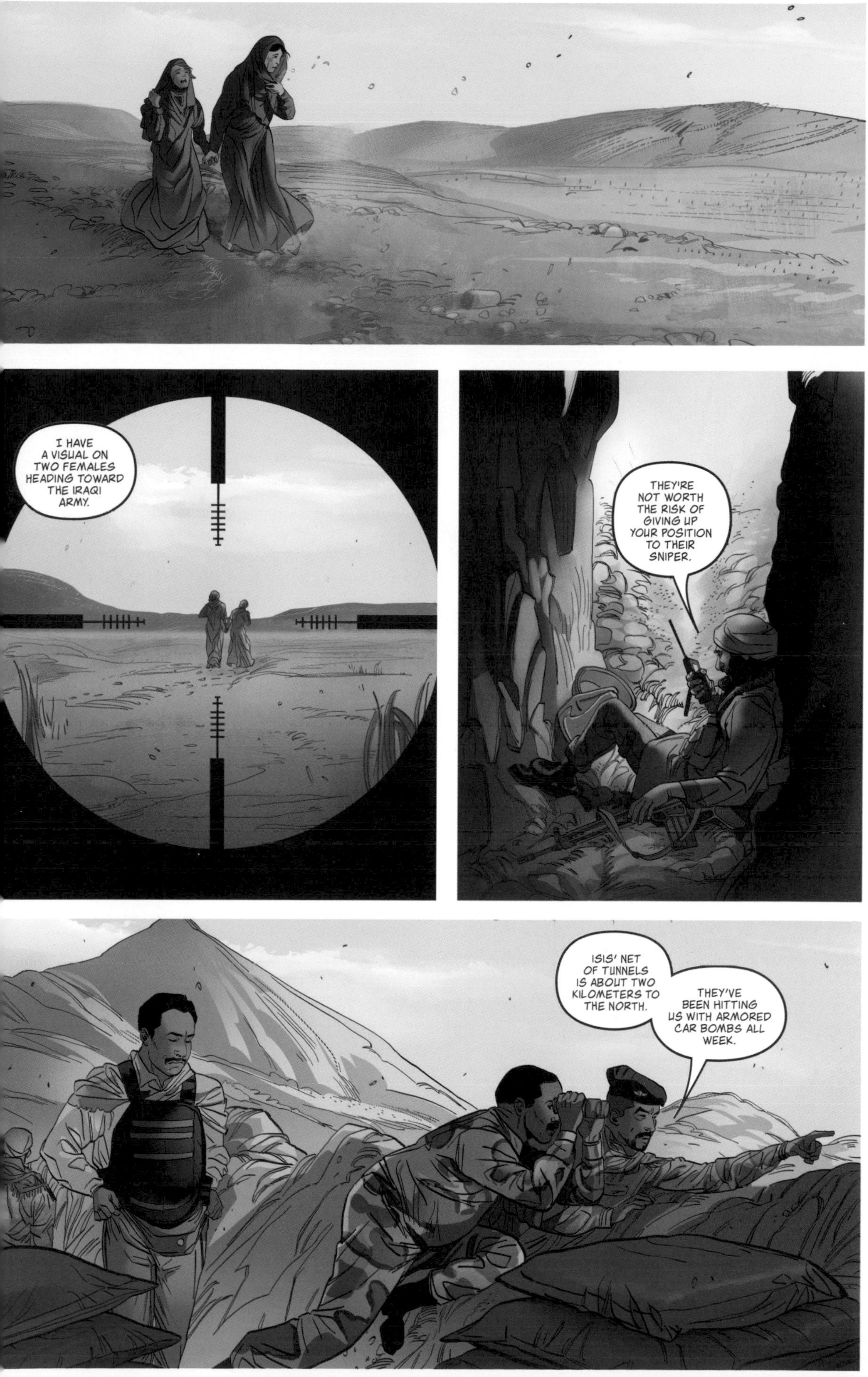
I HAVE A VISUAL ON TWO FEMALES HEADING TOWARD THE IRAQI ARMY.
THEY'RE NOT WORTH THE RISK OF GIVING UP YOUR POSITION TO THEIR SNIPER.
ISIS' NET OF TUNNELS IS ABOUT TWO KILOMETERS TO THE NORTH.
THEY'VE BEEN HITTING US WITH ARMORED CAR BOMBS ALL WEEK.

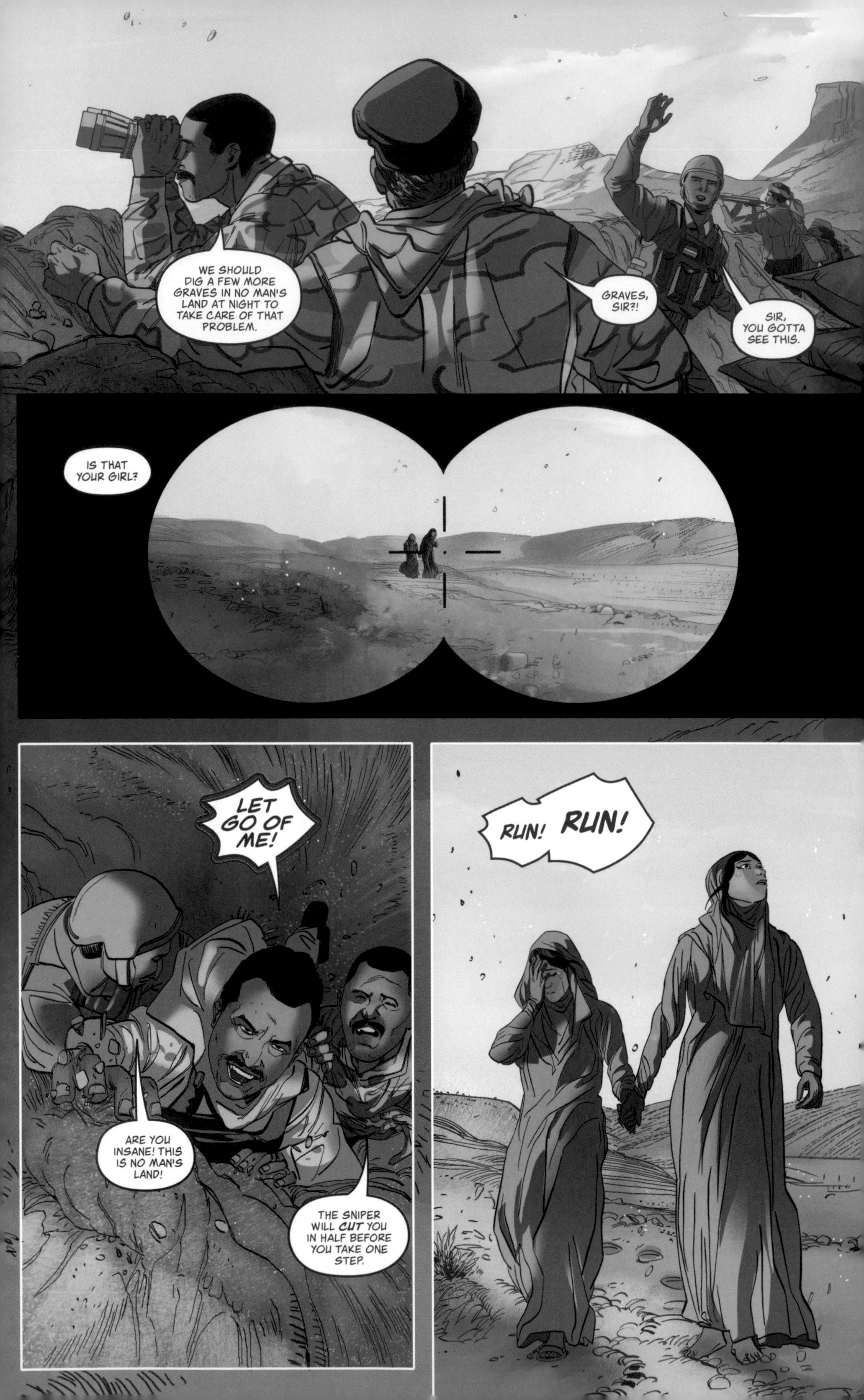
WE SHOULD DIG A FEW MORE GRAVES IN NO MAN'S LAND AT NIGHT TO TAKE CARE OF THAT PROBLEM.
GRAVES, SIR?!
SIR, YOU GOTTA SEE THIS.
IS THAT YOUR GIRL?
LET GO OF ME!
ARE YOU INSANE! THIS IS NO MAN'S LAND!
THE SNIPER WILL CUT YOU IN HALF BEFORE YOU TAKE ONE STEP.
RUN! RUN!

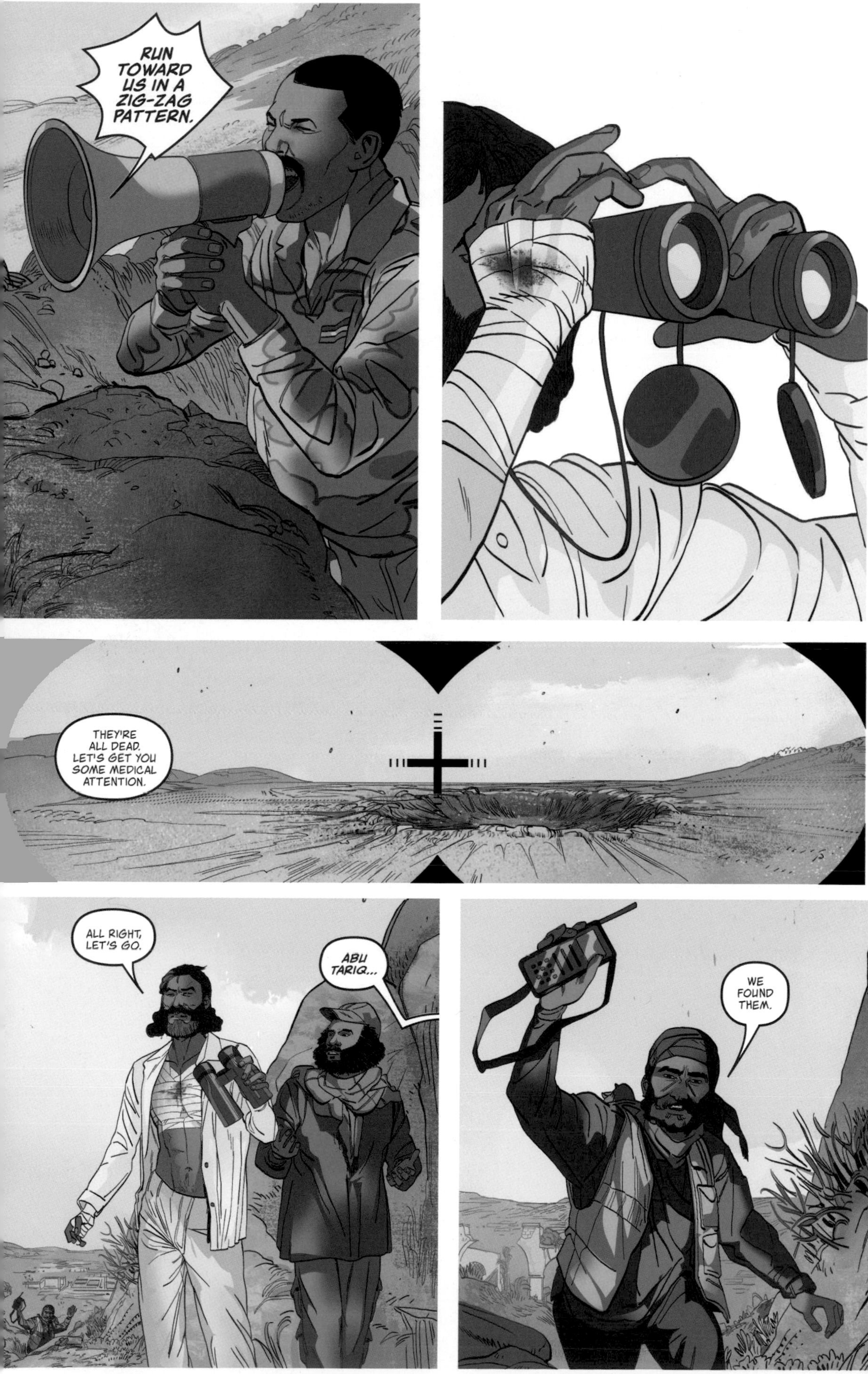
RUN TOWARD US IN A ZIG-ZAG PATTERN.
THEY'RE ALL DEAD. LET'S GET YOU SOME MEDICAL ATTENTION.
ALL RIGHT, LET'S GO.
ABU TARIQ...
WE FOUND THEM.

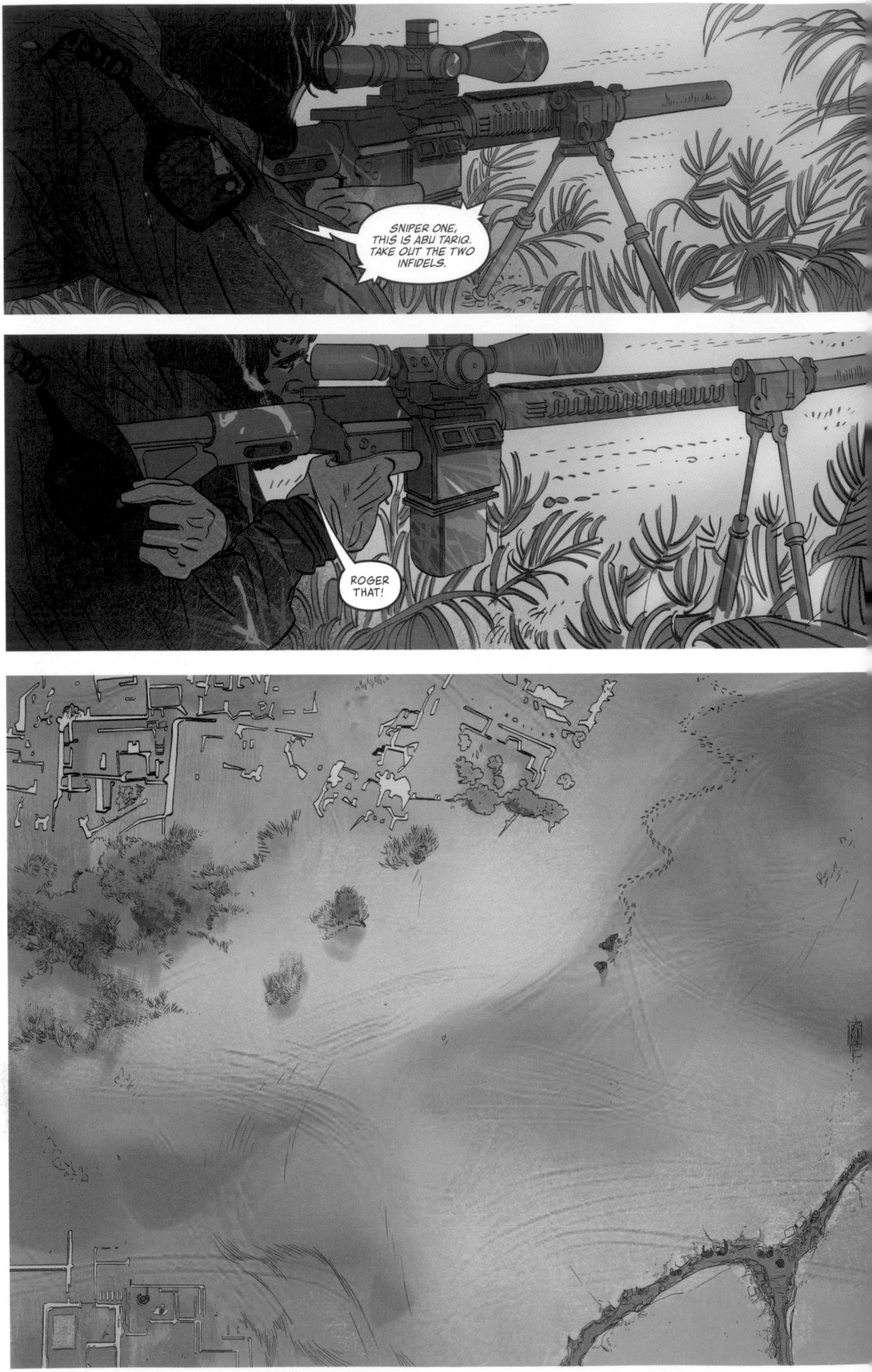
SNIPER ONE, THIS IS ABU TARIQ. TAKE OUT THE TWO INFIDELS.
ROGER THAT!

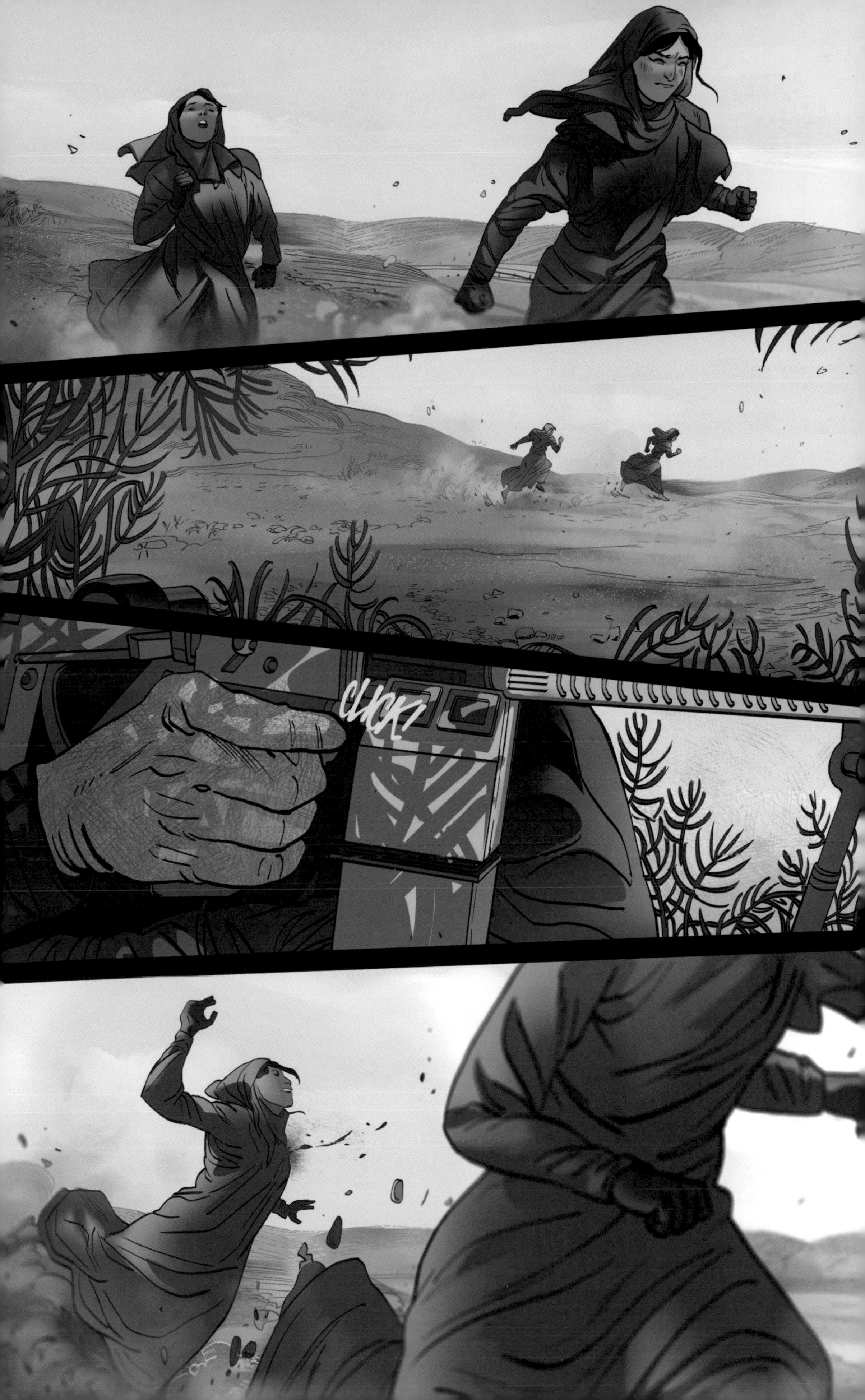
CLICK!

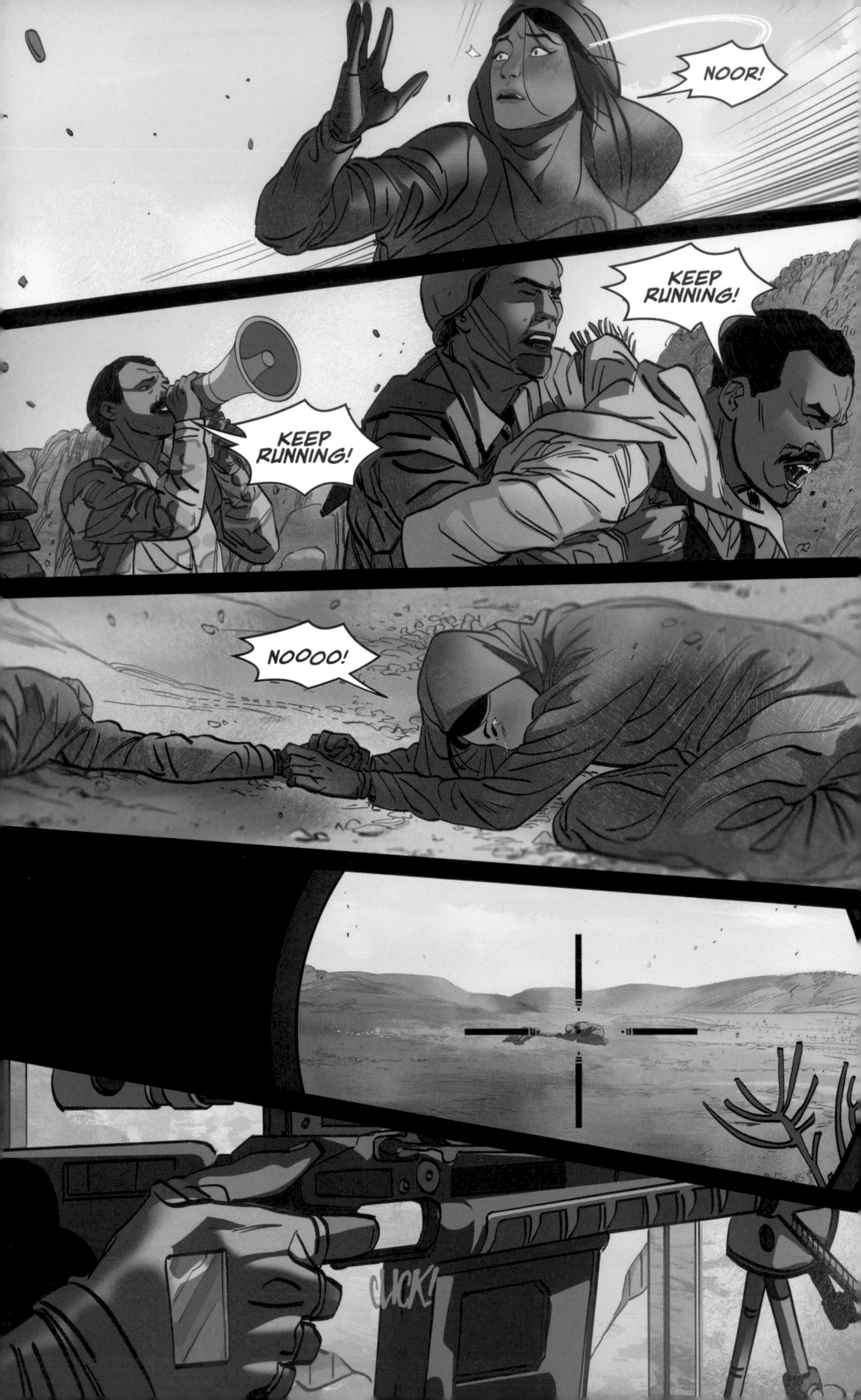
NOOR!
KEEP RUNNING!
KEEP RUNNING!
NOOOO!
CLICK!

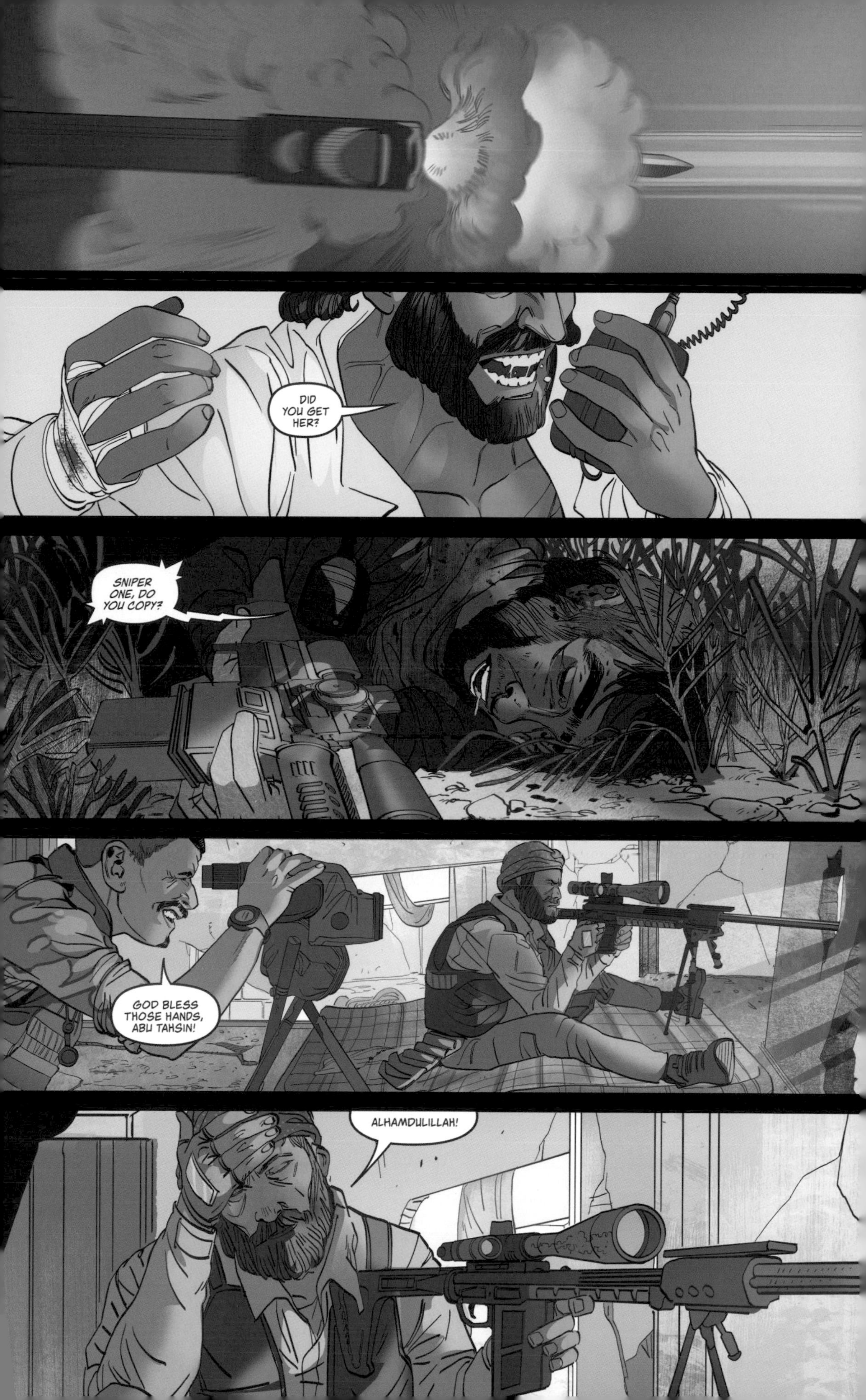
DID YOU GET HER?
SNIPER ONE, DO YOU COPY?
GOD BLESS THOSE HANDS, ABU TAHSIN!
ALHAMDULILLAH!

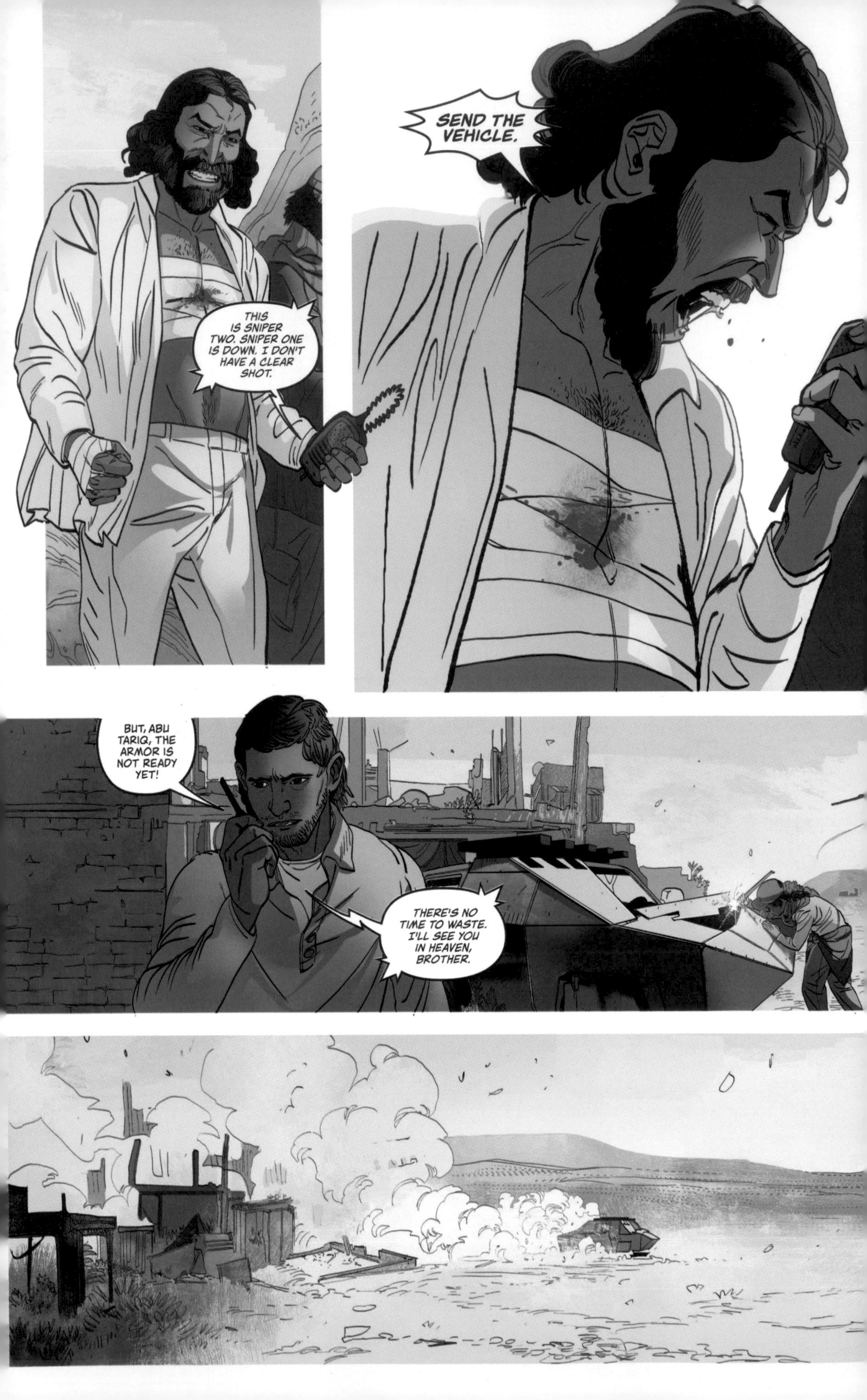
THIS IS SNIPER TWO. SNIPER ONE IS DOWN. I DON'T HAVE A CLEAR SHOT.
SEND THE VEHICLE.
BUT, ABU TARIQ, THE ARMOR IS NOT READY YET!
THERE'S NO TIME TO WASTE. I'LL SEE YOU IN HEAVEN, BROTHER.

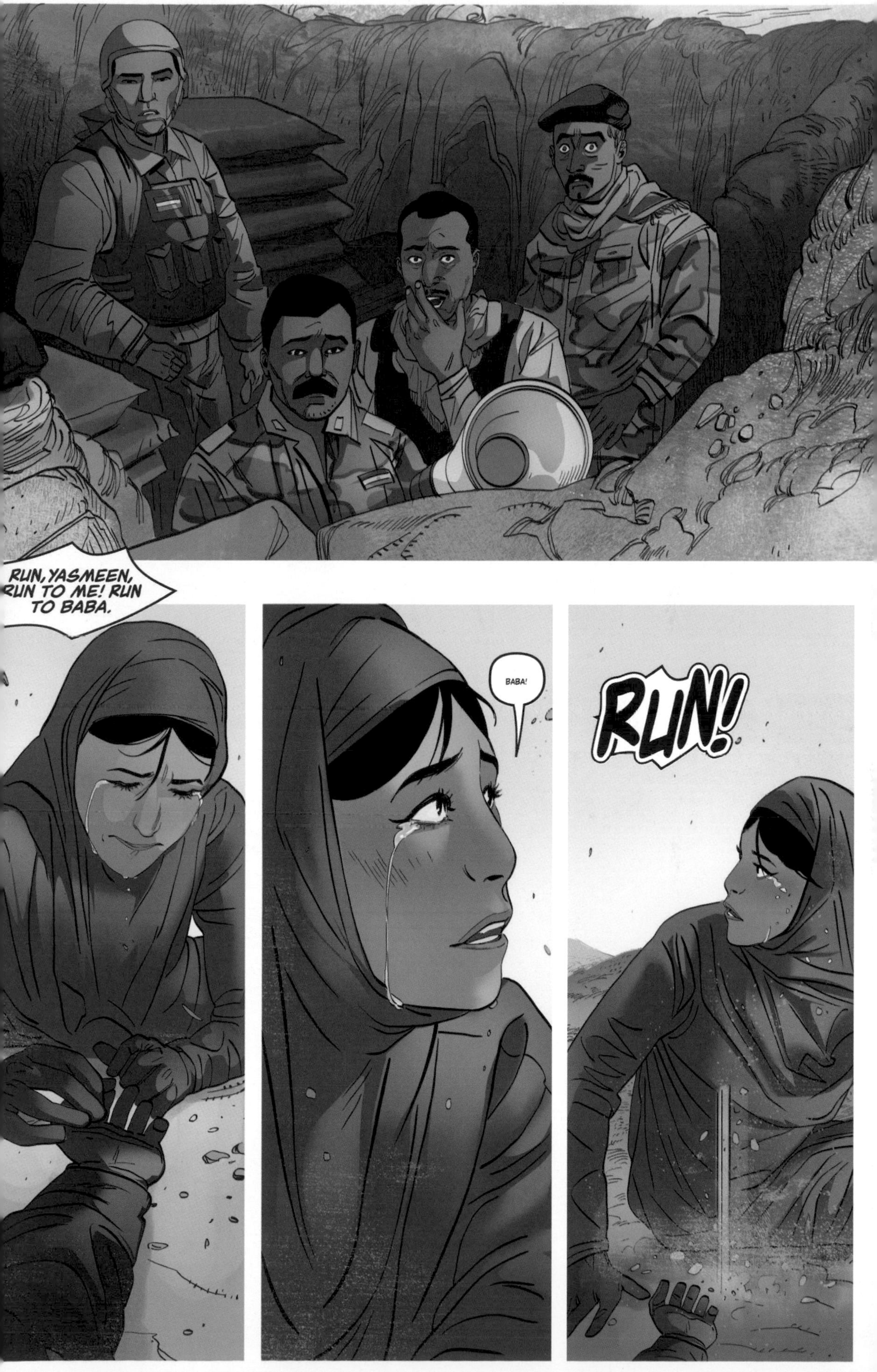
RUN, YASMEEN, RUN TO ME! RUN TO BABA.
BABA!
RUN!

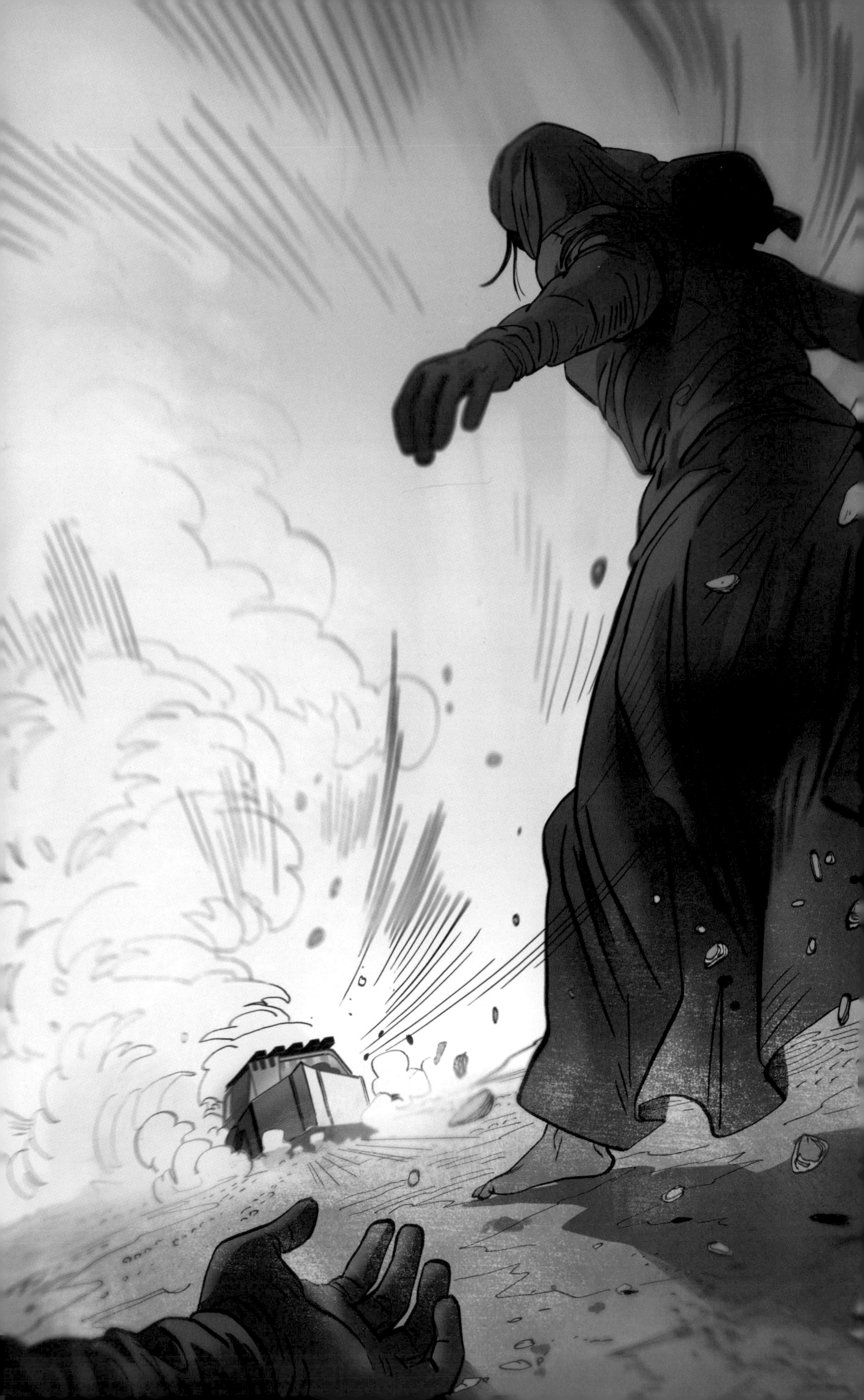

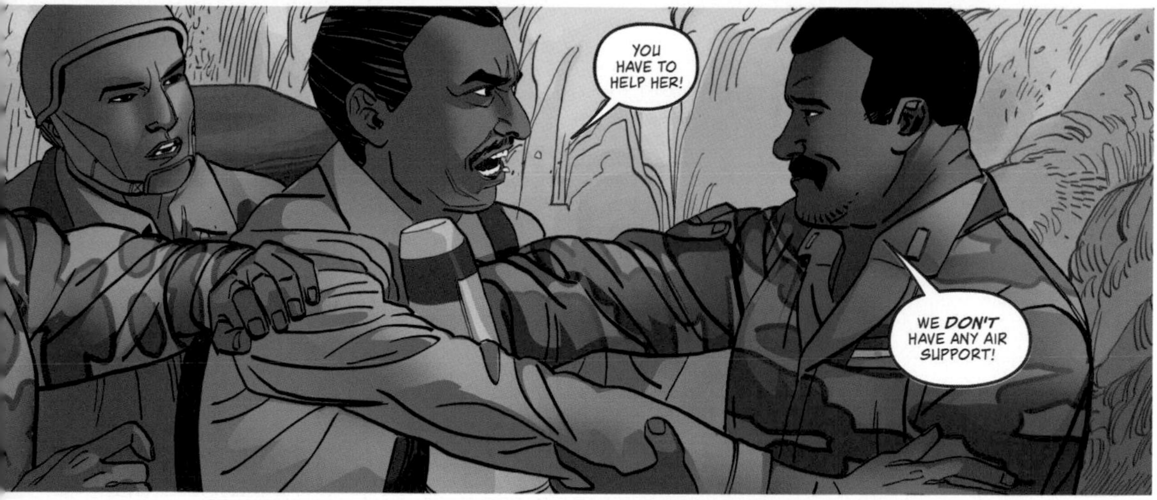
YOU HAVE TO HELP HER!
WE DON'T HAVE ANY AIR SUPPORT!

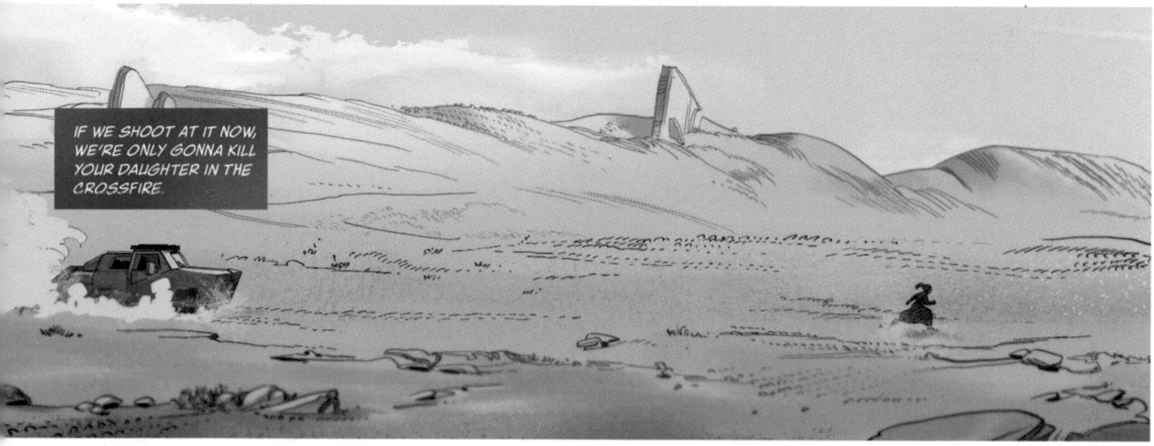
IF WE SHOOT AT IT NOW, WE'RE ONLY GONNA KILL YOUR DAUGHTER IN THE CROSSFIRE.

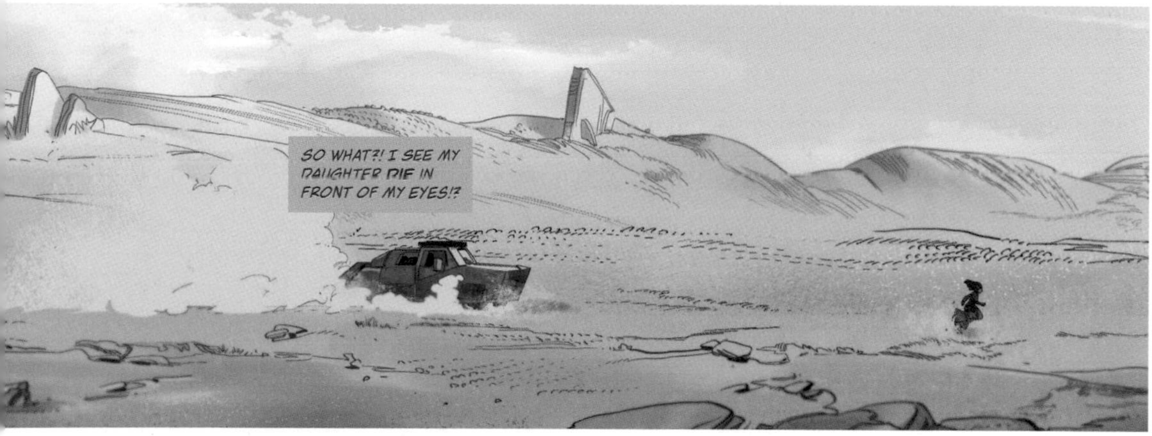
SO WHAT?! I SEE MY DAUGHTER DIE IN FRONT OF MY EYES!?

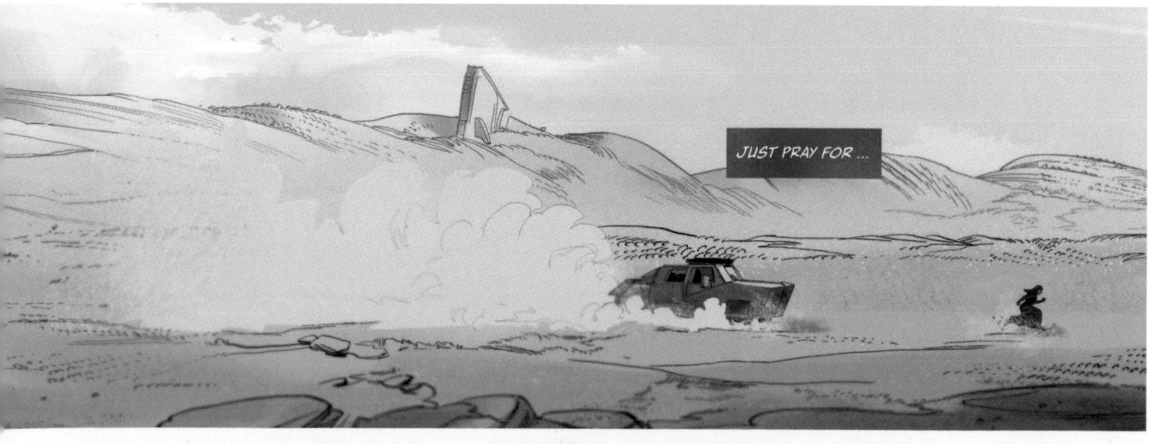
JUST PRAY FOR ...

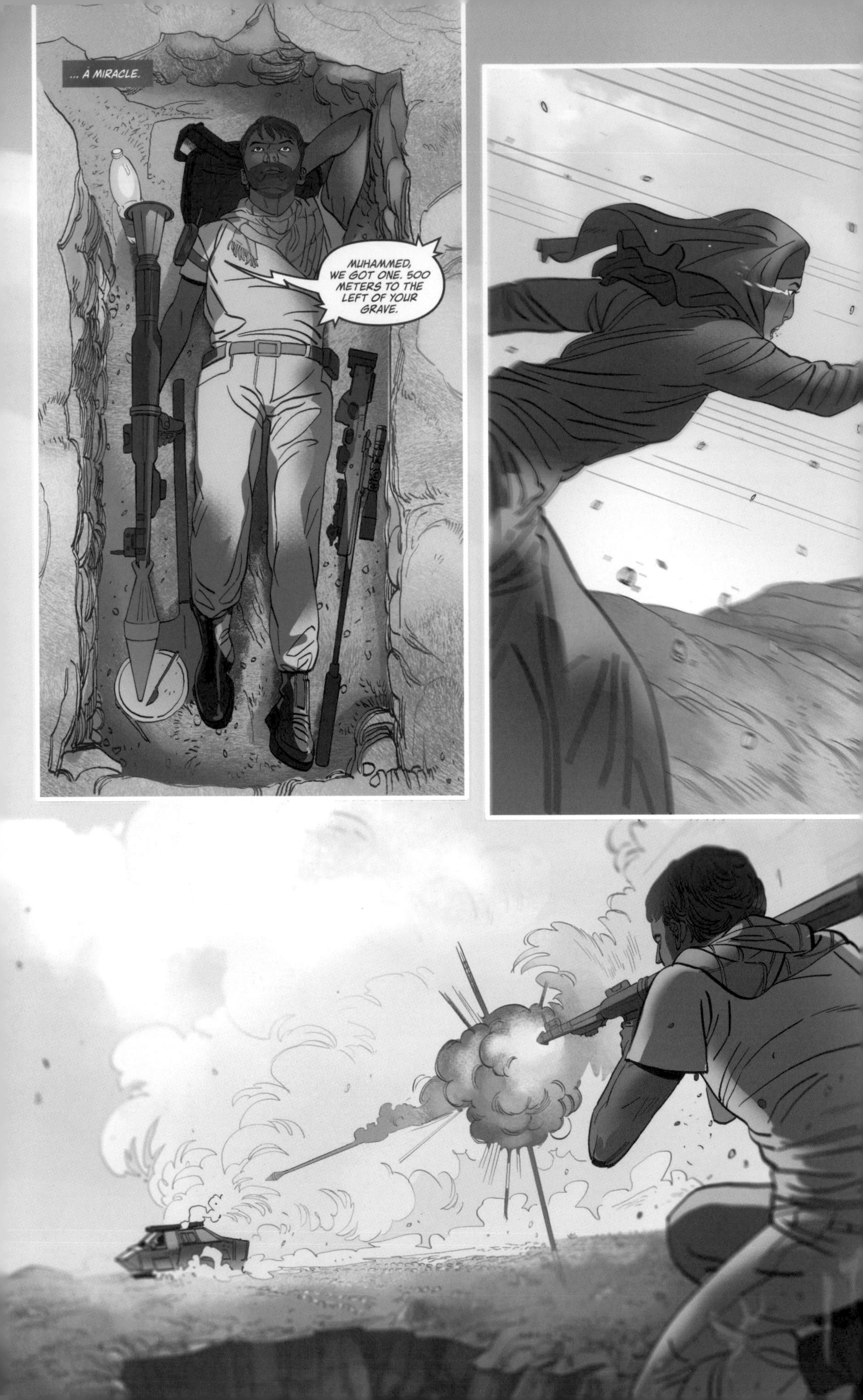
... A MIRACLE.
MUHAMMED, WE GOT ONE. 500 METERS TO THE LEFT OF YOUR GRAVE.

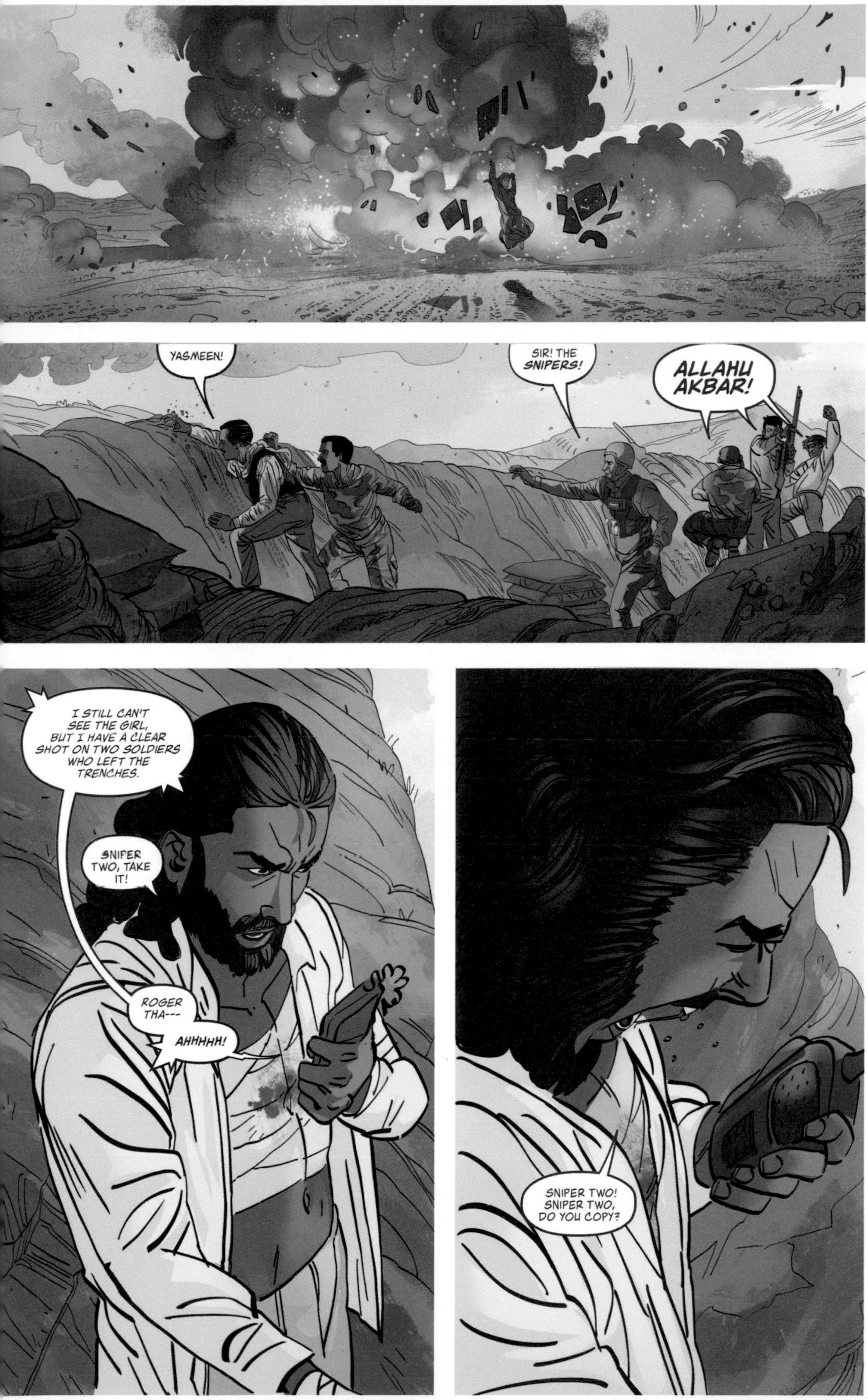
YASMEEN!
SIR! THE SNIPERS!
ALLAHU AKBAR!
I STILL CAN'T SEE THE GIRL, BUT I HAVE A CLEAR SHOT ON TWO SOLDIERS WHO LEFT THE TRENCHES.
SNIPER TWO, TAKE IT!
ROGER THA---
AHHHHH!
SNIPER TWO! SNIPER TWO, DO YOU COPY?

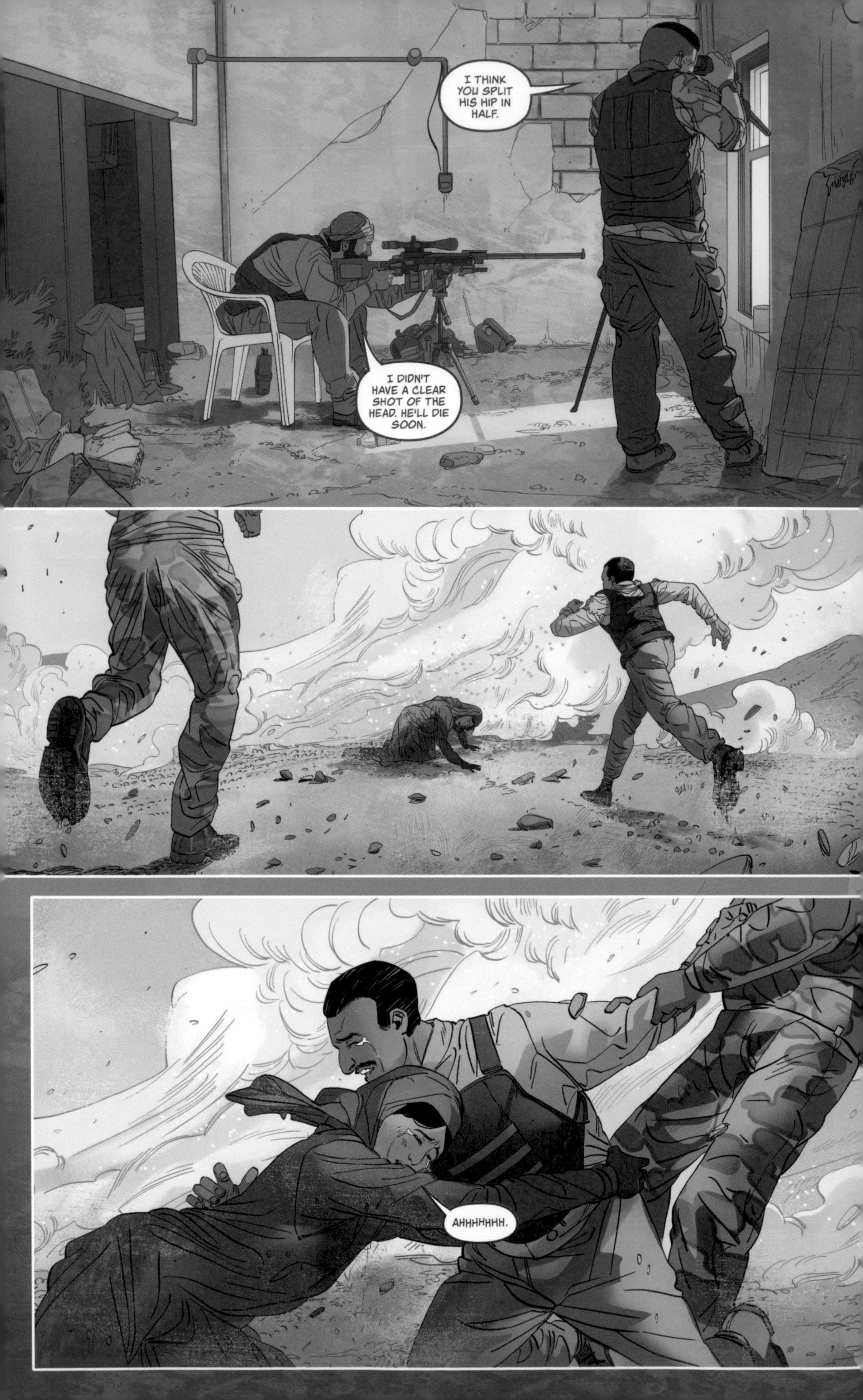
I THINK YOU SPLIT HIS HIP IN HALF.
I DIDN'T HAVE A CLEAR SHOT OF THE HEAD. HE'LL DIE SOON.
AHHHHHHH.

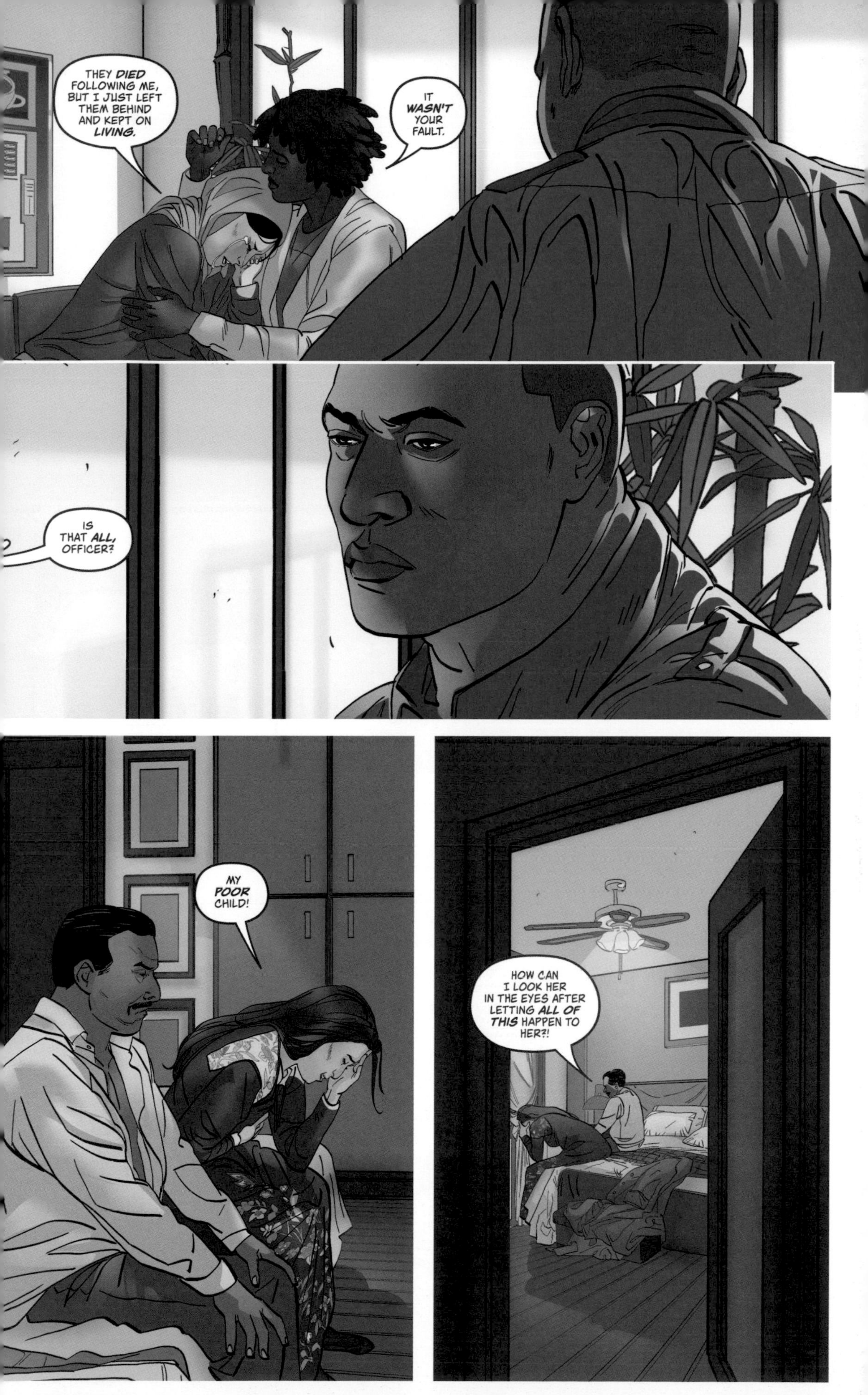
THEY DIED FOLLOWING ME, BUT I JUST LEFT THEM BEHIND AND KEPT ON LIVING.
IT WASN'T YOUR FAULT.
IS THAT ALL, OFFICER?
MY POOR CHILD!
HOW CAN I LOOK HER IN THE EYES AFTER LETTING ALL OF THIS HAPPEN TO HER?!

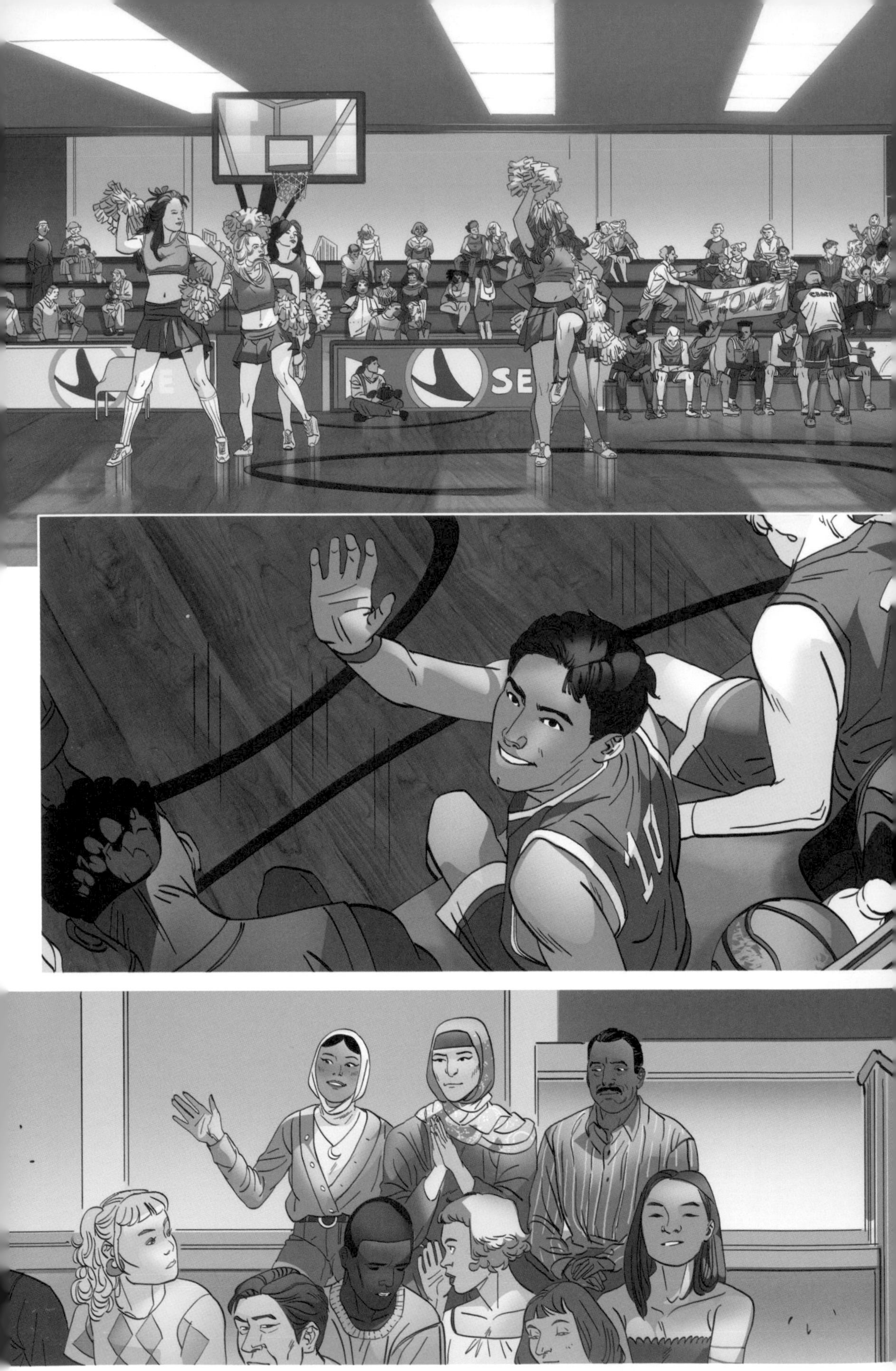
LIONS

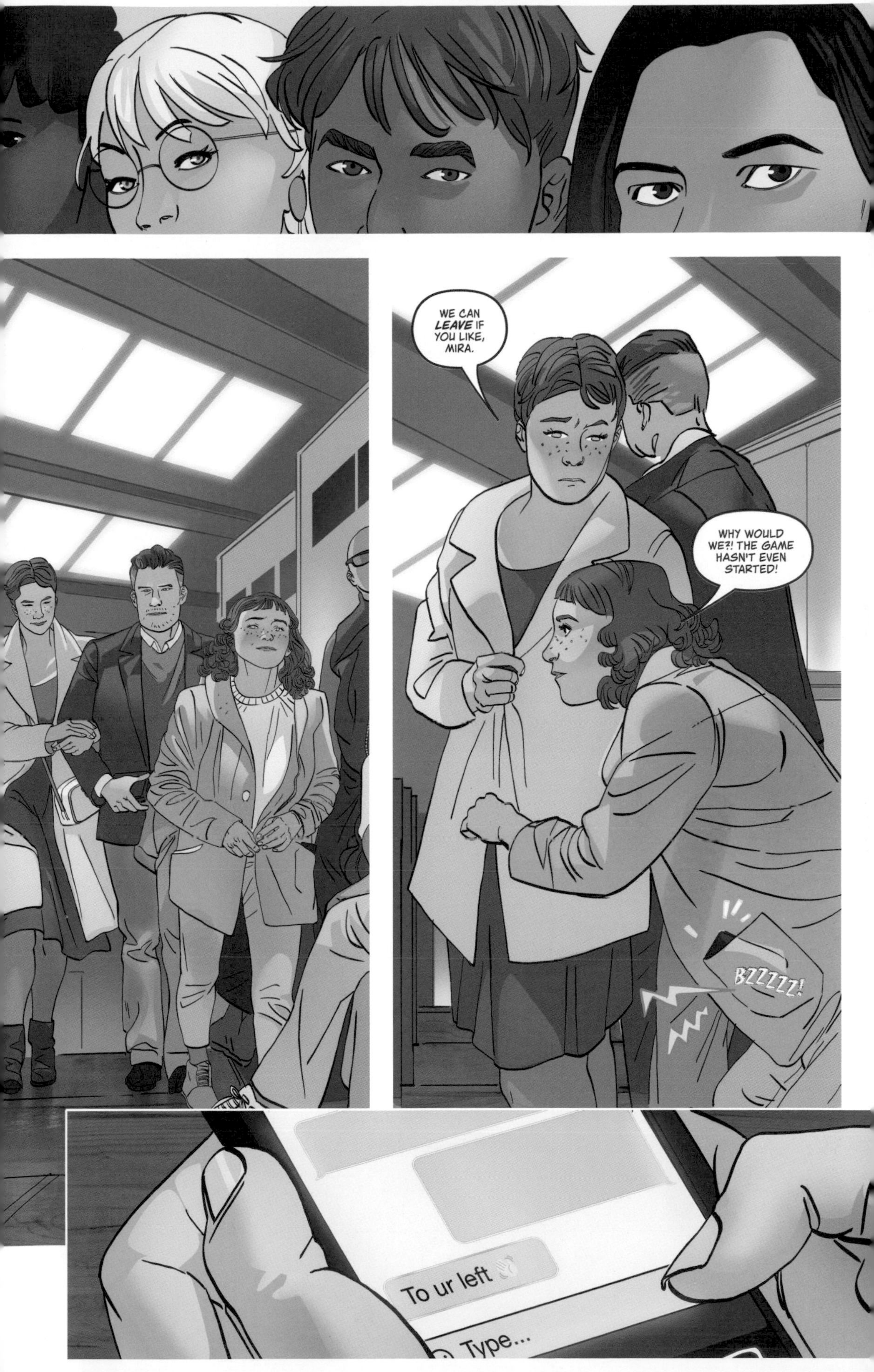
WE CAN LEAVE IF YOU LIKE, MIRA.
WHY WOULD WE?! THE GAME HASN'T EVEN STARTED!
BZZZZZ!
To ur left
Type...

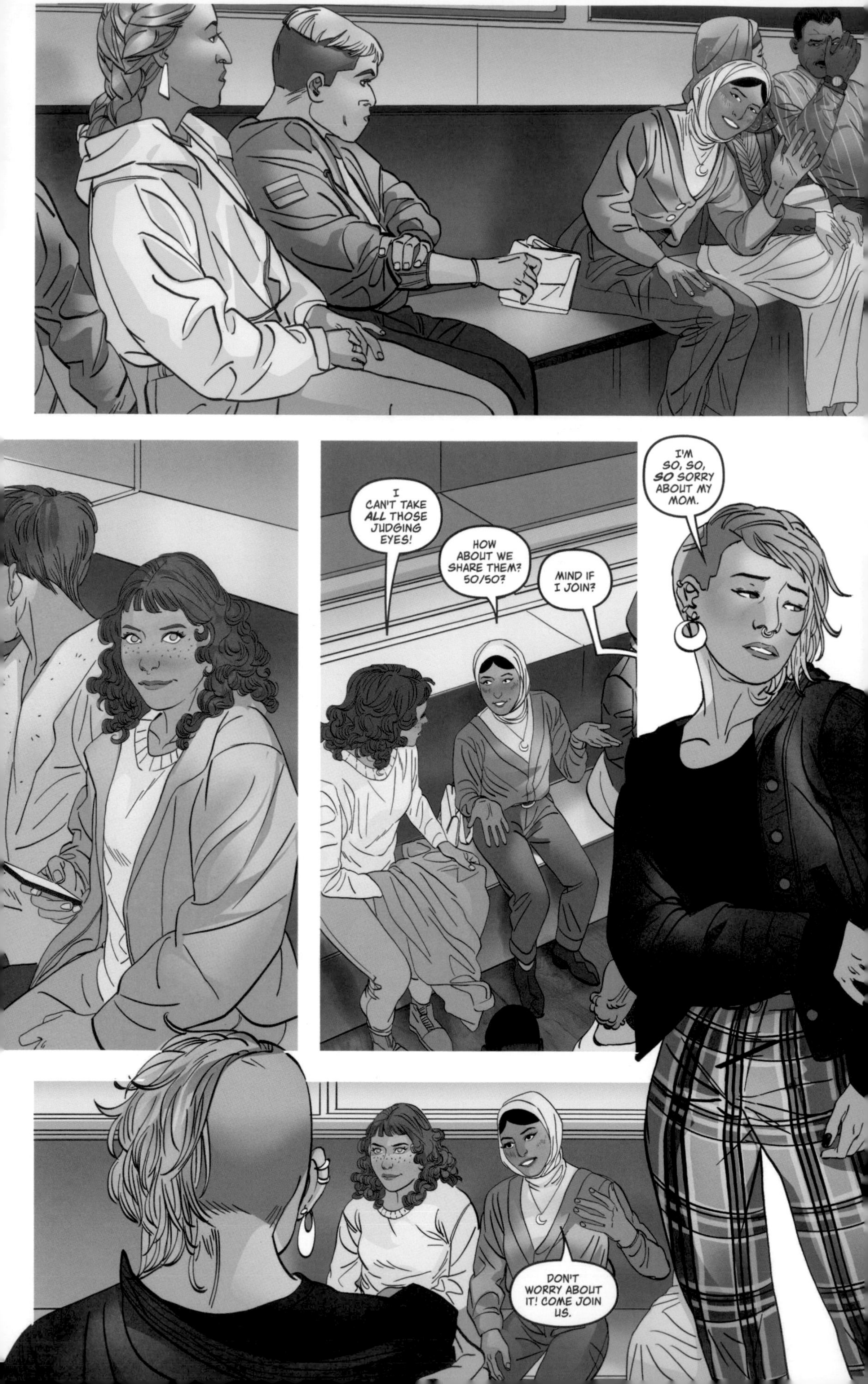
I CAN'T TAKE ALL THOSE JUDGING EYES!
HOW ABOUT WE SHARE THEM? 50/50?
MIND IF I JOIN?
I'M SO, SO, SO SORRY ABOUT MY MOM.
DON'T WORRY ABOUT IT! COME JOIN US.

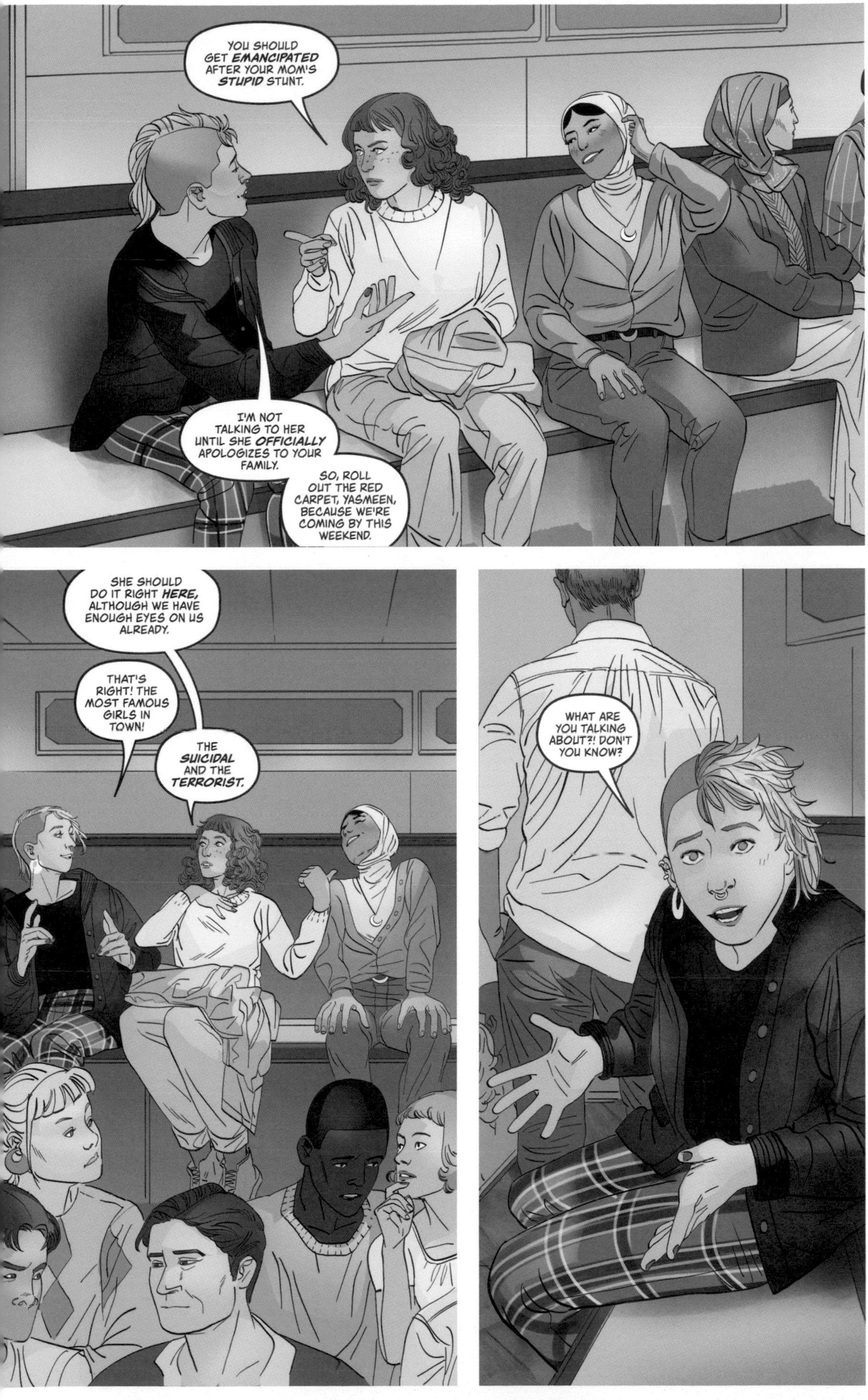
YOU SHOULD GET EMANCIPATED AFTER YOUR MOM'S STUPID STUNT.
I'M NOT TALKING TO HER UNTIL SHE OFFICIALLY APOLOGIZES TO YOUR FAMILY.
SO, ROLL OUT THE RED CARPET, YASMEEN, BECAUSE WE'RE COMING BY THIS WEEKEND.
SHE SHOULD DO IT RIGHT HERE, ALTHOUGH WE HAVE ENOUGH EYES ON US ALREADY.
THAT'S RIGHT! THE MOST FAMOUS GIRLS IN TOWN!
THE SUICIDAL AND THE TERRORIST.
WHAT ARE YOU TALKING ABOUT?! DON'T YOU KNOW?

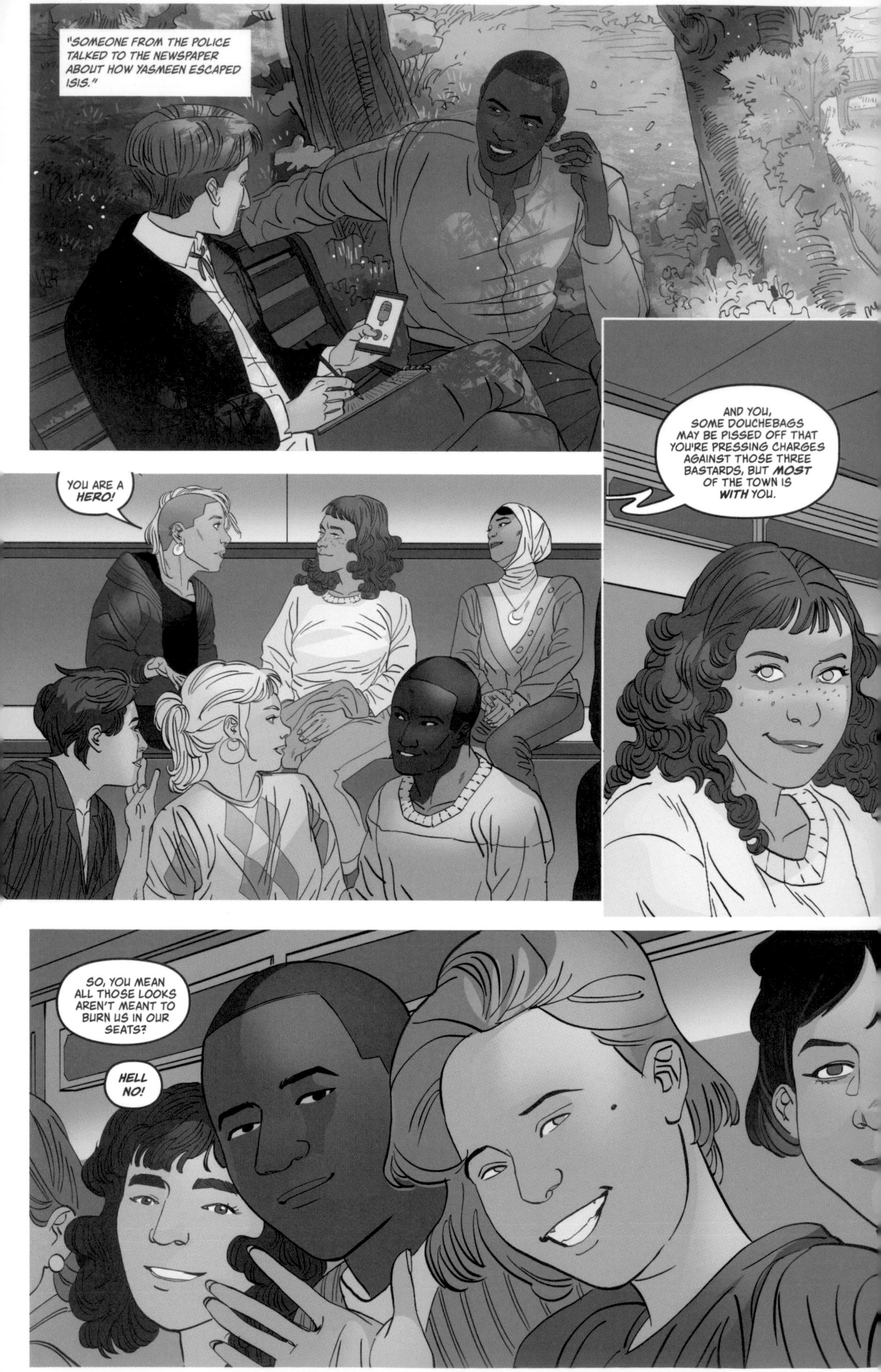
"SOMEONE FROM THE POLICE TALKED TO THE NEWSPAPER ABOUT HOW YASMEEN ESCAPED ISIS."
YOU ARE A HERO!
AND YOU, SOME DOUCHEBAGS MAY BE PISSED OFF THAT YOU'RE PRESSING CHARGES AGAINST THOSE THREE BASTARDS, BUT MOST OF THE TOWN IS WITH YOU.
SO, YOU MEAN ALL THOSE LOOKS AREN'T MEANT TO BURN US IN OUR SEATS?
HELL NO!

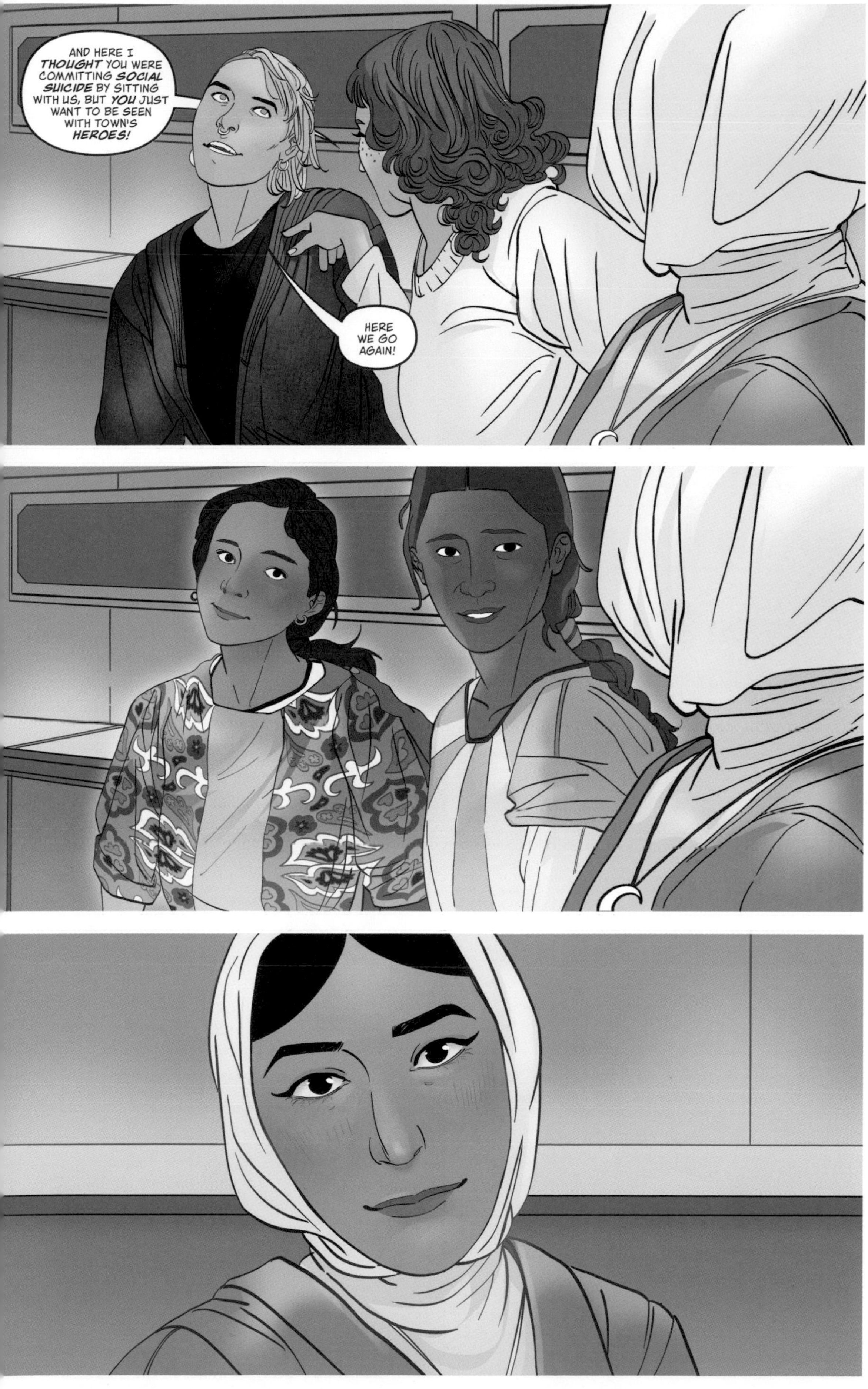
AND HERE I THOUGHT YOU WERE COMMITTING SOCIAL SUICIDE BY SITTING WITH US, BUT YOU JUST WANT TO BE SEEN WITH TOWN'S HEROES!
HERE WE GO AGAIN!

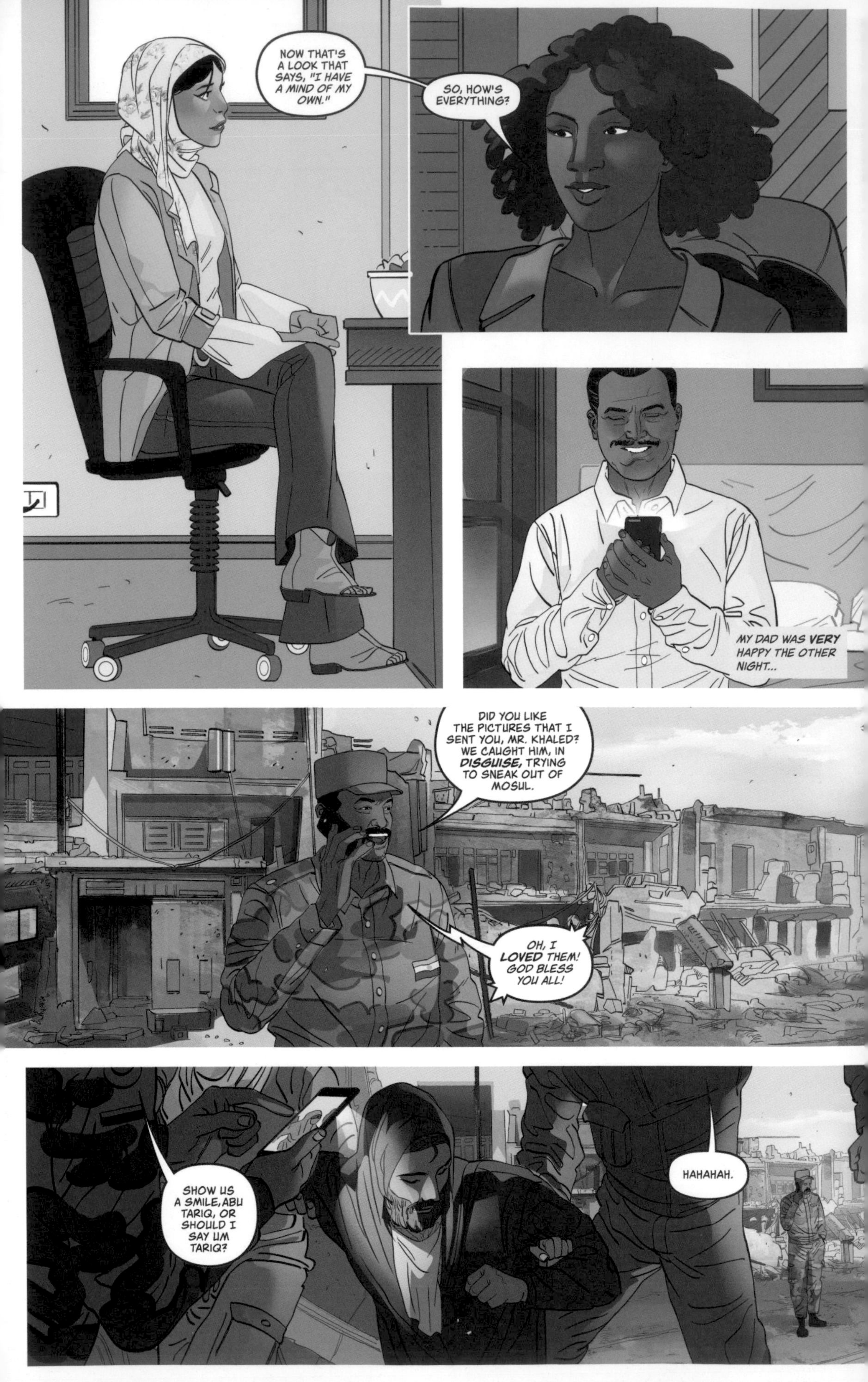
NOW THAT'S A LOOK THAT SAYS, "I HAVE A MIND OF MY OWN."
SO, HOW'S EVERYTHING?
MY DAD WAS VERY HAPPY THE OTHER NIGHT...
DID YOU LIKE THE PICTURES THAT I SENT YOU, MR. KHALED? WE CAUGHT HIM, IN DISGUISE, TRYING TO SNEAK OUT OF MOSUL.
OH, I LOVED THEM! GOD BLESS YOU ALL!
SHOW US A SMILE, ABU TARIQ, OR SHOULD I SAY UM TARIQ?
HAHAHAH.

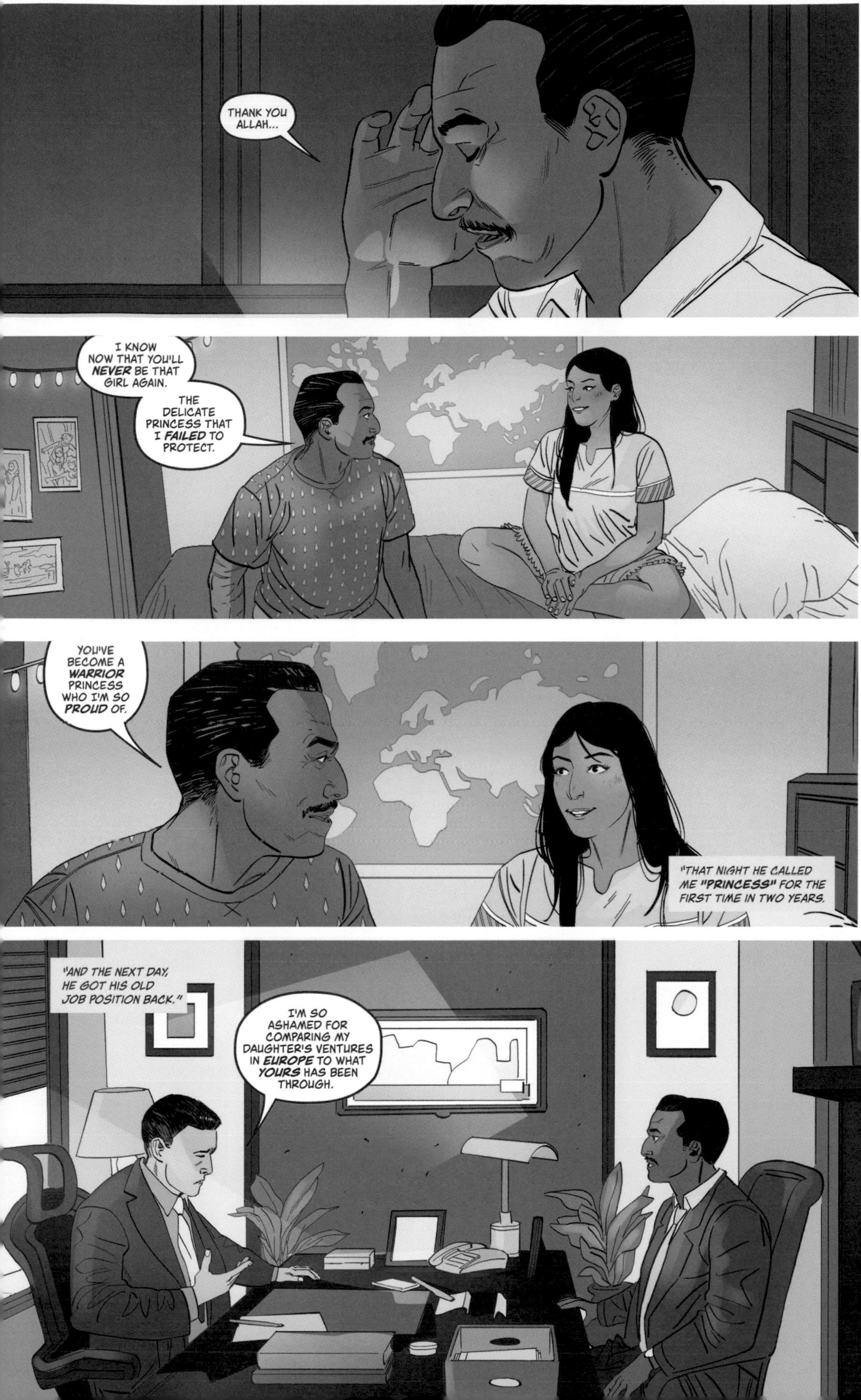
THANK YOU ALLAH...
I KNOW NOW THAT YOU'LL NEVER BE THAT GIRL AGAIN.
THE DELICATE PRINCESS THAT I FAILED TO PROTECT.
YOU'VE BECOME A WARRIOR PRINCESS WHO I'M SO PROUD OF.
"THAT NIGHT HE CALLED ME "PRINCESS" FOR THE FIRST TIME IN TWO YEARS.
"AND THE NEXT DAY, HE GOT HIS OLD JOB POSITION BACK."
I'M SO ASHAMED FOR COMPARING MY DAUGHTER'S VENTURES IN EUROPE TO WHAT YOURS HAS BEEN THROUGH.

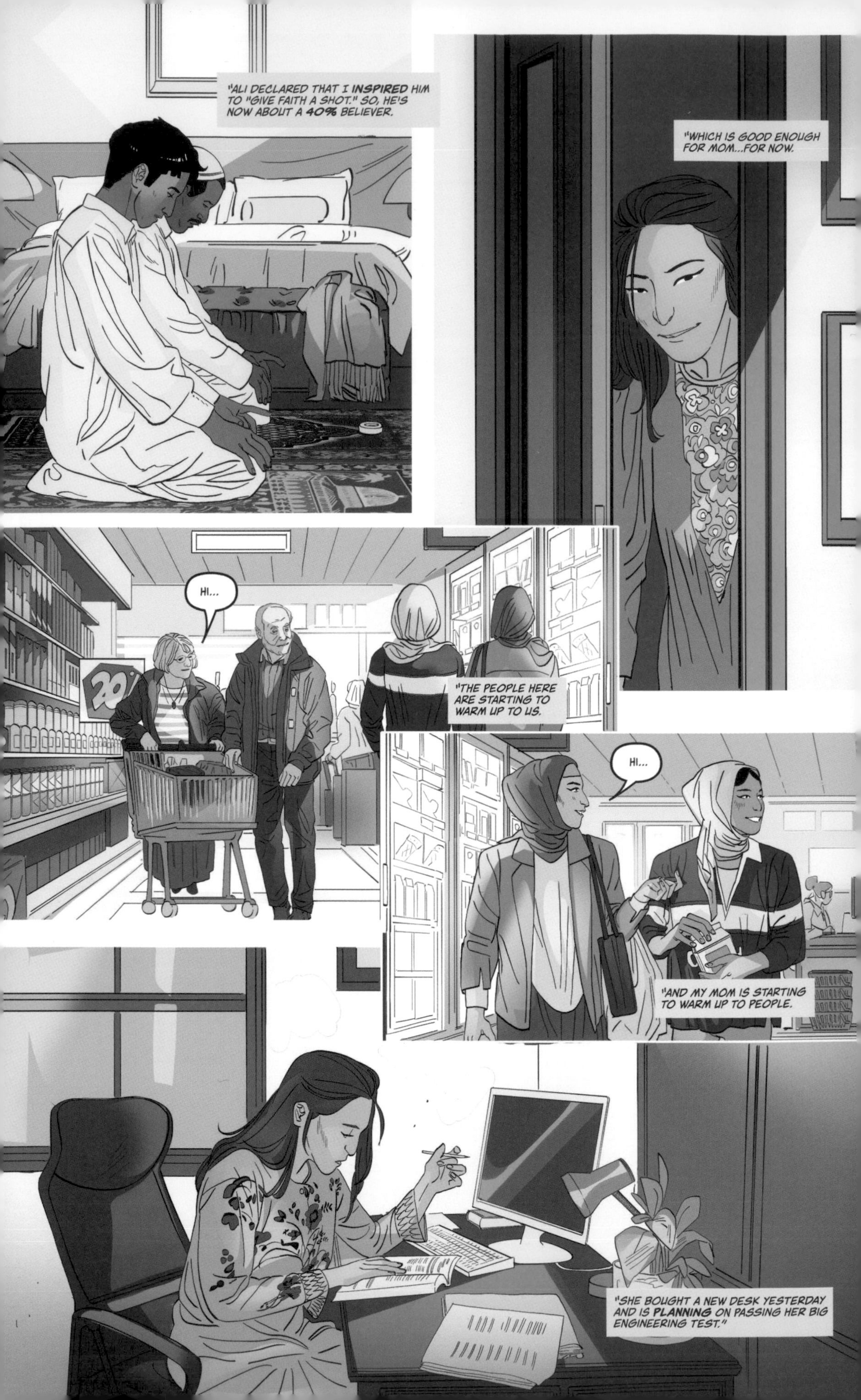
"ALI DECLARED THAT I **INSPIRED** HIM TO "GIVE FAITH A SHOT." SO, HE'S NOW ABOUT A **40%** BELIEVER.
"WHICH IS GOOD ENOUGH FOR MOM...FOR NOW.
HI...
20
"THE PEOPLE HERE ARE STARTING TO WARM UP TO US.
HI...
"AND MY MOM IS STARTING TO WARM UP TO PEOPLE.
"SHE BOUGHT A NEW DESK YESTERDAY AND IS **PLANNING** ON PASSING HER BIG ENGINEERING TEST."

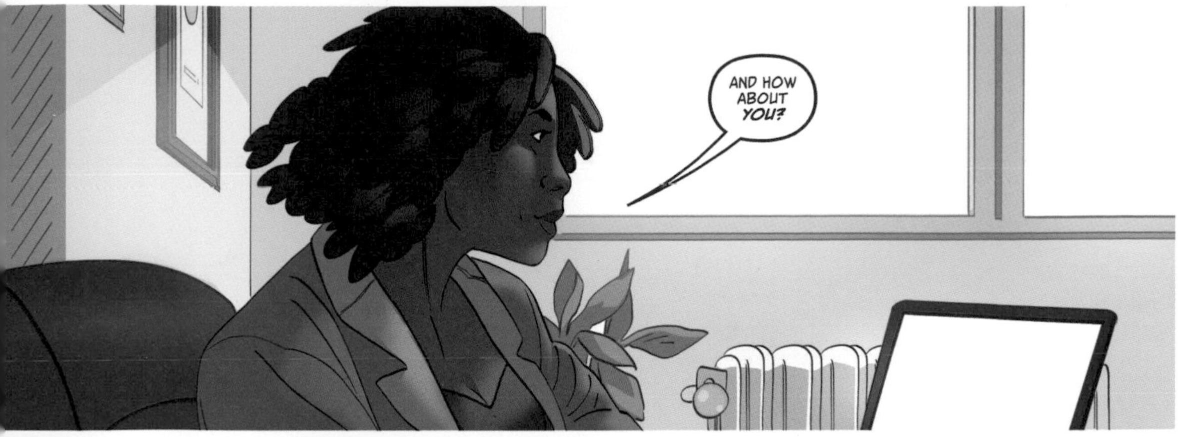
AND HOW ABOUT *YOU?*

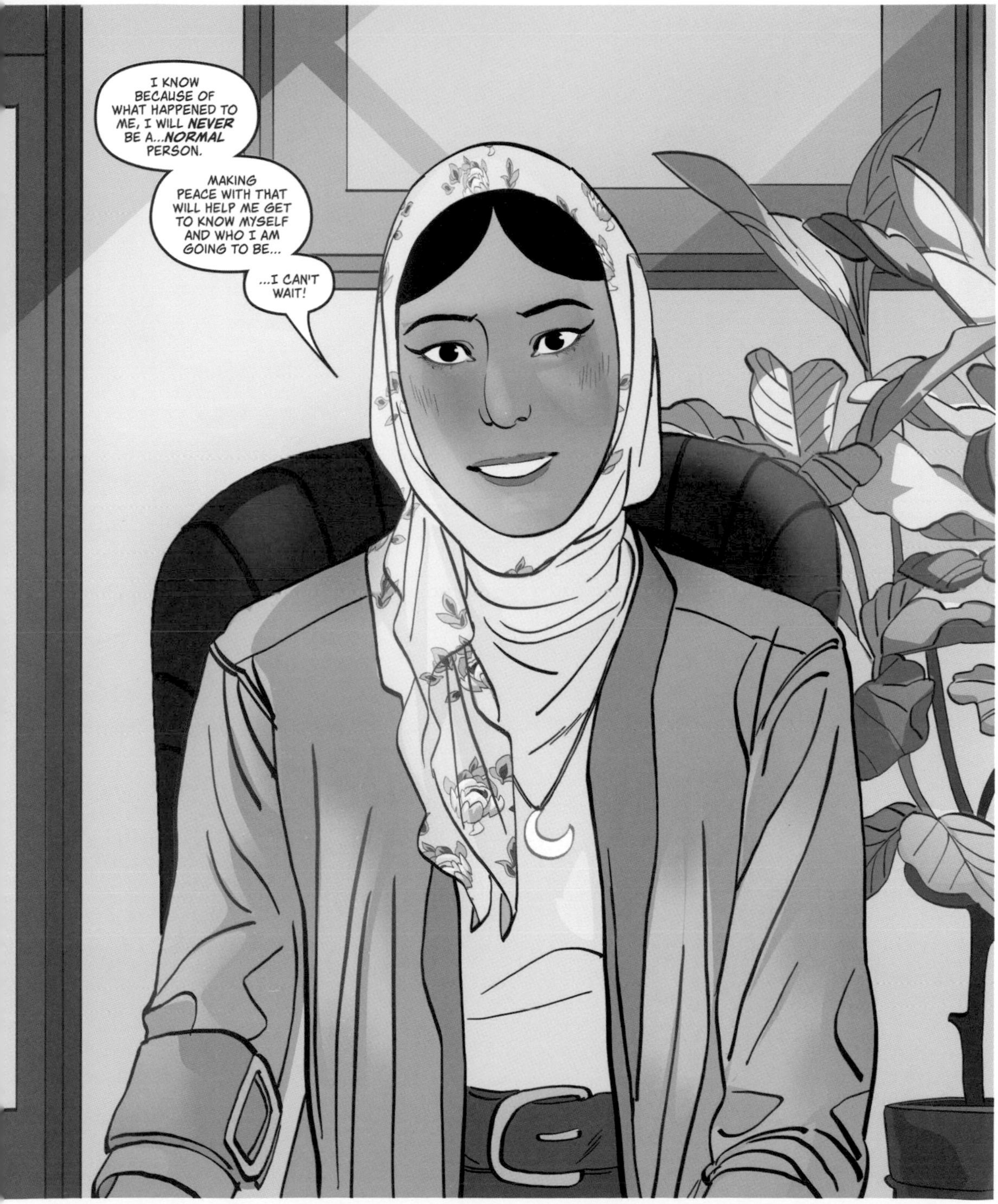
I KNOW BECAUSE OF WHAT HAPPENED TO ME, I WILL *NEVER* BE A...*NORMAL* PERSON.
MAKING PEACE WITH THAT WILL HELP ME GET TO KNOW MYSELF AND WHO I AM GOING TO BE...
...I CAN'T WAIT!

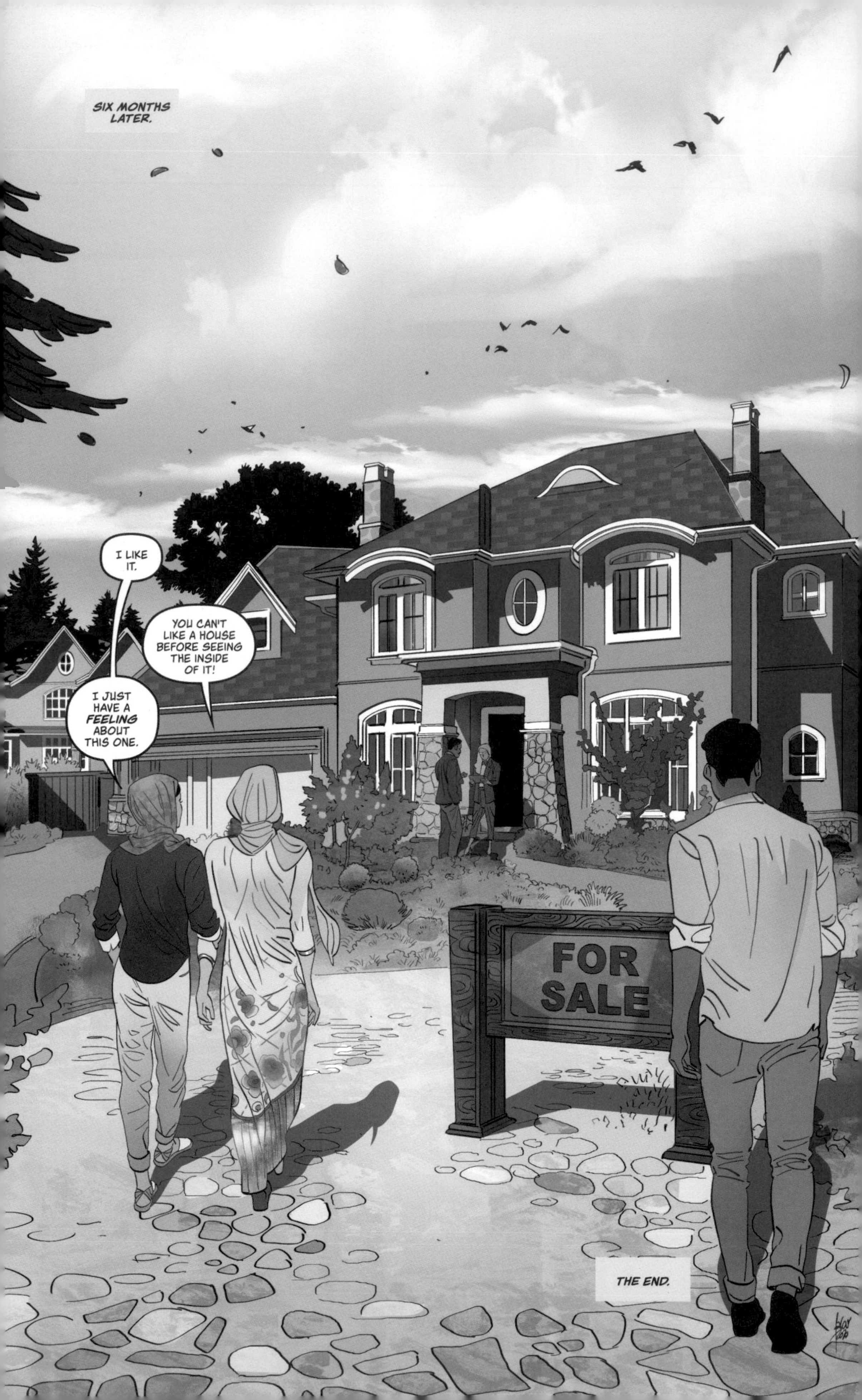
SIX MONTHS LATER.
I LIKE IT.
YOU CAN'T LIKE A HOUSE BEFORE SEEING THE INSIDE OF IT!
I JUST HAVE A FEELING ABOUT THIS ONE.
FOR SALE
THE END.

YASMEEN

COVER GALLERY

1
YASMEEN
Saif A. AHMED
Fabiana MASCOLO

1
YASMEEN
Saif A. AHMED
Fabiana MASCOLO

2
SAIF A. AHMED
FABIANA MASCOLO
YASMEEN

2
SAIF A. AHMED
FABIANA MASCOLO
YASMEEN

3
YASMEEN
Saif A. AHMED
Fabiana MASCOLO

4
YASMEEN
Saif A. AHMED
Fabiana MASCOLO

5
YASMEEN
Saif A. AHMED
Fabiana MASCOLO

6
YASMEEN
Saif A. AHMED
Fabiana MASCOLO

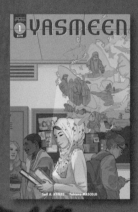

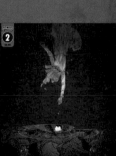

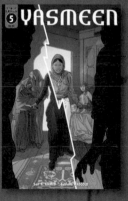

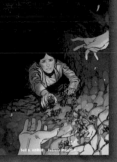

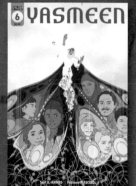

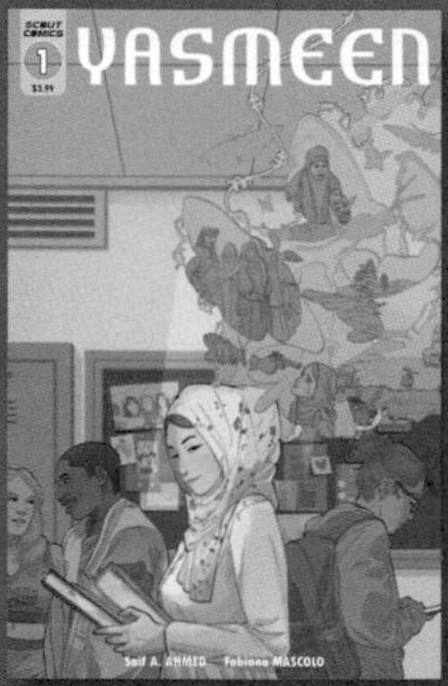

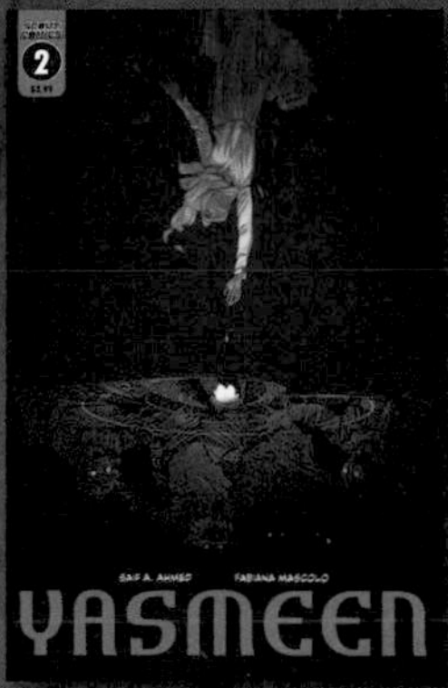

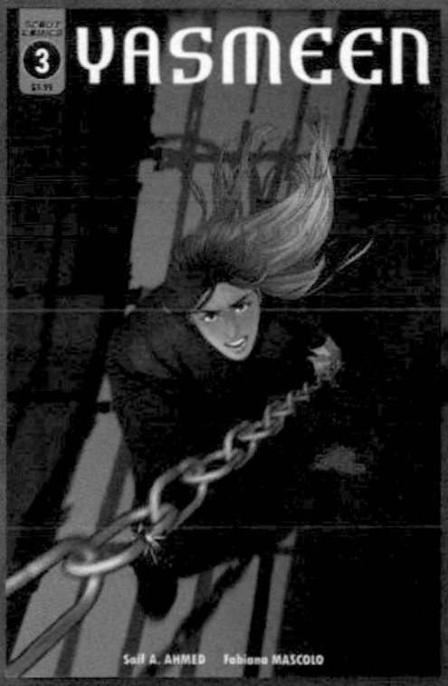

YASMEEN

BIOS

SAIF A. AHMED
Creator & Writer

Saif A. Ahmed is an Iraqi immigrant comic book creator and screenwriter. His short comic "THE DINNER" is featured in the Eisner Award-winning magazine "PanelxPanel."

FABIANA MASCOLO
Artist

Fabiana Mascolo is a freelance comic-book artist based in Rome. Upon graduating top of her class in 2015, she started working in the comics industry both as a penciler and colorist. Over the years she has worked for companies such as BOOM! Studios, Feltrinelli, and Edizioni BD. In 2019 she started her collaboration with Scout Comics for the mini-series YASMEEN written by Saif A. Ahmed.

ROB JONES
Letterer

Rob Jones is a writer and letterer of comics, he has lettered for such companies as Image Comics, Humanoids, Heavy Metal, DC Thomson, Behemoth, Scout Comics, Madius Comics, BHP, and many others. He can often be found spouting nonsense into the void on Twitter @RobJonesWrites or in a dressing gown in his local park.